Michael Rustin is the head of the Sociology Department at the North East London Polytechnic and a founder member of the Socialist Society. He is a frequent contributor to *New Left Review*.

Michael Rustin

Verso

For a Pluralist Socialism

**British Library
Cataloguing in Publication Data**

Rustin, Michael
 For A Pluralist Socialism.
 1. Great Britain — politics and government — 1979–
 I. Title
 320.941   JN237

First published 1985
© Michael Rustin 1985

Verso
15 Greek Street London W1V 5LF

Filmset in Times by
PRG Graphics Ltd Redhill Surrey

Printed in Great Britain by
The Thetford Press Ltd
Thetford Norfolk

ISBN 0 86091 074 1
     0 86091 774 6 pbk

Contents

Acknowledgements

Earlier versions of Chapter 2 appeared as 'The New Left and the Present Crisis' and 'Different Conceptions of Party' in *New Left Review* 121, May–June 1980, and 126, Jan.–Feb. 1981. A later version of the second article appeared in *New Socialist* 20, October 1984. Chapter 7 is a slightly revised from of an article of the same title which appeared in *New Left Review* 137, Jan.–Feb. 1983. Chapter 4 appeared as an article in *Marxism Today,* January 1983, and Chapter 9 as a Socialist Society pamphlet in 1982. Chapter 5 appeared in a slightly different form in *Dissent,* winter 1984–85. Chapter 9 has been substantially revised from an earlier article 'The Politics of Workers Plans' which appeared in *Politics and Power,* 2, 1981. I am grateful to the editors of these publications for their encouragement in the preparation of these articles.

Several of these essays were first given as presentations to seminars or meetings of the Campaign for Higher Education, *Radical Philosophy,* or the Socialist Society. Without these occasions and the discussions they made possible, many of the essays would probably not have been written.

I would like to acknowledge the help and encouragement of my colleagues in the Sociology and Cultural Studies departments at North East London Polytechnic, where many of these ideas have been explored in discussion. I was able to complete the manuscript for the book at the beginning of a year as a Visiting Member in the School of Social Sciences, at the Institute for Advanced Study, Princeton, and I am grateful to the Institute for making this possible. Peggy Clarke, Lucille Allsen and Lynda Emery at the Institute, and Jane Ward at NELP have provided exemplary secretarial help.

I am especially grateful for the help of Neil Belton at Verso, who at times seemed to understand the project of this book better than I did myself.

Finally I would like to thank my wife Margaret for the large contribution she has made to this book, by much careful reading and editorial work, and by her sustaining support for the project as a whole.

1

Introduction:
A Strategic Perspective

The component parts of this volume were written as separate articles during the period since Mrs Thatcher's election victory in 1979. Nevertheless, they develop several unifying themes, which this chapter will attempt to summarize. They argue for a pluralist conception of socialism in modern British society, both as a matter of principle and theory, and as a matter of agency, because of the range of different social interests which any socialist politics now has to address if it is to have any hope of success. They assert the priority of class in socialist politics, but also suggest an approach to class which acknowledges actual differences of interests among potential allies, and requires their compromise and synthesis rather than expecting their transcendence in the discovery or recovery of an essential working class consciousness.

The essays are nearly all exercises in a kind of 'practical reasoning'. That is to say, they address problems of programme and political agency, not, primarily, the more academic tasks of description, analysis and explanation. They are concerned to think about what should be. There has been a scarcity of such informed practical reasoning on the left in recent years, despite a proliferation of radical academic literature in the social sciences and other disciplines. One might almost say that socialist preoccupation with the past has, in British national character, increased in proportion to the unattractiveness of the present. Programmatic writing without theoretical resources or content is a thin and abstracted genre, but theoretical writing which does not tackle questions of what should be done lacks engagement with actual politics. It is hard to find a viable synthesis of these contrasted modes of thought.

I hope that each of these essays has at its core a fruitful idea, whether drawn from sociological reasoning or from applications of moral or political principle, which gives some theoretical context to the arguments and links particular cases to the more general problems of British society. Although I believe that the thinking which has gone into this book is consistent, each of its claims is argued (and has been evolved) separately, and not as an instance of some general view. Certain of the essays are speculative proposals for unlocking particular intractable problems, perhaps in unexpected ways, and some of the solutions will probably turn out to be more adequate, and to meet with more agreement, than others. At any rate, in Britain's current deep crisis, we need to allow ourselves to think without too many inhibitions of orthodoxy. Through public discussion we may again come to feel that problems are after all as amenable to political solution as they have been before, in not-too-distant memory.

Political Time-Scales[1]

A distinction can be drawn in political analysis between the immediate tactical situation (the time-scale of a week which Harold Wilson, in a well-known phrase, saw as a long time in politics); the medium-term scale of parliaments, five-yearly elections, and party programmes; and the longer periods during which substantial political changes, such as the coming of electoral democracy, or the growth in the role of the State, take place. About the first of these this book will say little, except to point out that one of the besetting weaknesses of the new Labour leadership appears to be its over-absorption in the day-to-day routines of parliamentary and television politics, at the expense of more substantial kinds of tactical or strategic thinking. At least, this is so far as anyone can see from public debate: Neil Kinnock and his team have scarcely yet made much effort to wrest the intellectual initiative from their Tory and Alliance opponents. One of our implicit arguments will be that such a preoccupation with political immediacy is likely to prove fatal to Labour and socialist hopes if it continues.

The second time-scale, that of the election cycle and the period in office of elected governments, has recently seen an unparalleled defeat for the Labour Party and the left more generally, since the election of 1979 and the loss of direction and momentum of the second Wilson government in about 1976. Any political argument which hopes to influence events at all directly must situate itself in relation to these real necessities of fighting elections and attempting to form, influence or resist governments. Many of the following chapters are addressed directly to these problems. In fact this book will attempt to be programmatic at just this level, of seeking to identify issues and positions which would provide favourable grounds for socialist intervention within the framework of a feasible politics.

Within this time-scale, the outlook remains ominous, and the beginning of political sense is, as Eric Hobsbawm[2] pointed out in his *Forward March of Labour Halted?* article of 1978, to recognize this. Labour's 28 per cent share of the vote in the 1983 General Election, the loss of much of its support to the Liberal–S.D.P Alliance, and the consequent impotence of the opposition parties (and of the Tory left) to exercise any restraining influence on the Thatcher Government, have been nothing short of political disasters. Nor, despite the moderately encouraging evidence of public opinion polls, can one have confidence that Labour has yet found the basis for a solid recovery. Some more profound adjustment and rethinking will be needed to prevent the further advance of Labour's centre-party rivals and a resulting consolidation of Conservative rule for a further term. A number of chapters directly address the problem of Labour's lost support: this is attributed in part to long-term weaknesses in the traditions and organization of the Labour Party, and to the failure of the movements loosely described as the 'new left' to modify these. But it is also due to a fragmentation of the electorate and its political allegiance, with which Labour has been slow to come to terms, and which has now produced a volatile and multiparty pattern of support in place of the duopoly of the earlier post-war period. The response which is proposed to these problems is three-fold. Firstly, in the perspective of an organizational regeneration of the Labour Party, arguments are put forward for an open and participatory concept of party democracy against, on the one hand, the old oligarchy of parliamentary leaders and trade union bosses, and on the other hand an unrepresentative and narrow vanguardism. Secondly, proposals are made for a broad programme which could recapture the political and ideological initiative against Thatcherism and oblige the centre to argue on Labour's own terms. Democratization is an important theme of this programmatic discussion. Thirdly, likely limits are suggested for Labour's actual recovery of its electoral position, and it is argued that Labour has to contemplate the necessity of a politics in which the defeat of Thatcherism would be the first priority. A crucial issue in the isolation of the radical right is the reform of the electoral system to some form of proportional representation. This is argued not only on the normative grounds required by an authentic belief in democracy (the 1985 distribution of seats between Labour and the Alliance cannot conceivably be justified, given their respective 28 per cent and 25 per cent distribution of votes) but also on grounds of political advantage to Labour and the working class. A dual strategy is advocated, in which Labour attempts to strengthen the legitimacy and support for its own political positions, as a class party, and also makes realistic adjustment to a new pluralist party system in which it cannot count on a return to an absolute majority of parliamentary seats, still less a majority of votes cast. It will be suggested that consistent arguments for democratization, which require acknowledging the strength of the case for P.R., will help rather than hinder Labour's electoral prospects.

The third and longest time-scale is one in which there are grounds for greater political optimism. In the very long term, the transformation of the means of production — which Marx cited as the basis for the overcoming of scarcity and thus of the necessity for class domination — continues with accelerating speed. While the immediate effects of this process on many social groups and even national economies are often extremely damaging, there seems no doubt that the long-term trend, even for many parts of the Third World, is towards an increase in material production and in the length and material standard of life. Marx's account of this as a process of growing socialization of the economy seems also to be substantially correct. Systems of production become more integrated with one another and require greater measures of planning and coordination, whether these are undertaken by multinational corporations, by national governments, or by international governmental cooperation. The enhanced role of the state in economic production — which has developed since the Second World War, and for many countries long before that — does not seem likely to be thrown back by the current ascendancy of free-market-oriented government in most of the Western world. As a result, large-scale economic forces become evidently subject to conscious decision, and not merely the automatic outcome of impersonal market mechanisms. The Republican government of President Reagan has been able to defend the appearance of a market-regulated economy only by the pursuit of covert budget-deficit strategies which depend on the Administration's expenditure and taxation decisions (and especially on military expenditure). Just as important as these economic processes is the accompanying rise in human expectations and aspirations, for societies in which basic rights of political self-determination, material subsistence and social self-expression are available to all. This worldwide transformation of expectations has after all destroyed most of the overt structures of colonial rule in the period since the Second World War (though many less direct forms of economic and military domination by major powers continue). Electoral democracy, as Göran Therborn[3] has recently reminded us, did not become a universalist and inclusive institution until the twentieth century. And it is only in the last few years that virtually the whole of Western Europe has been subject to formally democratic governments. Within many states such as Britain, one can point to an extension of the concept of 'citizenship' from initially political and legal definitions of rights, through economic norms of minimum subsistence and full employment, to broader social rights to education, health, cultural access, and so on. The claims of women in many of these spheres are evidence of a continuing dynamic of demands for social justice.

Each of these elements of what Raymond Williams described as Britain's 'long revolution' has become in recent years a matter of crisis for the ruling classes of the West. The rise of state expenditures and regulation of the economy appeared to indicate an irreversible process of creeping socialism. Thus,the use of political powers to advance social rights and interests was held to be threatening to 'overload' the political system, and to be bringing about a 'crisis of governability'.[4] Demands for personal and expressive liberation, evident in the youth culture of the 1960s, seemed to undermine the work ethic and the norms of sexual restraint and family life on which orderly, conservative society depended. The reaction of the radical right in America, Britain, and elsewhere in the West is to be understood as in its own way a rational response to the severe pressures stemming from democratization and mass access to the political, economic and cultural arenas. Arguments for the restoration of market forces (and thus the distinctive power of the propertied), for strong government (against collective demands from trade unions and new social movements such as those of blacks or women), and for a re-establishment of traditional values in the areas of the family and sexual life, were moved by real anxiety about the threats which the prosperity and characteristic claims of the post-war era posed to the prerogatives of property and to the minorities associated with its rule. To be sure, there were many actual difficulties and contradictions in the management of so rapidly changing and conflictual a society. The neo-conservative programme could appeal to many whose existence or peace seemed threatened by such manifestations of economic competition as inflation or industrial conflict, by the cultural dissonance apparent in youthful hedonism and violence, or by the demands of blacks, for example, for political equality of access to social goods. But the deliberately reactionary strategy of the new right was an attempt not merely to slow down and moderate the pace of social transformation, but also to undermine the underlying moral, political and economic conditions of this collective advancement. We should not be so discouraged by the local successes of the right in exploiting these contradictions as to forget the positive long-term social forces which originally created the conditions for democratization and mass participation in the world's goods.

A similar pattern of social advance and assertive counter-action can be seen in the West's relations with the Third World since the rise of the New Right, especially in the United States. Fred Halliday[5] has shown that it is the real undermining of US influence — through reverses in Vietnam, Mozambique, Angola, Iran or Nicaragua — and the interpretation of these essentially anti-imperialist struggles for self-determination as Cold War losses to Communism, which have led to the renewed drive for military superiority by the West. The possibilities of disengaging social revolutions in the Third World from the global struggle for hegemony between the USA and the USSR have rarely been pursued since the later years of the Carter Administration, though it can scarcely be doubted that in some cases at least — Nicaragua, for example — the option has been, and remains, available. In the international as in the internal politics of the capitalist powers, the policy manifestos of the new conservatives have sometimes lucidly set out their counter-revolutionary intentions and their analysis of the changing balance of social forces which has provoked them.

A dominant means of reasserting an equation of capitalism and freedom, and of defending the boundaries of capitalism especially in the Third World, has been the renewal of Western hostility towards the Soviet bloc. The campaign for human rights in the East has been a powerful weapon of this Western strategy of increased pressure — which has taken military, economic and ideological forms — and can therefore rarely be taken at its face value. Nevertheless, the reality of the demand for fuller democratic and civil rights by the populations of the Eastern bloc states can hardly be doubted after the successive conflicts in East Germany (1953), Hungary (1956), Czechoslovakia (1968) and Poland (1980-81). These demands have been repressed by force, and in the long time-scale we are here considering it cannot be doubted that they will continue to find expression until they are met. Far from being a means to advance such freedoms, as its protagonists claim, the Cold War serves to bolster the power of both major antagonists against their subordinate allies, and is thus collusively sustained by each side in the conflict. The revival of the process of detente remains among the most pressing causes for democratic socialists in both East and West.

The long-term perspectives on which the arguments of this book are based are therefore by no means pessimistic. The global transformation of the means of production — the basis of the optimistic teleology of both liberal and Marxist traditions — and the accompanying revolution in human aspirations and expectations continues with unabridged force, whatever temporary curbs are imposed by regimes determined to defend local class privileges. Only the shadow of nuclear war must massively qualify any reasoned and hopeful perspective for human societies. This threat ultimately emerges from political institutions, and particularly from the powers of the privileged in the two rival world systems. One must hope that the pursuit of democratization, and of constructive solutions to the (intractable) problems of our own society, may make some small contribution to a political climate in which the overwhelming claim of the protection of human life is more seriously respected. That is to say, a climate in which the paranoid and megalomanic phantasies of the nuclear arms race ('the bombing of the Soviet Union will commence in five minutes') will be universally unacceptable as a political stance.

Britain: The Post-War Consensus

Many of the detailed arguments in this book draw on a neo-Gramscian analysis of the politics of class alliances. Gramsci,[6] at least according to some interpreters, sought to identify the distinctive problems of socialist strategy in liberal democratic societies, where a dense network of 'civil society' stood between the individual and state power. Gramsci also recognized, in relation to his contemporary Italian society, but with subsequent relevance to many others, the range and complexity of class formations that had to be taken into account in the development of a socialist politics. He saw that political and ideological domination had a reality of its own, not reducible to the direct and immediate expression of class interests. It was the attribute of successful ideological hegemony, whether of left or right, that it unified disparate class interests through normative constructs and definitions whose immediate reference might not be to economic issues, even though the ultimate roots of ideology lay in class interests and powers.

Gramsci's ideas have been among the most important in a thoroughgoing revision of Marxist political theory which has taken place in the West in recent years and is one of the most positive achievements of the new left. This theoretical revision has focused specific attention on the effects of state forms (including bourgeois democracy) and of ideology and mass communications in politics; and it has led to a rejection of the crude forms of economic and class reductionism as guides to political action. The most influential empirical studies within this perspective have been analyses of Thatcherism and the cultural basis of the politics of the new right. These studies have traced the development of a populism of the right, in whose rhetoric class interests have been transformed and encoded in more traditionalist and rooted appeals. The values of race, territory and family have figured as issues in a politics of law and order whose principal motive nevertheless lies in the conflicts of class. Dominant class anxieties about the 'ungovernability' of a society in which the trade unions had defeated three successive governments (Wilson's over *In Place of Strife* in 1969; Heath's in the miners' strike of 1974; and Callaghan's in the 'winter of discontent' of 1978-79) were projected as more diffuse anxieties about disorder in the streets, immigration and threats to traditional sexual standards. This analysis has made the popular resonance of Thatcherism intelligible; and it should have enabled us to predict that an adventure such as the Falklands war would be its most potent means of mobilizing conservative feeling. However, such an analysis of populism has been less fully deployed in thinking out an alternative radical strategy. This will be one of the main preoccupations of this book.

Neo-Gramscian concepts provide a theoretical framework for assessing the gains and losses of the post-war period, and the significance of the populist alliance of the left that was forged during the Second World War as an exemplary case. In the 'war of position' between classes and class interests (to use the phrase by which Gramsci characterized conflict in social formations with a highly developed 'civil society'), who has gained and lost what ground? Analysts of Thatcherism have neglected these more 'structural' dimensions of institutional power, in a preoccupation with its cultural or 'superstructural' aspects. But it is in this perspective of a 'war of position' that the post-war consensus and its breakdown can be best understood.

The historic meaning of the post-war consensus was a compromise between the dominant capitalist order and the working-class movement and its allies. The popular mobilizations of two world wars had raised levels of expectation and increased the organized power and leverage of the working class. The achievement of universal suffrage, complete only in 1928, became effective in returning an absolute Labour majority only in 1945, though the terms of the post-war settlement had already been set during the war-time Coalition Government, as the price for trade-union co-operation. For the working class this involved recognition of a national minimum income, following the Beveridge Report; a commitment to full employment, which lasted for twenty-five years; nearly universal public services of education and health; and a substantial public stake in housing provision.[7] The growth of the state, as a source of employment, as a spender of a higher and higher proportion of GNP, and as a regulator of economic life, established a large institutional sphere not directly subordinate to capital, and subject, more than the private sector, to electoral and trade-union pressures from the labour movement. Trade unions gained in the post-war period through legal protection and saturation of the employed population. The nationalized sector of the economy, which grew even during the Heath government, constituted a zone of capital partially neutralized or taken out of the struggle between capital and labour, at least until the efforts of the Thatcher governments, in steel, motors and mines, to subject it to more stringent market discipline. Public sector industries were more highly unionized than the private sector. They were precluded from engaging in the private sector's anti-socialist and anti-working-class agitation, and tended to favour a 'corporatist' and socially responsible management orientation. The significance of the public sector for working-class interests may be gauged by the fact that electoral support for Labour has come to be increasingly correlated with public sector employment.

The benefits for capital of these arrangements were also very considerable. The growth of public investment, and even the nationalization of basic industries, underwrote capital's infra-structural costs, and the growth of welfare expenditure secured both the reproduction of labour power (at lower direct cost to firms) and the organizing of consent to the market economy. Keynesian techniques of economic management did succeed in achieving, in the context of global economic expansion, higher rates of consistent economic growth and greater improvements in living standards than had previously been known. Clearly the hope, expressed in the politics of 'Butskellism' (the Labour right and the moderate Tory leadership which was dominant in this period), was that the working class could be successfully incorporated into the structure of the new welfare capitalism, and would abandon any fundamental ideological challenge to capital. This incorporation appeared to have been accomplished in West Germany with the repudiation of Marxism in the 1959 Bad Godesberg programme of the SPD. It was this objective to which Anthony Crosland's major revisionist work, *The Future of Socialism*, was devoted — the vision of a social democracy compatible with private ownership of the means of production. Hugh Gaitskell's unsuccessful attempt to revise Clause Four in 1959 was intended to mark out precisely this change of epochs.

But though many processes were set in train by 'affluence' which did erode the communal base of the working class — a predominantly consumerist and private definition of affluence, major re-locations of population away from the older urban centres, etc. — the hoped-for incorporation of the working class, or 'embourgeoisement' as it came to be called by sociologists,[8] did not occur. Class identifications proved obstinate in Britain, both among the organized working class whose trade unions were instrumental in defeating revisionism in the Labour Party as a formal programme, and among the bourgeoisie, which was reluctant to open up the closed world of private education, recruitment to top positions, and generally status-segregated ways of life to competition from below. The effect of 'affluence' in Britain was not to produce a general conversion to bourgeois individualism and a withering away of the unions and claims for State provision. What came instead was a more powerful expression of 'instrumental collectivism' — that is to say, the vigorous prosecution of their own claims by trade unions and, following their example, professionals such as doctors and teachers, and interest-groups of collective consumers (e.g. social security claimants, or neighbourhood conservation groups usually of the middle class). Governments during the 1960s and 1970s became dominantly occupied with the management of these competing and escalating pressures. 'Corporatism'[9] — the attempt by the State to integrate trade unions and employers into measures of tripartite economic management, for example in the control of prices and incomes — was the characteristic response of the MacMillan, Wilson and post-Selsdon Heath governments to this state of disruptive conflict. The fact that the incorporation of the working class into a less class-divided and class-conscious society had not occurred, and that the working class seemed to enter increasingly, in the late 1960s and early 1970s, into what Ralph Miliband described as a 'state of de-subordination',[10] was the most important failure of the post-war consensus from the point of view of capital. The increased intensity of industrial conflict, and the dissension on other moral and sectoral frontiers that opened after 1968, were (temporarily) encouraging to the left and had a considerable influence on its subsequent development.

The right was able to gain control of the Conservative Party as a result of Heath's defeat at the hands of the miners in 1974. The failure of this phase of consensus government — a combination of State interventionism and expansionary policy more radical than the previous Wilson government's economic programme — had brought disillusion in the employing class with the policies of class conciliation. An element of governing class panic now made it possible for the Thatcherites to reshape the strategy for capital in Britain.

Thatcherism[11]

The right has developed a consistent and lucid analysis of the failure of the post-war consensus. Thatcherism gained much of its strength of purpose from its clear view of what, from capital's point of view, went wrong in the post-war period, and from the availability of an alternative theoretical scheme — the model of a laissez-faire economy, a minimal though strong State, and a culture of individual self-interest and responsibility under a punitive system of law — to set against the pragmatic and incrementalist compromises of the Welfare State. The Thatcherite Conservatives saw the cumulative rise in social spending and in the powers of trade unions, the 'inflationary' expectations of public expenditure generated by the Welfare State, and the growth of State intervention in the economy, as a process of creeping socialization which would prove irreversible if not halted in time. The State's submission to one set of demands — from a collapsing firm or industry, from a group of employees, from a new kind of collective consumer — would merely make it easier for the next claimants to legitimize their own claims. 'Inflation' itself evolved from a technical economic term into a general metaphor for excessive expectations and demands. A right-wing view of capitalist crisis and 'overload' of government was the subject of many books and articles. The left's own typical political techniques were appropriated by the right, and research institutes such as the Institute of Economic Affairs and the Centre for Policy Studies proved fertile in developing policy-related applications of neo-liberal theory. There is no likelihood that the Thatcherites will run out of ideas: the neo-liberals, and not the Fabians, have become the successful permeators of our day. Intellectuals such as Hayek and Friedman, previously regarded somewhat as fossils of a discredited ideology, came to have a critical role as sources of the fundamental conservative ideas and values on which practical political thinking could be based. The political opponents of the MacMillan and Heath governments within the Tory Party (Thorneycroft and Powell, for example) were retrospectively vindicated, and returned to influence, inside or outside of the party. Both in the United States, through writers like Daniel Bell and Nathan Glazer,[12] and in Britain, writers and academics who had formerly had commitments to the left proved important in this intellectual counter-revolution. The methods of moral mass mobilization previously characteristic of the left (for older conservatives, popular mobilization by the right was almost a contradiction in terms) were also appropriated by the new right. At the level of individual prophecy and charisma, the seminal figure in Britain was Enoch Powell. Mass campaigns, such as the anti-abortion movement, mobilizations against pornography and alleged radicalism in the media (often making skilful use of the media themselves) and appeals to crucial interest-groups who felt threatened by progressivism (for example, the Black Paper campaign on educational standards which succeeded in shaping the Callaghan government's educational attitudes) together brought substantial participation in support of traditional values. This cultural offensive has extended across a wide range of issues: the Prince of Wales's recent denunciation of the modern movement in architecture is taking up a prolonged counter-attack against modernism in the architectural profession. One of the most important theorists of this anti-modernist position, Roger Scruton, represents a counter-appropriation of radical ideas at the level of theory.[13] His defence of tradition and convention in art and architecture depends on an understanding of the social meanings of symbolic forms which has in recent years been a foundation of socialist aesthetic theory.

What will be the consequences of two or more periods of Thatcherite government for the balance of class powers in Britain? It is clear that a coherent series of measures will have the effect of weakening working-class, democratic and egalitarian claims of many kinds. The maintenance of unemployment at a level of three or four million will weaken trade unions and the rights of working people, without the countervailing advantages of the past 'corporatist' arrangements which conceded benefits — the 'social wage', legislation on health and safety, equal opportunities, trade union recognition — in return for wages limitation. The dismantling of the nationalized sector through privatization will establish regimes of capital more hostile to trade unions than public employers have generally been, and able to enter the field of battle against welfare provision or modes of economic planning in ways in which public corporations have not been free to do. Public corporations cannot make contributions to Conservative Party funds. The Conservatives are engaged in a major attack on the autonomy and powers of local government, through rate-capping and the abolition of the metropolitan authorities. The effect of these measures is both to weaken specific areas of influence of the working class and its allies, and to lessen the autonomy and neutrality vis-à-vis capitalist interests of an important sector of State power.

The Conservatives have had a significant success in one previously established area of public provision, through their sale of council houses. As the majority form of housing tenure has come to be private ownership, one ground of support for collectivist social policies is undermined, with serious implications for Labour's support. This is due in part to the fact that Labour policies have been rather out of touch on these issues. An obvious problem has been Labour's reluctance to recognize the insensitivity of many bureaucratic authorities toward their tenants. But perhaps more important is the failure to grasp the material superiority of the 'middle-class Welfare State' for its beneficiaries in the housing sector over the working-class sector of council housing. The privileged forms of saving made possible by tax-relief on mortgage interest, and by exemption from capital gains tax on owner-occupied properties, have probably been more important factors in the growth of home ownership even than questions of housing choice, decor and petty regulations. House ownership has simply become the most advantageous form of saving, and there have been strong tax inducements for families and individuals to take out a mortgage if they can afford to do so. Labour's emphasis on physical standards, such that council housing achieved an enormous improvement in the housing stock over a generation, blinded the party to the changed economic and social climate which it had helped to create. A hard-headed attention to the economic interests of its working-class voters is necessary if Labour is to retain their support.

Attacks are also in preparation by the Thatcherites on other fields of welfare provision. Public support for the more universal services of education and health has so far held firm against privatizing ideology, and opposition has succeeded in extracting a commitment to continued provision in these areas. Where the welfare system is nearly universal, and redistributes resources across phases of the life-cycle rather than between classes, it has been more difficult to discredit. The consensual basis of these aspects of welfare policy, though previously a ground of criticism by the left, has to some extent protected them against neo-liberal attack. But given time, these services will be subjected to such resource starvation and favouring of private-sector provision as to weaken their consumer base. The growth of occupational pensions is another area where private-sector insurance, aided by tax concessions, has been able to take an increasing share. Though the funds come in part from employees' incomes, the investment of these lies outside the influence of trade union representutives and removes another potential for democratic intervention in the economy, with significance for employment and industrial regeneration. Transport is a similar case, where against the logic of the social costs of energy, transport congestion and safety, public systems have had the greatest difficulty in securing investment support.

The right's attack on ethical approaches to inequality and injustice, and on the use of social policies to ameliorate them, has led to a prioritized strengthening of the state's means of violence. Moral consensus and force are contrasting means of conflict-resolution available to ruling classes, and each has its predictable consequences. Thatcherism means an increasingly armed and policed society, and a more violent one. The higher levels of violent crime in the United States, especially among the more marginal sectors of the population, are a product of its more mobile and individualist, and less contained, social structure. In the more solidaristic and class-divided society of the United Kingdom, violence takes a more collective form, whether in Toxteth or on the

Chelsea football terraces. The recent proposal by a government committee of enquiry for a league table of clubs responsible for football hooliganism gave this unhappy trajectory an unintended humour. Who would have expected even twenty years ago that Britain would become internationally noted for the levels of collective violence on its streets?

The radical measures designed to 'roll back' the Welfare State are securing profound changes in the balance of class power in Britain. The weakening of local government, welfare services, civil liberties, the nationalized sector and trade unions, entails that any future progressive government will no longer be able to start from the ground won in its last period of office, but will have to begin from a much weaker base of state power, social provision and class organization. The demographic opportunity of the period of numerical majority of the industrial working class, and the historical opportunity brought about by the anti-Fascist victory of 1945, will have been missed for good. Both the working-class movement and its middle-class allies, largely employed in the public sector, are being damaged by the Thatcherite offensive, and their numbers, confidence and institutional power are being eroded. The moral and intellectual basis of 'socialism' as a conception and a vision have also been sapped by these defeats. It is a matter of critical importance to conceive a strategy which can turn back this apparently irresistible tide of defeat. Otherwise, the idea of democratic socialism in Britain may have to be considered dead for all realistic purposes.

What combination or coalition of class forces does Thatcherism itself represent? Is this a stable and viable formation, or a self-contradictory one? We argued above that the historical opportunity for the new right arose as the employing class began to panic about the long decline of the British economy and the increasing problems of accommodating trade union power. It was in this context, and amid the recriminations following electoral defeat, that an ideologically tough-minded leadership was able to seize control of the Tory Party, and to carry a broader coalition behind its negative programme against welfarism. Even so, it took time for the Thatcherites to establish their ascendancy in the party, and the government needed the Falklands War to revive its electoral popularity after the disillusionment of the first years of recession and rising unemployment. The immediate 'class base' for this formation lies in social strata particularly threatened by 'inflation' and social conflict. It has offered many short-term benefits to its supporters, both financial, in tax-reductions for example, and moral, in a strong triumphalist celebration of employer and middle-class power. There has been a cult of 'strong men' — for example, Michael Edwardes at British Leyland, and Ian MacGregor at British Steel and the National Coal Board — with Mrs Thatcher herself as the embodiment of the 'resolute approach'. (Perhaps this radical departure from gender stereotype may have played a role in subtly discomposing the natural resistance to such authoritarian leadership.) But the vision of removing the obstacles to successful entrepreneurship fits the local and short-term horizons of the petty businessman much better than it does the perspectives of long-term planning and interlocking decisions of large corporations. For these, the role of governments has for forty years been critical in establishing a positive environment for growth. While the Thatcher Government has protected itself from capitalist attack by its attention to financial interests (through high interest rates, an overvalued pound, the early removal of exchange controls), its programme is poorly adapted to the 'real economy' of industry and services within Britain. Those employed in British-based companies, at almost every level save the highest, can only benefit from resources invested within this country. Here we should recall the old argument about a separation of owner and managerial interests. For although this was refuted for times of economic growth, when a company's prosperity also benefits its senior employees, it is more persuasive in a period of disinvestment and decline. Whereas shareholders can protect their savings by shifting them elsewhere, and especially overseas, employees must depend on work within Britain. To the extent that it fails to generate investment and economic growth, therefore — and there is little sign of any lasting success so far — Thatcherism is a self-contradictory programme.

The Break-Up of the Centre

The hegemony of Thatcherism has depended in part on the failure and loss of confidence of an earlier dominant political formation that was responsible for management of the post-war consensus. In an important article, Gareth Stedman Jones[14] drew attention to the break-up of a particular class alliance which had provided the backbone of Labour's periods of post-war rule. This was the alliance between a still mainly docile trade union movement, subordinated under strong union bureaucracies, and an Oxbridge-educated upper-middle-class political leadership who were the spiritual descendants of the philanthropic collectivistic liberalism of the Edwardian period. The regimes of Attlee and Gaitskell, and the influence of figures such as Dalton, Cripps, Strachey, Crossman and Crosland over two generations, represented this form of upper-middle-class leadership. The Fabian Society was the collective intellectual vehicle for this stratum, whose own occupational interest was in the rise of rational scientific administration and of the educated State-salaried service more generally, for which it provided the manpower. Its later eschewal of partisanship or collective position-taking brought the 'objective' attitudes of the higher civil service into Labour policy-making.

Accommodation to the rising power of the working class was the political prescription of influential Conservatives and Liberals as well as of those who opted for gradualist socialism. We can discern a political centre, with representatives in both dominant parties and among significant Liberal intellectuals such as Keynes and Beveridge, whose identification was with an educated, enlightened, salaried professional class more connected with the state than with business. This 'class fragment', whose role in the State and political apparatus gave it an importance far in excess of its numerical weight, was committed to 'modernization' of the British economy and society, and to the diminution of the divisive effects of inherited and traditional class divisions. Keynes even wrote of the 'euthanasia' of the rentier. The ultimate aim, then, was to incorporate the working class into a socialized capitalism: the state would provide a level of material security and other forms of social benefit and opportunity (health, education, housing, pensions, etc.) which would assure popular consent to the capitalist economy, and dissolve ideological and class-based threats to the social order. Clearly there were important value differences between members of this stratum who had identified themselves with the working-class movement (like Anthony Crosland) and were therefore egalitarian in outlook, and those (like MacMillan) whose outlook remained more that of enlightened and far-sighted members of the employing class. But the deep distaste of the Labour right for fundamental changes in the relations of ownership (however rationalized in terms of electoral necessity or the dangers of state bureaucracy) showed how difficult it was even for socialist members of this stratum to imagine an extension of the process of democratization and equalization beyond the level it had already reached in their own experience.

In office, the representatives of this modernizing stratum faced many institutional obstacles. In the economy, there remained a preponderance of financial and overseas-oriented institutions over those of modern manufacturing. This produced a characteristic preoccupation with the strength of the currency that reached a new level of destructiveness with the Thatcher government, but which had been an object of radical criticism for years before. Many British industries were backward in their orientation, and had maintained since the 1920s a traditionalist and coercive style of management which produced its own typical trade union response: the docks and shipbuilding were two industries that were substantially ruined by this history; and coal-mining was only saved from it by early nationalization. In the government service, especially in the ministries responsible for the economy, technical, managerial and scientific competence was minimal. Wilson's 'white heat of technological revolution' rhetoric, though disappointing in its results, therefore spoke to a genuine problem. 'Consensus' governments attempted both statist and liberal-market methods of industrial modernization, sometimes at the same moment: anti-monopoly legislation and the abolition of retail price maintenance on the one hand, forced industrial mergers, state subsidies and reconstructions on the other. They also sought to rationalize major areas of the state's activity on modern administrative lines, and local government, the National Health Service, and secondary and tertiary education were all subject to major reorganizations. They developed conciliatory 'corporatist' strategies of economic management, through agencies such as the National Economic Development Council, the Prices and Incomes Board, the Advisory Conciliation and Arbitration Service (ACAS), and through incomes policies such as the 1975 Social Contract. Eventually, entry into the Common Market was negotiated as a means of stimulating competition, but at a stage so late that many British industries were already at a huge relative disadvantage, and continued to lose markets. Recurrent balance-of-payments crises, rising inflation and unemployment rates in the 1970s, mounting industrial conflict, rates of economic growth lower than in most comparable countries, a declining share of world trade — all this indicated a cumulative failure of the 'modernizing' strategy. Thatcherism was made possible by this economic crisis, which it has proceeded to deepen. The declining and crisis-ridden British economy established the preconditions for the breakdown of consensus. But also important in the break-up of the post-war reforming alliance of the centre were the *social* dimensions of the British crisis. A critical early moment was the failure of Gaitskell and Crosland's revision of Clause Four, which gave notice that the programme of turning Labour into a 'modern' social democratic party would fail. Gaitskell's successors, manoeuvring after this defeat, were never able to call on the unquestioning commitment from the social democratic wing of the Labour Party that Gaitskell's crusades against the left had mobilized. The defection of the SDP began at this point.

A decomposition of the older structures of class consciousness did take place during the years of relative prosperity, but not in the way in which the reformers and modernizers of the managerial centre had hoped. Class solidarism was replaced not by a consensual agreement to slow advances towards relative social justice, but by increasing sectionalism and militancy. Deference, in the more conservative elements of the working class, was replaced by more individualist calculations of interest. Stable political allegiances began to diminish from 1951 onwards, as voters made up their minds increasingly by reference to government performance rather than class loyalty.[15] White-collar and professional employees, previously protected by a privileged status and economic advantage, responded to the demands of the manual trade unions by abandoning their ethos of respectable superiority to the trade union methods of strike action. The public sector generated a growth dynamic of its own. New and old consumer and producer interests, from the declining industries and regions to the inner-city twilight areas, were able to demand government action in response to their problems. New areas of moral and cultural difference and dissent began to make themselves felt. While this could to some extent be celebrated, as in the phenomenon of the Beatles, as a creative and benign emergence of ex-working-class youth into cultural flower (with parallels in fashion, theatre, cinema and writing), it always had a more sinister and disturbing aspect for the respectable, because of the associations of youth culture with drugs, sexual promiscuity and experimentation, street violence, attacks on parental and official authority, and other unacceptable forms of expression. The later development of a new sexual politics, and the assertion of different gender interests and life-styles — feminist, gay, or simply more libertarian and hedonistic — brought another dimension of differentiation with which the conventional political rhetorics could not cope. It was as if emancipation into relative prosperity and release from the mundane constraints of sheer hardship had lifted the lid off a bubbling cauldron of new social forces.

1968 saw the explosion of one generational element of this new brew.

The pace of social differentiation and fragmentation was rapid. British society found itself with burgeoning sub-cultural differences superimposed on its established class cultures. These differences — generational, sexual, ethnic, nationalist, educational, ideological — go some way to explaining the paralysis and division of a Labour Party faced with the political problem of integrating divergent social forces into a coherent bloc. An instrumental and consumerist politics, with whose advance Labour had colluded since the mid-fifties, eroded the ethical basis (derived in part, after 1945, from the collective memories of war-time sharing and sacrifice) by which Labour governments could exact loyalty and restraint from their supporters. Jack Jones's 'social contract' of the 1970s was a brave attempt to make such a commitment to social justice work. But the destruction of two Labour governments at the hands of the trade unions was as telling evidence as Labour's declining share of the vote of its increasingly shallow roots in the working class.

One fundamental weakness was the institutional and cultural limitations of British Labourism. The Labour Party lacked in-dividual membership, cadres, organizers, intellectual resources, political culture and 'outreach' through civil society, to match its earlier pre-eminence in voting support. The trade unions, as separate, mutually competing bodies (though not as a unified move-ment coordinated by the TUC — another problem for the modern-izers) were by contrast defensively strong. Labour was thus able to give relatively feeble expression to working-class interest when in office, and had little internal strength with which to resist the pressures from capital and the State machine in determining its economic priorities. Parliament and the Constitution, as Anthony Barnett has recently pointed out,[16] were something of a fetish that cut Labour off from its necessary base outside. The trade unions in these conditions were always available, if governments failed, as an alternative channel for working-class demands, however incom-patible these might be with one other and with broader political goals. Though minor participants, the groupings of the far left were always ready to support economistic demands of any group of workers, however relatively privileged, without regard to their implications for competing interests. Just as it is the role of bour-geois governments to further the collective interests of capital where necessary over those of particular capitalists, so socialist governments have to further universal and not merely particularist working-class interests. Labour governments in Britain were rarely able to do this.

The contrast with Sweden is most graphic.[17] There workers have retained a general commitment to class goals, and to the redistribution of wealth and power: the Social Democrats have held their support as reliable supporters of these interests. The Swedish trade unions, on the other hand, have been prepared to depend on political and universalist, rather than on merely sectionalist and economistic strategies to advance their members' interests. The current Swedish proposal for Worker Funds, designed to bring about a new element of social ownership of the means of production, has been pressed by the LO trade union federation on the Social Democratic Party as a strategic political demand, though it transcends and might ultimately inhibit the conventional wage-bargaining role of trade unions. In Britain, by contrast, the trade-union attitude to participation in decisions over the disposition of capital — as revealed, for example, in the response to the Bullock proposals or to the alternative plan movement — has usually been negative.

Just as the defeat of the Heath government by the miners (and by Heath's own misjudgements) put an end to the hegemony of the centre in the Tory Party, so did the demise of the Callaghan government after the public service workers' strikes produce a parallel disenchantment with consensus politics in the Labour Party, on both left and right. While the long-term factors discussed above were important in determining the 'break' of the SDP 'gang of four' from the Labour Party, also significant was the response of this group to the rise of the new Labour left. It is to this latter phenomenon that we now turn.

The Break from the Left.

The emergence of a new and younger membership in the Labour Party, especially drawn from white-collar and professional employment in the public sector, from the products of educational expansion, and from inner-city areas which were poorer and socially more mixed and marginal than older working-class communities, produced a militant 'new left' cadre. Labour parties in older working-class areas had in many cases become mere shells held together by small caucuses of councillors operating as local bosses, but with little remaining active membership. In turn, new memberships either captured these parties or forced the older leaderships to share power with the newcomers.

These new forces were substantially influenced by the experience of the extra-parliamentary movements and grassroots trade union militancy of the 1960s and 1970s, and by the role of the various Trotskyist groups in stimulating and organizing these. The Vietnam Solidarity Campaign, the Anti-Nazi League, and the short-lived student revolutionary movement of 1968 are the most important instances. These extra-parliamentary movements failed to generate independent revolutionary parties of the left, as some of their leading cadres had hoped, but they provided an effective social-ization into activist and somewhat vanguardist political organiz-ation for many young people. This then made possible a form of entryism and disciplined internal organization within the Labour Party of a quite new kind. These new political forces were in touch with many constituencies of radical politics — the peace move-ment, the anti-fascist campaigns, feminist and gay politics — and it would be a mistake to see them merely as conspiratorial cadres, without substantial social roots. It was fundamentally necessary to achieve some stronger form of political and even factional organiz-ation among Labour Party members if the weakness of the party under the pressures of office was ever to be remedied. The isolation of the old *Tribune* left in Parliament, and its lack of connection with any organized political force outside, had reduced it to little more than ideological posturing over many years. This was a model of leadership that the new left had to reject.

Nevertheless the new Labour left had a somewhat simplistic idea of the mechanics of power, at least until the second election defeat of 1983. There was a curious amalgamation of the 'parliamentary centralism' of the *Tribune* tradition, with the Leninist concept of the disciplined cadre party, in the idea that a Labour government could be made effective if only it were put under the firm control of party activists. The main strategy of the new forces was to increase activist influence, through the constitutional reforms which are discussed in Chapter Three. These were automatic reselection, a broader elec-torate for the party leader's election, and greater powers for the NEC over the party's election manifesto. The second aim was to radicalize the manifesto itself so that the new model party would have a socialist programme to implement when it took power. These goals were pursued in a climate of great bitterness, without much regard for their wider political effects on Labour's support. Inexperience, perhaps, gave rise to unlimited and unrealistic hopes of the changes that could be achieved, and to a denial of the actual diversity and indeed conservatism of much of Labour's support. There was some instrumentalism too in the attempt to exploit, and organize around, the personal popularity of Tony Benn, who was by no means an organic representative of these new tendencies, and whose greatest potential strength lay in a 'broader' democratic appeal. There seemed to be an underlying idea that a Gramscian 'war of position' could be transformed into a decisive 'war of manoeuvre' if only the organizational preconditions within the party could be met. The wider dysfunctions of open party conflict, superficial programmes, and patently opportunistic policy compromises in any electoral contest were not sufficiently recognized.

The parliamentary and electoral vanguardism of the post-1979 period has subsequently been enacted in industrial and trade union terms in the miners' strike of 1984–5. There was a visible shift within the NUM to a more centralist mode of organization — not only ballots but also other procedures of national discussion were apparently suspended during the strike. The formation of disciplinary committees headed by the national union officers was an ominous side-sign of an authoritarian drift of thinking among the leadership. The issues at stake in the strike — mass unemployment, the threat to old-established working-class communities, anti-trade union laws, recession and economic decline, national energy policy — lent themselves to a broad argument and campaign to which a miners' struggle could uniquely force attention. But the choice was made to fight the battle on a narrower front, within the mining communities and the 'old' working class, through attempts to solidify and intensify the strike and to seek support for its picket lines. Liberal concerns about ballots and mass picketing and intimidation of working miners were shrugged off, though these issues lost the miners much public support. A dominant memory was of the successful miners' strikes of 1972 and 1974 — a period of militant sectionalism in which determined collective force (the mass pickets at Saltley) had been able to overcome cautious governments in the conditions of post-oil-crisis energy shortage. The NUM's objectives in the 1984 strike seemed deliberately pitched as demands which were not amenable to the usual kinds of trade union negotiation and compromise. A victory for the miners would mean humiliating defeat for the National Coal Board and the Thatcher government. This was a defiant war of manoeuvre, an attempt to restore working-class confidence through mass struggle and to achieve a decisive class victory.

From the outset of the strike it has seemed improbable that such a victory could be won, despite the immense resolution and fortitude of the striking miners, and the strength of community feeling against unemployment. The prepared strength of the government's position, and the failure to obtain solid support within the miners' union, have counted heavily against the NUM leadership. It seems likely in any case that a lesser victory would have been possible, more swiftly and at lower cost, if the union had set itself such specific objectives as withdrawal of the original five closure proposals, negotiated criteria for closure, and alternative investment funds, rather than in principle excluding economic criteria. A broader and more outwardly-oriented campaign might then have been able to unify rather than divide the labour movement and other anti-government opinion. It was surprising that the TUC and Labour Party leaderships, who must be committed to this kind of conception in principle, did not argue more outspokenly during the strike for the pursuit of a more attainable victory.

Foundations for an Alternative to Thatcherism

Social Ownership

The underlying argument of this book is for a broad class alliance which can resume the post-war advance towards a more democratic, egalitarian but also pluralist society. It is the essence of a socialist politics that this must encompass the social ownership and control of large-scale capital. There can be no equal citizenship in a society where large-scale capital is in the control of private property-owners, and where economic decisions affecting great numbers of people are not democratically accountable. Market mechanisms, given the powers accruing to large-scale producers in modern capitalist economies, do not themselves 'democratize' economic decisions: 'consumer choice' is qualified as an instrument of socially just distribution by the vastly unequal powers and bargaining resources of different consumers; while patterns of inheritance and the means of allocating current incomes from labour ensure that the actual division of income and wealth has no ethically defensible foundation. The model of a market economy in which participants compete on a relatively equal basis, which is the idealized framework of neo-liberal theory, has little correspondence with the facts of a late capitalist economy. Such a hypothetical society of equal competitors, regulated by a State which merely maintained the rules of fair competition, would have some moral attractions if it were feasible, and arguments for a free labour market and an active small business sector pay some tribute to this conception. But an economy which depends on long-term, large-scale investments of capital, and in which there is a high degree of interdependency between the decisions of different economic actors, has of its nature already been socialized and collectivized. Planning has become the essence of the operation of modern capitalist economies. The question at issue is whether this should be undertaken mainly by private industrial and financial corporations, or in ways to which workers, consumers and elected governments have effective access. Those who attack the power which trade union organizations or even majorities of members sometimes exercise over trade unionists invariably neglect to criticize the power wielded by shareholders and managers over employees. There is no reason why it should be just to be subject to the power of the owner of capital, but unjust to be subjected to the collective decision of owners of labour power. Arguments for democratic procedures which are relevant in the one case are equally applicable to the other. The recession, and the problems of managing the reconstruction and modernization even of advanced Western economies in ways not damaging to the standards of life of these societies, have demonstrated in the last decade how fundamentally capitalism has depended for its success on an increasing measure of social regulation and control.

The argument for 'Socialization' is then both ethical, insofar as it concerns the economic dimension of democracy and civil rights, and also more pragmatic, insofar as it seeks to restore the conditions of full employment and rising material standards. There is reason to be cautious and undogmatic about specific mechanisms of social ownership and control. Few Western socialists now favour a 'command economy' of the Soviet kind, or a monopoly of economic powers in the hands of the state. There has been increasing recognition, even in Communist countries, of the value of market mechanisms in measuring comparative economic performance and in assuring the efficient allocation of resources. The time-scale of 'social ownership' of the economy has to be a long one, and will require the development of many different skills, methods and strategies by socialists. But this conception of the transformation of a capitalist into a social mode of production, and the abolition of the distinction and contradiction between a class that lives and rules by ownership and a class that lives by labour, is the basic heritage of the Marxist tradition. It must be defended in principle by any socialist party.

Four of the chapters which follow relate to these objectives in specific and medium-term ways. *A Statutory Right to Work* argues for the 'socialization' of one important dimension of the mixed economy — namely, the labour market — in such as a way as to guarantee a basic right to employment. It proposes specific interventions through both the public and private sectors to secure this. *The Politics of Workers' Plans* examines the workers' plan movement as an innovative attempt to shift the emphasis of trade union activity away from bargaining over wages within a market system, towards determination of investment decisions. This reorientation of trade unions away from their present functions of 'collective capitalism' within the labour market, towards the more social functions of participation in the regulation of the broader economy (both through corporate bargaining and through the agencies of the State) is a common theme of both chapters. It is also consistent with the argument of *The New Left and the Labour Party*, which is that the weakness of a political party vis-à-vis the trade unions as representatives of the working class has been one of the major long-term limitations of British Labourism, and needs to be addressed seriously if any way out of the current impasse of the left is to be found. Finally, the chapter *Power to the Regions* argues for a stronger economic role for elected regional authorities as an intermediate form of public economic agency, which might allow for the development of a more decentralized and competitive model of public enterprise.

A Socialist Populism

A second, neo-Gramscian, assumption of these essays is that an alternative hegemony to that of the neo-liberal right will depend on the construction of a *normative* basis for a socialist programme. Unity is effected in the formation of a dominant bloc not by mere aggregation of discrete economic interests, but by appeals to common social definitions and values. (Paradoxically this also explains the importance to the right of the issue of 'law and order' — revived prominently in the miners' strike — as it does the 'Falklands factor' in the fortunes of Thatcherism and the weight of anti-Communist rhetoric in Britain and America.) The development of a vigorous intellectual life of the left in the past three decades should have provided some resources for the renewal of a socialist populism, though in recent years the initiative in fashioning appeals to popular convictions and sentiments has lain with the radical right. The repudiation of merely 'ethical' and 'humanist' arguments in influential segments of the Marxist left has attacked a necessary dimension of any popular socialist ideology. But the revival of Marxist intellectual work, and the development of the social sciences more generally, does make possible a more adequate and complex theory of social transition. It is no longer the case, as was plausibly suggested twenty years ago, that neither a sociology nor a Marxism is available as indigenous resources to British intellectuals, a deficiency of culture and ideology which might explain the relative failure of the British labour movement.

An alternative hegemony is not, however, to be fashioned merely from an orthodox Marxism, joined through the forced march of a determined sectarian vanguard to the institutions of the labour movement. Such attempts become more difficult as the structures of 'corporate' class consciousness and the older working-class communities and sub-cultures are eroded. The 'Bolshevik' model of leadership and revolutionary transition, which is still important to orthodox Marxist political groupings, grates with the democratic and pluralist aspirations of contemporary societies. Individuals expect to be consulted — for example, by vote — on issues which concern them, and are usually unamenable to the definition of themselves as passive masses waiting to be led from above. Leaders claiming to represent class interests seem increasingly to risk being seen as the 'over-political' and even oppressive members of a prescriptive minority, and not as natural spokesmen. The roles of party caucuses and union organizers may be so vulnerable to criticism because they claim more legitimacy than many union members or Labour voters are willing to accord to them. The diminution of the spokesmen of a universal class, to the perceived advocates of sectional or merely 'ideological' interests, has placed great difficulties in the way of a movement whose procedures and working assumptions have been based on a belief in its actual or potential representation of a class majority. It is one thing to place a picket to ask support for the decision of an established majority, and another when the democratic basis of decisions is deeply contested. The manual working class from which the imagery and consciousness of a socialist politics has historically derived now appears to be a declining class formation (though still a large one) not a class in the ascendant. The decline in the number of coal miners from 750,000 in

1945 to 200,000 today (and of dockworkers by a similar proportion) explains in quantitative terms why the mobilization of the 'old' working class has become a less than decisive industrial and political weapon, and inevitably gave the miners' strike the quality of a desperate if heroic last stand.

It is truly extraordinary that the ideology of rights has been appropriated by conservatives, by the party of private property, in an individualist reaction to the apparent excesses of bureaucratic power. In the process, economic participation has been redefined as access to the opportunities of the market, and political participation as the opportunity to vote individually and privately rather than to be a participant in more collective or deliberative procedures. This has come about through a loss of legitimacy of collective forms of provision (for example in housing), and of solidaristic forms of decision-making (e.g. by unions) which formerly seemed able to presuppose more basic loyalty among members than they now can. But while rejection of the injustices of the market mechanism is fundamental for socialists, opposition to individual choice in the 'political' market of votes is not a tenable position. Socialists will be rightly hostile to the imbalance of electoral influences — apparent in, for example, the weight of commercial or government powers in the mass media — and properly prefer deliberative and face-to-face modes of decision-making to privatized ones. But the ballot, unlike the economic market place, gives each voter equal weight, and has historically been the means by which subordinate classes have been able to overrule the unjust claims of property. Socialists should be seeking to extend the writ of the suffrage to decisions over the disposition of capital, and not to protect forms of bureaucratic power (even if these happen to be locally in the hands of the left) which have already lost their popular legitimacy. The essays which follow are for this reason uniformly favourable to democratic electoral procedures, in the areas of party, regional government and national elections.

In other historical and societal conjunctures, it might be possible to argue for a more directly class-based politics which could hope to unify the great majority of workers by hand and by brain against the irresponsible powers of the capitalist economy. Indeed, since capitalism will not, in the absence of major mobilizations, concede powers of ownership, of bargaining, of taxed income and wealth, or of political control, it is evident that an explicit class politics of economic democratization and redistribution remains necessary, as a central part of contemporary socialist strategy. But the recent past in Britain gives no reason to hope that such a politics can succeed by itself. The earlier language of class solidarity, which did provide the explicit basis of voter identification with Labour until 1951, is no longer available. Labour's 'core constituency' has diminished, with the decline of the manual workforce and with the migration and relocation of inner city populations. This support is now increasingly concentrated in the north of England, Scotland, Wales and inner London. While it is possible theoretically to assert an identification of interests between manual and non-manual workers in opposition to the owners and controllers of capital, the idea of a unified working class (an 'us' united against 'them') now has little purchase in common culture. Membership of the sub-cultural working class in the older sense, which implied an experience of common hardship, subordination and imposed inferiority, may be just what large numbers believe they have (or had) escaped from. The move towards a less status-divided society in the post-war period is seen by a majority as a gain, not a loss.

Socialists in Britain are therefore now obliged to formulate their conceptions and proposals in universalist terms, and not by reference to the solidarity and values of a subordinate class. As John Westergaard has pointed out,[18] 'corporate' class consciousness has been a source not only of positive solidarity but of limitation of aspiration and rational capacity for the labour movement. A more universalist politics, evoking the common rights of citizens, should provide a less closed rhetoric and frame of reference. The paradoxical strength of Thatcherite populism is that it *has* been universalist in this sense, proclaiming in its own way a 'classless' vision of individual but universal self-interest against what it has chosen to represent as merely sectional collective interests. Neither a return to traditionalist class politics, nor an attempt to aggregate separate interest groups each with its own specially targeted policy proposals, will suffice as a counter to this universalist populism of the right. The debris of consensus, and the absence of intellectual coherence and moral principle in its latter years, provides an opportunity for theoretical reformulation on the left as well as the right.

The breadth of the class alliance now needed to defeat Thatcherism makes this universalism particularly important as a minimal condition of progress. An argument of this book is that Thatcherism has to be defeated, before the conditions for a longer-term advance towards a socialist society can be restored. Almost as important as the unification of subordinate class forces, therefore, becomes the division and defection from Thatcherism of significant elements of the bourgeoisie: not only elements of its salaried service class, most readily in the public sector, but even some of the possessors and controllers of fractions of capital itself, where this is deployed within the UK. It is not, of course, that these strata can be persuaded to support socialist programmes: this they will not do. But they can be persuaded to recognize that 'Thatcherism' is a self-contradictory and damaging strategy for the British economy and society, and to give support to fractions of the centre for whom it would be crucial to find some compromise with working-class interests in order to regain influence over the British State. This is a far from improbable development. Major sections of capital did support or tolerate the 'corporatist' strategies of the 1960s and early 1970s, through such institutions as the NEDC.

The terms of such a progressive compromise have to relate to the indigenous ideological traditions in which earlier advances towards citizenship and social democracy have been accomplished. It cannot be just through the rhetoric of a theoretical Marxism whose effective base in the British class structure is confined to a younger intelligentsia and to small though important cadres of trade union activists among the working class. While the renewal of a Marxist tradition has been important to political and economic under-standing, and should be defended as such against academic and other attacks, this theoretical utility is still distinct from its restricted normative purchase in everyday political debate.

Collectivist liberals and reformist socialists successfully contested the ideology of possessive individualism and the free market in ethical terms, both in the pre-First World War period of reform, and in the radical populism of the Second World War and after. This led eventually to an influential advocacy of the moral ideal of equality (Tawney and subsequently Crosland); of an extended concept of social and economic citizenship (T.H. Marshall); and of altruism as the basis for universal social services such as the NHS (R.M. Titmuss). The concept of democratization is particularly crucial, since it summarizes a history of advances towards political and social democracy, and is yet capable of conceptual extension into the economic domain. A political programme which gave emphasis to democratization would, however, cut against the left as well as against its enemies, in certain important respects. To succeed on this terrain will require a programme of political renewal by socialists themselves, and not merely an insistence that others should mend their authoritarian ways. One reason why the advocacy of greater democracy sometimes makes little headway is because of confusion between genuinely universalist arguments for democratic procedures, and more partisan and partial attempts to invoke the value of democracy to legitimate more sectional causes. It is an unfortunate paradox that the framework of discourse which ought to be the left's most powerful argument against capitalism has recently been so successfully deployed by the right and centre against the labour movement's own procedures. This is sometimes made possible by the left's retention of forms of minority leadership which presuppose a passive class majority which no longer exists in reality. In the absence of actual majorities whose decisions can be demonstrated by overt procedures, reliance is placed upon 'essential' majorities, who are represented by a small number of leaders or activists in a classic substitutionist version of class politics. The chapter on *The New Left and the Labour Party* contains a fuller critique of this position, and advocates a more thoroughgoing democratization of the Labour Party against both vanguardist and oligarchic 'parliamentarist' conceptions of democracy managed from above.

It is a painful paradox of this argument for the centrality of democratic principle that it will only have credibility and effectiveness if its consequences for the left's own powers and methods are also accepted and acted upon. Labour does not now represent a 'real' majority, merely distorted by the mass media and capitalist power. While challenging these specific inequities, it has to acknowledge that it is now a party which in 1983 held less than a third of the national vote. Acceptance of the implications and limitations of this actual position of a strong minority is now a prerequisite for any persuasive advocacy of socialist principles in Britain. This should affect the way Labour thinks of its relationship with potential rivals and allies (including the nationalists and the two centre parties); its attitude to the electoral system, which now seriously overrepresents its actual support and sustains illusions of an imminent majority which might usher in an era of socialism; and also the internal political organization of the Labour Party and trade unions. Unless principled positions are taken in these spheres, arguments for greater democracy will be discounted as special pleading.

The effectiveness of Ken Livingstone's campaign to defend the GLC against abolition, and its mobilisation of very wide support, shows the potential of an argument for democracy when this is deployed consistently by the left. The political courage involved in putting up four candidates for re-election and thus risking Labour control of the council, was important in demonstrating fidelity to the principle of majority choice. This contrasted with the difficulties encountered by the miners' and dockers' leaderships with their own members, when they refused to allow ballots on strike action.

Democratization of the political system provides a significant safeguard to liberals of the centre against 'authoritarian' tendencies from the left or right. It is thus an important issue in the construction of any explicit or de facto anti-Thatcher alliance. In this book the chapters *Political Arguments for Proportional Representation* and *Power to the Regions* put forward specific 'democratic' preconditions of a 'broad alliance' strategy which is intended to maintain a secure power-base for socialists and the left as well as to defeat Thatcherism. The chapter on Northern Ireland makes a case for a democratic solution to this problem, through a concept of self-determination which acknowledges the legitimate (and in any case militantly defended) rights of both Northern Irish communities. The concept of democratic access and control has potential leverage on other programmatic areas — for example, on policies for more pluralist access to and control of the communications media, where there might be some common ground with radical liberals, and for the democratization of capital, where there might be little. There is scope, within the broad concept of democratization, for socialists to work in parallel both for minimal agreements with the centre, and for support for more far-reaching changes. A more confident socialist movement would assume, from the long-term developments of a hundred or more years, that increasing popular access to decision-making in all its forms would be to its benefit, even if not always in a direct and instantaneous manner.

A second concept with significant resonance in recent British progressive and reformist history is that of social rights, or citizenship. The roots of this are in an idea of the common good, which was itself the product of an earlier idealist critique of possessive individualism. This way of thinking had a specific national resonance in a society which prided itself on its relatively peaceful and evolutionary progress towards democracy, and which had avoided in modern times the most bitter forms of class struggle such as had occurred in France, with the suppression of the Paris Commune in 1871, and in Germany in the inter-war period. While ideologies of national harmony can have a merely tranquillizing effect, there are many positive aspects to the identification of the British with conceptions of non-violent and peaceably resolved conflict. This national image has been important in the British view of decolonization which, inasmuch as it does correspond to some reality of peaceful transition and adjustment, has probably ameliorated (despite Powell) the savageness of the British backlash to the loss of empire. In relation to this ideal state of acknowledged social relationship and mutual obligation, Thatcherism is vulnerably divisive and violent. The polarization of the country by region, the contrast of inner city devastation and peripheral growth, and especially the proliferating life-tragedies of long-term unemployment, are morally unacceptable facts in a society whose self-conception has been one of social peace. Just as pre-capitalist values remain active in the 'social Catholicism' of Italy and France, so in Britain ideas of moral obligation even in an unequal society remain rooted in political thought and practice. Higher levels of collective violence are an inevitable consequence of a more competitive and coercive regime. Not only new methods of policing are being learned in Belfast and translated back to civil conflicts on the mainland, but also images of collective hatred and despair which are then acted out on the streets with fire and stones. Belfast is on the road to becoming a generic condition. 'Law and order', like democracy, is a rhetorical token which ought, in the different terms of civility and social peace, to be capable of being turned against the right. Possessive individualism generates conflict and the necessity for its forceful repression. The contrary concepts of common membership and morally sanctioned rights and obligations ought to be capable of renewal in a counter-hegemony of the left.

The idea of social membership requires a more extensive theoretical justification in contest with competitive and individualist concepts of man. This was the basis for Durkheim's sociological critique of individualism, and for the development of his major critical concept of anomie. In a differentiated and mobile society, attention to the social needs for emotional relatedness and containment is a necessary part of a socialist vision. These have tended to be neglected in an uncritical endorsement of the benefits of large-scale organization and bureaucracy, against which the right has been able to rally some traditionalist discontent. Elsewhere[19] I have explored the relevance of psychoanalytic concepts of relationship for a socialist view of man, and the conception of the family and other institutions devoted to primary relationships which might follow from this. These concerns, which also involve questions of gender equality, will be developed more fully in a subsequent book. Normative concepts of social rights need to be more than pioussounding substitutes for political action. Workable compromises and alliances have to be constructed in definite policy, and not merely be the subject of that kind of feeble adjuration to 'nego-tiated solutions' which has substituted for more trenchant thinking by Labour leaders in several recent crises, from the Falklands to the miners' strike. The plausibility of the view that conflicts can be resolved by political means depends on courage and clarity in spelling out the grounds for defensible compromises. This book makes two proposals intended to exemplify the potential benefit of arguments from social rights. The most far-reaching of these is in the chapter on *A Statutory Right to Work,* which advocates the legal enactment of a right to employment and a strategy in which this would be made actual over the period of one parliament. Its achievement would require, in return, a significant change in the wage-bargaining role of trade unions, most probably in the direc-tion of a more centralized and coordinated system. This is because the right to work would oblige governments (and the employing class) to forego the collective sanction on working people of the threat of unemployment, although individuals and categories of worker would still be subject to the loss of particular jobs. The reform would also have major implications for tax and welfare policies, in the redistribution of income to the newly employed or re-employed, and in the greatly reduced incidence of poverty and social security support which would then result. A commitment to full employment would generate resources for private and social investment, which would have many consequences for the quality of life of local communities, and for decision-making structures to develop appropriate projects where these are needed in the public sector. (On a patchwork and piecemeal basis, some of these have already been begun by current employment-generation pro-grammes.) Access of all members of society to work (or to the acceptable equivalents of education and training programmes, voluntary early retirement or part-time work, 'Sabbaticals' etc.) would also have deep implications for the moral and social order. It would make possible a strengthening of the social texture, and reduce the probable incidence of collective and individual disorder. This proposal, which both seeks to restore the earlier basis of the post-war consensus on full employment, and also to advance from it in the means of social planning and coordination, is the most funda-mental put forward in this volume. The chapter on *Power to the Regions* makes the related case for a stronger decentralized level of economic decision-making, especially important in relation to a socially planned labour market.

A second proposal involving the idea of extended social rights is set out in the chapter on *Comprehensive Education after 18*. This argues for an extension of educational rights to include an entitlement to at least one year's full-time (or part-time equivalent) education in adult life. It seeks to break the existing link between possession of academic credentials (mainly held by children of the middle class) and entitlement to education and its funding, proposing instead a broader range of educational programmes for the majority of post-school age, which should include instruction in basic skills, vocationally related courses, and the development of personal aptitudes and interests. This chapter also imagines universities as comprehensive and popular institutions, which make cultural resources and facilities available to the whole community.

Pluralism

An important theme of this book is that socialists have today to be pluralist, and to acknowledge the diversity of interests and life-styles which political programmes must reconcile. It is a difficult paradox that radical programmes must now be both universalist, in seeking a common definition of social rights and obligations, and pluralist in recognizing unavoidable and indeed desirable differences in social values. The process of differentiation, described first by liberal-individualist theorists of the division of labour such as the classical economist Adam Smith, and later in the more holistic tradition of classical sociology (Durkheim, Weber, Simmel and Tönnies), has had an irrevocable and beneficial part in the construction of contemporary social forms. Socialists have to take account of this diversification of the social structure, as well as of the grosser phenomena of class subordination and class conflict more familiar to them from the main socialist and Marxist traditions. There is no possible return in democratic societies to simple prescriptive communities of 'mechanical solidarity', except as one available choice (e.g. a self-sufficient commune) among many. An important dimension of this pluralism is in the moral and cultural domains. The overcoming of scarcity creates the preconditions for an increasing diversity of life activities, whether expressed in the proliferation of specialized fields of knowledge, the practice of new kinds of participatory physical sport or expressive art, or the development of distinctive kinds of social community.

Such a pluralism need not be merely an anodyne resignation in the face of gross inequalities of wealth and power. The only chapter in this book which is mainly theoretical in content — *A Theory of*

Complex Equality — argues that it is possible to support both a definition of common rights of political membership and economic citizenship, and a diversity of separate spheres of social and cultural value. Freedom is not only defined in individual terms — though individual freedom should of course be underwritten by universal civil rights, and is enhanced by a diversity of available social alternatives. What is distinctive about this argument is the recognition that choices are socially constructed, and that particular ways of life and spheres of value need to be defended from invasion. The one-dimensional values which typically threaten invasion in modern societies are those of capital and monolithic political or religious ideologies. Justice consists in respect for the autonomy of different spheres of value — and indeed it is necessary for a contemporary socialism to celebrate the variety of socially made forms of life. The regional decentralization and autonomy discussed in a later chapter is one example of such a desirable social diversity. In London, a large metropolis where there is no single dominant culture, the GLC has pursued a cultural policy and a defence of diverse ethnic and sexual values which explicitly recognizes the variety of the constituencies and social movements that it represents, and in so doing it has pointed to the way in which a pluralist socialist politics might be developed. Certainly the equation of socialism with a monochromatic and coercive uniformity bears little relation to what most people in a modern society now want.

A pluralist approach is necessary in terms of the 'broad alliance' strategy required by socialists, as well as for more basic reasons of principle. The fragmentation of the electorate, and the clear diversity of values and identifications involved in party allegiances, make a capacity to unify and orchestrate different interests fundamental to the work of a modern socialist party. The achievement of this aim, to the extent of reconstructing an electoral majority, may no longer be within the power of the Labour Party, as its electorate has fragmented and polarized. For this reason the possibility of some measure of combination of Labour and one or more centre parties against the right is explored in this book. The chapter *Political Arguments for Proportional Representation* argues that the existing 'first past the post' system is ill-adapted to a fragmented electorate (especially when left-wing parties are poor at articulating and unifying different interests) and suggests that socialists would do better with a more plural system in which they could pursue distinctive goals and programmes without allowing the right to benefit from the division of opposition parties. It will nevertheless be necessary to compete within a pluralist system for the maximum support and leverage for a socialist programme, and to improve the Labour Party's capacities to organize its forces for this contest. The role of the party in this struggle is discussed in the chapter on *The New Left and the Labour Party*.

The enrichment of the discourse of social science and especially sociology in the last twenty years — an advance in which socialists and Marxists have taken a leading role — provides the means to think about the social system in more complex terms than was previously possible. Thus the ideological lacunae which the editors of *New Left Review* identified in the early 1960s as major weaknesses of the British left have been substantially repaired in the subsequent expansion of radical culture; while the renewal of the Marxist and sociological traditions in Britain has supplied the materials for a politically engaged socialist theory. The recruitment by the Greater London Council of many socialist intellectual workers, as a means of strengthening its policy-forming capacity, gives some idea of what could be done by other Labour authorities and by a Labour government centrally. In London this has enabled the GLC to produce substantial policy analysis in many areas (e.g. the London economy, the implications of cable technology) where this would not otherwise have occurred. The experience of the Lucas Aerospace shop-stewards and CAITS, which is discussed in the chapter on *Workers' Plans and Industrial Democracy*, shows that it is possible for planning to take a more facilitating form than in the earlier Fabian administrative model, supporting workers and others in the development of their own initiatives.

The lead in deploying politically committed researchers and planners has been taken by the Thatcher conservatives in Britain, whose think-tanks have been important in giving the government a coherent purpose and momentum. Information and research of all kinds are inexpensive commodities, relative to their potential benefits, and a measure of 'redundancy' in the supply of data and new ideas is desirable insofar as it allows many alternatives to be considered. In an 'information society' the left should not be backward in supporting a greater availability of information of all kinds, scientific, technological and social. The model of recruiting politically attached staff-workers to government originated in the United States, where substantial changes of personnel are customary when a new party takes office. The adoption of this model both by Thatcherites on the right, and by the Greater London Council on the left, is an indicator of the subtle influence of 'pluralist' assumptions as these become more applicable to the British social structure. Ken Livingstone's informal 'meet the people' style, his skill with television and broadcasting media, and his attraction of a personal following, make him incidentally the most American of British politicians, in his mode of operation rather than in any superficial imitation.

From the increasing sophistication of the social sciences, it is now possible to recognize the complexity of interests which a modern class structure generates. From Weberian sociologists, socialists can learn that collective conflict and its resolution is an inevitable condition of society which can never be wholly overcome. Conflicts between different groups of producers (even in conditions of workers' ownership or control), between competing consumer interests, and even between the immediate interests of the present generation and the long-term benefit of the next, will remain to be resolved by political or other means in any conceivable dispensation. The socialization of capital will not remove the necessity for choices between present consumption (wages) and investment for the future (which requires the appropriation of some form of surplus). Conflict between the existing institutions of labour and capital must not be confused with a rejection of the need and function of investment as such. The development of a social theory which is able to reflect the complexity of present society is a necessary precondition of an advance towards socialism which is not continually forced into crisis or forms of coercion by the inadequacy of its own social maps.

What follows from a greater recognition of inherent collective conflict (for example, between workers with different bargaining powers, between richer and poorer regions, or between strata with different resources of 'cultural capital') is a heightened priority for politics as the typically rational and deliberative means of resolving differences of interest. Critics of electoralism must not forget that the system of 'one person one vote' uniquely equalizes the formal powers of individuals in society, in contrast to the greater inequality of resources which derives from the market or from the claims of technical competence. A preference for political mechanisms over all others should therefore be a signal mark of socialist values. This book suggests a number of means of strengthening the system of political decision-making, within parties, in the electoral system, in the system of local government, and in the idea of a second chamber of parliament which represents functional and regional interests rather than hereditary or aldermanic ones.

A broad alliance strategy depends on a careful estimation of the real interests of different strata, and of the ways in which they can be reconciled in political programmes. To emphasize normative and universal definitions of citizenship is not to deny that conflicts of interest will persist and must be dealt with by compromise or in the last resort by decision in favour of one side. Concretely, the project of a broad alliance will have to reconcile the relatively privileged interests of the credential-holding professional workers, officials and managers of a complex society (strata becoming more numerous and powerful in late capitalism) and the interests of a majority of wage-earners and their dependants. The relative bargaining strength of the participants in the earlier alliance of middle-class professionals and industrial workers has been changed in favour of the former in recent years, and a politics which ignores this division (which is approximately reflected in the split between Labour and the Alliance parties) is unlikely to gain much purchase. The argument for compromise is not derived merely from aggregation of hypothetical votes: the leverage exercised by different class fractions depends not only on their voting strength in elections, but also on their collective capacity to define the political agenda and to sustain or undermine particular programmes. The middle-class components of a centre-left formation will inevitably have more weight than their numbers per se would indicate. The aim of socialists must be to reduce the autonomy and weight of capital and property, through an alliance between the classes of worker and functionary. This is the only plausible democratic strategy for the gradual socialization of large-scale private property — one which makes possible the continued operation of modern industrial organizations and the advance of high living standards, while changing their ultimate ownership and legitimation. This is a potential consequence of the increased power of the state, of the 'socialized capitalism' of pension funds and insurance funds, and of the bargaining power of trade unions. Capitalism is being 'socialized' through the marginalization of the individual capitalist and his replacement by the custodians of a large-scale impersonal capital many of whose rights of ownership, even without workers' funds, are actually derived from the pension and insurance funds of employees. The recurrent role of predatory individual capitalists (for example, in the newspaper industry in Britain and elsewhere) might seem to suggest the fragility of this 'socialization' thesis, but it would clearly be quite feasible for governments to insulate the press from such gross interventions, through some kind of 'ownership trust' concept. While the Thatcher government's policy of encouraging building societies to enter the financial markets on a more competitive basis is part of its drive towards privatization and laissez-faire, this also draws attention to an important alternative model of corporate ownership and control which could be extended and encouraged by socialists.

The dispute between 'revisionists' and their opponents in the 1950s had the 'managerial revolution' thesis as one of its major issues. The revisionists assumed a degree of social responsibility of capital which subsequent history has not vindicated. But in the goal of transforming the service class of large-scale capital and establishing a more accountable management of socially owned forms of production, there may be more common ground between the advocates of a progressive technocracy (Galbraith is its leading exponent) and socialists committed to develop forms of democratic ownership and control. A theory of 'mega-capital' underpinned Labour's strategy for 'planning' agreements and nationalization of a number of leading corporations after 1974. Such a direct assault now seems unlikely to succeed, though in those many instances where government determines the conditions of operation of a monopoly or near-monopoly producer (British Airways, British Telecom, BNOC, for example) the case for public ownership should be sustainable. But more plural and indirect means of increasing social accountability also need to be developed. At any event, until and unless the Labour Party and the trade unions train a cadre of planners and managers capable of taking a more effective part in corporate decision-making,[20] programmes for greater public control may in any case founder on a lack of social commitment among the expert, and of technical expertise among the committed.

Such an economic strategy of the 'centre left' is in conflict with the new right's reassertion of the interests of the individual capitalist and the rentier-shareholder. But we have already suggested that Thatcherism may in reality be the ideology and programme of a declining class fraction, whose historical opportunity to exercise class leadership was provided by the intensity of the British crisis. As the self-contradictory effects of Thatcherism as a strategy for British economic revival become more evident — through disinvestment, rising unemployment with its eventual consequence of 'under-consumption', and civil conflict — it should be possible to achieve majority support for an alternative reforming programme.

In this process it will be important both to pay regard to the conciliation and incorporation of middle-class interests, and to ensure that a long-term strategic conception of Britain's future is renewed and argued. Thatcherism has shown that the definition of social conflict does not merely reflect but also profoundly shapes it. In Britain a party of the left without working-class and trade-union roots would be condemned to remain a minority fraction, no matter how energetic and skilful its leadership, and to this extent Labour still has a long-term advantage in its contest with the SDP. Holding the middle classes' commitment to universal provision in the crucial sectors of health and education will require a sensitivity to their high demands of these services, and a consequent strategy of incremental improvement rather than of radical redistribution within them. But it should be possible to defend the egalitarian principle of universal public services, and to continue it to new areas of necessarily public provision (the environment, for example). Once again the Labour GLC, at least in its later phase, has shown itself to be intuitive in its response to these dilemmas of 'balance'. It has been able to ensure, in its public transport and cultural policies, that it meets the interests of both working-class and middle-class consumers (the latter probably making disproportionate use of both these amenities), and also to involve new minorities in council-initiated programmes. It has by these means extended the usage and support for these services, and enhanced the reputation of a socialist public authority.

The problems of sectionalism and conflict among the various segments of potential support for an alternative hegemony become less crippling when they are admitted to rational discourse. Socialists will have to assert the priority of universal over partial interests where this is necessary, and this will be more feasible if they are candid about the conflicts of purpose and interest which their politics must reconcile. This has implications for political style and leadership. Labour needs to set out a longer time-scale of discussion and to introduce its own historical perspective into the political debate. Just as Thatcher gained some credit from her early insistence that there were no easy solutions to Britain's economic problems, so the left needs to make clear its own awareness of a long-term crisis, and the difficulty of reconciling all short-term competing interests in an immediate programme. Labour will need to stretch and not underestimate the capacity for reflection of its electorate.

In recent years the process of cultural democratization seems to have worked against and not for the left. The increase in formal and higher education, and in the number of people trained at work in more objective and impersonal ways of thinking, might have been expected to raise the 'rationality' of political debate, as it has augmented the sales of serious newspapers and books. But the decline of 'deference', and the rise of a brash commercial culture in competition with the status-bound cultural forms of the established middle class, provided an alternative opportunity which Thatcherism has seized. This is the potentiality for a populist simplification of politics which undercuts the previously dominant middle-brow modes of political discussion. The influential commitment to Thatcher's cause of the vanguard of the popular press — *The Sun* the *Daily Mail* et al. — has reinforced her gut instinct that effective communication can take place at a very basic emotional and intellectual level. This 'gift' is easier for a 'conviction politician', who articulates the passions of a specific following, than it is for politicans more sensitive to the need for compromise. The left has little choice but to seek more thoughtful modes of discourse, and more effective techniques than the lecturettes through which policy has usually been expounded. Livingstone's skill with the 'conversational' medium of the interview and chat-show has shown one way of communicating with publics which is informal and accessible without being intellectually degraded or empty of political substance.

International Policy

Finally, what are the implications of the broader political argument of this book for a socialist international policy? It is mistaken to separate foreign policy from the analysis of competing class interests which is the basis for socialist strategies within particular states. Fundamental as the issues of peace and nuclear war are to the prospect of *any* future, they cannot be resolved simply in terms of ethics or the aim of national self-preservation. The threat of nuclear weapons is now such that survival would no longer be assured even by neutrality in a world war. It seems likely that major climatic disaster and a catastrophe for world food supply would follow from a major nuclear exchange.[21] And moral categories, though essential in deciding on a policy with the least risk of suffering, do not have sufficient explanatory purchase on the dynamics of international conflict to form the sole policy criteria.

The concluding chapter — *Towards a Feasible Socialist Foreign*

Policy — argues that a similarity in the configuration of powers and geo-political interests of the nations of Western Europe (both in and out of the Common Market) should provide the main grounds for the orientation of a socialist foreign policy for Britain. All of these states are now parliamentary democracies, of one kind or another — not an insignificant historical fact in itself, nor without some wider potential for the further evolution of social and economic rights. Most Western European states also have highly developed labour movements, each with some socialist tradition, and have established some kind of 'welfare compromise' with the interests of the working class (and peasantry where it survives), whether on a social democratic or 'social Catholic' basis. They have withdrawn from their former colonial empires, for the most part, and their influence in the Third World now depends more on trade and political ties than on the possibility of direct military intervention which, despite the Falklands and Chad affairs, is now mostly closed to them. The Western European economic region is in competition with the United States and Japan, and its best hope of advancing its material standards lies in greater regional and financial cooperation, for example in a common expansionary economic programme. In defence, Western Europe is more at risk of finding itself the victim of an East-West conflict that breaks out in some crisis and is fought over its soil, than it is of being directly invaded from the East. While the Americans have been using the return of cold war to pursue their goals of renewed military superiority and increased influence in the Third World, the West Europeans have a clearer interest in a renewal of detente and more stable relations with the East.

The East European states find themselves in a position of some similarity vis-à-vis the USSR to that of West Europeans vis-à-vis the United States. Their internal social structures are inherently more pluralist than those of the USSR, as may be seen from the survival and expression of various oppositional traditions — Catholic, nationalist, democratic socialist or humanist Marxist. They are also kept under firm control through the military imperatives of the Cold War which, as E.P. Thompson has been arguing since 1956, enforces the grip of both major powers over their allies and client States. There are regional and cultural reasons for much closer association between the peoples of eastern and western Europe, and the economic viability of the whole region would be assisted by increased trade and investment. For a variety of reasons, therefore — libertarian, socialist and pacific — a disengagement of the military blocs in Europe and friendlier relations between western and eastern European states should be a central objective of socialist international policy.

Nevertheless, the balance of forces in the Cold War cannot be ignored as a factor in determining foreign and defence policy. The final chapter suggests that the contradiction of 'unilateralist' strategies for Britain lies in their possible and perceived effects on the balance of East–West power, although their intention is rather to achieve disengagement and a lower level of tension. It is argued therefore that a much stronger emphasis on European-wide policy-making and cooperation, even with limited immediate goals, may be more successful both in winning support and in influencing the international climate, than the pursuit of implicitly isolationsist objectives. This is not to say that some unilateral 'refusals' in the present climate have not been and would not be of great value in opposition to the renewal of the arms race and the Cold War.

Conclusion

I hope it will be evident from this introduction that the programmatic proposals developed below are based on some consistent theses about British society and its post-war development. The author's engagement in these issues has been in various phases and initiatives of the British new left, and I hope the book expresses some of the good qualities of moral and practical commitment which characterized its earliest years. But it has also been influenced by the fuller theoretical resources which developed in the new left's later phases, in fruitful debates between a renewed Marxist tradition and competing social-scientific perspectives. The intellectual complexity and level of these discussions have usually exceeded their direct political application, especially in regard to interventions concerning agency and programme rather than to analysis, explanation and commentary. The second chapter suggests that the new left was able to flourish as a cultural movement throughout the 1960s and 1970s while remaining largely on the political margins. Anyway, the book is an attempt to cross this gulf, and to think about what socialists need to advocate and to do if they are to make an effective contribution to shaping the political future of Britain. While these essays may be satisfactory neither to social scientists nor to political activists, I am certain that their objective of finding a coherent basis for a feasible socialist programme could hardly be more necessary than at the present time.

NOTES

1. B. Crick, *Socialist Values and Time*, Fabian Society, 1984 discusses this issue in a useful way.

2. E. Hobsbawm, in F. Mulhern and M. Jacques (ed.) *The Forward March of Labour Halted?* London 1981. See also E. Hobsbawm, 'Labour's Lost Millions', *Marxism Today*, October 1983,

3. G. Therborn, 'The Rule of Capital and the Rise of Democracy', *New Left Review*, 103, May–June 1977.

4. References to the debate on the 'crisis of ungovernability' are as footnote 9 to chapter 6.

5. F. Halliday, *The Making of the Second Cold War*, London 1983.

6. The literature on Gramsci is too extensive to list. For two interesting recent articles see J.V. Femia 'Gramsci's Patrimony', *British Journal of Political Science*, Vol. 13, 3, 1983, and P. Gibbon, 'Gramsci, Eurocommunism and the Comintern', *Economy and Society* Vol. 12, 3, 1983.

7. On the rise and multiple functions of the welfare state, see Ian Gough, *The Political Economy of the Welfare State*, London 1979.

8. The classic article criticising the 'embourgeoisement' thesis was J.H. Goldthorpe and D. Lockwood, 'Affluence and the Class Structure', *Sociological Review*, Vol. 11, 2, 1963. See also their three-volume study, *The Affluent Worker*, London 1968–9.

9. For an overview of the debate of corporatism, see L. Panitch, 'Recent Theorisations of Corporatism; Reflections on a Growth Industry', in *British Journal of Sociology* Vol, 31, 2, 1981.

10. R. Miliband, 'AState of Desubordination', in *British Journal of Sociology*, Vol. 29, 4, 1978.

11. See S. Hall and M. Jacques (ed.) *The Politics of Thatcherism*, London 1982; also S. Hall et al., *Policing the Crisis*, London 1978.

12. The journal *The Public Interest* in which Bell and Glazer were prominent was important in providing a theoretical basis for neo-conservatism in the U.S.A.

13. I have developed a critique of Scruton's architectural aesthetics in a forthcoming article in *Radical Philosophy*.

14. G. Stedman Jones, 'Marching into History?' in J. Curran (ed.) *The Future of the Left*, London 1984.

15. See the references to electoral de-alignment in footnote 7 to chapter 6.

16. A. Barnett, *Iron Britannia*, London 1983.

17. See W. Korpi, *The Working Class in Welfare Capitalism*, London, 1980.

18. J. Westergaard, 'The Withering Away of Class: a Contemporary Myth', in P. Anderson and R. Blackburn (eds), *Towards Socialism*, London 1965.

19. M.J. Rustin, 'A Socialist Consideration of Kleinian Psychoanalysis', *New Left Review* 131, January–February 1982; M.J. & M.E. Rustin, 'Relational Preconditions of Socialism', in B. Richares (ed.) *Capitalism and Infancy*, London 1984.

20. It would be a long-term investment for Labour authorities to set up postgraduate educational programmes to train economic planners and managers for future work in public authorities and publicly funded companies. Such a development, which might involve both college courses and in-service experience, is made feasible and necessary by the growth in economic planning functions performed by the metropolitan counties and by some city councils.

21. As it becomes more widely understood, this probability may provide the strongest argument from self-interest for the United States to abandon its quest for strategic superiority over the USSR, which is now the greatest destabilizing factor in the arms race.

2

The New Left and the Labour Party

This chapter is an exploration of the forms of political organization and action through which socialist goals might be advanced in contemporary Britain. It reflects on the development of two different kinds of political formation. The first of these is the British New Left, which the author originally encountered in its earliest days in 1956–57 while he was still at grammar school, and with which he has been associated in one way or another ever since. The second is the Labour Party, of which the author has been a member (sometimes an unenthusiastic one) for most of his adult life, and whose difficulties in and out of office have given rise to the bleak political environment confronting socialists today. I shall argue that the separation between the various currents of the new left, and the political organization and culture of the Labour Party, have been a major impediment to political progress by the left over two decades. Once the early attempt by the founders of *New Left Review* to maintain an active dialogue with and influence upon the Labour Party had been abandoned in crisis in 1962, the Labour Party and the currents of political life which were finding expression in the 'new left' diverged. The Labour Party, for various reasons, began an organizational and intellectual degeneration, masked by the occupancy of office, which has only recently (and in far from ideal ways) been contested. The emerging strata of educated professionals, white-collar workers, students and academics who provided the main social base for new left politics put their energies variously into 'single issue campaigns', sectarian parties or groupings, or intellectual work of a Marxist or Marxist-influenced variety. While there were many positive outcomes from this growth of a new radical culture, lasting influence on the mainstream of British political life has not been one of them. The development of a vigorous political counter-culture (with its numerous magazines, organizations, campaigns, conferences, courses, demonstrations, and bookshops) has been accompanied by two major electoral victories for the right, the reversal of many social advances, and the struggle of the Labour Party for its very survival. Some of the efforts to reverse these setbacks, in the new left's bid for power in the Labour Party after 1979, seem even to have made matters worse. A certain reappraisal is thus called for, both of the internal evolution of the new left, and of the political assumptions and institutions of the Labour Party. The emergence of new formations within the Labour Party, especially at local and municipal level, has brought some convergence of these two traditions, sometimes through the roles of key individuals. This, despite a number of early mistakes and reverses, has been a positive development. What is now needed is that this convergence should recover an earlier openness and pluralism of political approach, which alone can bring success in democratic politics in Britain.

The New Left before 1962

The early new left attempted to hold together the theoretical and practical dimensions of socialist work. Though many of its members came from a Communist tradition, it rejected 'vanguardism' and 'substitutionism' in all its forms. It intuited, years before anyone else on the left, the incipient fragmentation of the British social structure under the influence of 'modernity' and 'affluence'. It saw the need to identify and crystallize the forms of the new politics as they emerged and to link them to a 're-thought' socialist vision. While the 'early new left' and Anthony Crosland were the principal intellectual adversaries of left and right in the late 1950s and early 1960s, they at least shared a serious commitment to rethink or revise socialist ideas, and to face the realities of a society whose rapid changes were rendering or soon would render much of traditional Labourism irrelevant.

The issues of *New Reasoner*, *Universities and Left Review* and the 1956–1962 *New Left Review* initiated, among other things, discussions of 'revisionist' Marxism; the problems of East European socialism; the implications of social theory (in many forms) for a re-thought socialism; literature and politics; 'committed'
and theatre; the contradictions of affluent capitalism; the
the Cold War; the Cuban revolution; the mass media; the
and potential of the new youth culture; the nature of wor

problems of certain British industries. For four or five years this very broad agenda of political and social issues, of a kind which socialists now take for granted, was an enormous and thrilling advance on the then-existing social democratic or communist modes of political debate. This discussion also took an open and democratic form. Academic boundaries were not important. Meetings were open. There was a wish to encourage people to join or rejoin a political culture which had become attenuated during the period of the Cold War.

On the more negative side, the early new left was to learn painfully about the institutional difficulties facing independent socialist formations in the British political system. It attempted to stimulate and speak for a rebirth of socialist thinking and culture (the early meetings of the Universities and Left Review Club in London in the late 1950s had the heady quality of a renaissance of political feelings and ideas last visible in the 1930s) and to bring together a political and organizational movement. But it found it impossible to fulfil both roles. Differences between the two tendencies which had contributed to the merger of *ULR* and the *New Reasoner,* and to the launch of *New Left Review,* brought underlying conflict. The Campaign for Nuclear Disarmament stimulated but also took energy from the new political grouping. The effort to maintain both an open, locally based movement and an intellectual journal (and sometimes the beginnings of post-university jobs and families) proved wearing. The original project of *New Left Review*, and the coordinated movement of New Left Clubs, eventually failed, in financial and collective crisis. A new editorial board took over the journal, and changed and narrowed its aims. The left clubs movement died away, though some individual clubs or nuclei of members did continue to function independently. Such groups were in some cases the centre of response, in particular areas, to later campaigns or initiatives on the left. But a consequence of the general failure was that cultural and more strictly political modes of activity, which had been unified in the first conception of the New Left, now took separate roads.

The New Left after 1962

A number of leading participants in the movement, including founders of the two journals and their successors in the new editorial board of *New Left Review,* devoted themselves to intellectual and cultural renewal, regarding the work of political organization as simply unfeasible, or incompatible with the resources actually available. While certain forms of this intellectual work (e.g., History Workshop, The Centre for Contemporary Cultural Studies) translated the open and participatory modes of the early new left into a distinctively cooperative and collective style, they nevertheless did not pretend to be political in the more direct sense. A recently published review on the history of the Centre for Contemporary Cultural Studies, by its current Director, Richard Johnson, refers to the uncertain and undeveloped political implication of its 'cultural politics'. Others, such as *New Left Review*, adopted without apology a high intellectual style, and undertook a substantial and demanding work of theoretical renewal, the political and historical rationale for which they soon explained in cogent and solid statements of position.[1]

The theoretical and cultural side of the 'new left', as a movement of ideas, burgeoned after this 'break' in the early 1960s, sometimes taking the forms indicated by the original journals' synthesis of writings. Journals of the 'new left' kind serve as places where ideas cross-fertilize and incubate before developing a life of their own. This is explained partly by the point of their development at which writers are often most active in these collective forms of work. The expansion of post-school education after 1960, and of the welfare professions and the academic disciplines (the social sciences and humanities) in which their new entrants were trained, produced a rapid boom in the amount of intellectual work being done, and in the number of academic and kindred jobs available. This also provided a large constituency receptive to radical ideas and publications. Radical intellectual work developed in such fields as social history, popular culture, mass communcations, politics, literature and sociology, where it was often greatly influenced by the work of the first generation of new left writers (e.g. Raymond Williams, Edward Thompson, Stuart Hall, Raphael Samuel, Richard Hoggart and John Rex).

The somewhat different intellectual programme of the new editors of *New Left Review* (notably Perry Anderson) also had produced a major development. Their serious attention to the work of the Western Marxist tradition, and to the Third World, had considerable influence. Partly through the impact of NLR's programme of publishing and translation, Marxist work became an important current in most of the social sciences and humanities. *New Left Review* Mark II unashamedly thought of itself as a journal of an *intelligentsia*, oriented at first as much towards Paris as London, as E.P. Thompson wittily pointed out at the time. The earlier grouping had on the whole avoided this self-definition, preferring for reasons of politics, and in some cases social origin, to hold on to a more populist and less exclusive social identity, with affinities with an 'English radicalism' of the Cobbett–Morris–Orwell kind. The later discovery of Gramsci's work, and his conception of the organic intellectual, has now provided some bridge between these different identities. Certainly the theoretical project of the later NLR was highly successful, even while its political interventions remained uncertain an ill-based on any consistent practice. England was during the late 1960s ripe for some opening-up of its culture to international and especially European influence, after a period of suffocating and self-regarding insularity after the Second World War. This offered one solution to the problem of national identity following the loss of Empire, though unfortunately, as Anthony Barnett has recently demonstrated, 'Churchillian' conceptions died hard even in the Labour Party.[2] The explosion of 1968 generated a more cosmopolitan intellectual climate, which was receptive to Marxist writings of many tendencies, from the Frankfurt School to the structuralist Marxism of Althusser. It became possible to escape from the piecemeal and empiricist tradition which had hitherto characterized much British intellectual work, in sociology, for example. Cultural concerns became central to socialist work. The generation of students who were taught in the late 1960s and early 1970s were widely influenced by a generally critical, and then a more explicitly Marxist climate of ideas. The evolution of these rapidly changing intellectual fashions can be followed through the annual conference reports of the British Sociological Association, or some of the course books of the Open University, which registered these shifts of interest very rapidly. Professional fields, especially in the state sector (social work, planning, education) close to the social sciences, were also influenced by these developments, and the new left acquired and permeated these particular areas of 'civil society' in a manner which Gramscian ideas were later to theorize.

But the specifically political side of this movement had a much less positive trajectory. The early new left had adopted a stance of 'one foot in and one foot out' in relation to the Labour Party. This ambivalent commitment, like the equivalent position for CND, had made possible a significant role in the Labour Party's debates. It had the merit of recognizing, on the one hand, that there were social and cultural forces which, though not mobilizable by the Labour Party itself, were still crucial to socialist advance; and, on the other hand, that without a relationship to a major working-class party, these new formations could have little influence on government. The Campaign for Nuclear Disarmament was a particularly important channel of influence for the early new left, several of whose leading figures played a major role in its broader thinking and analysis. The decline of CND after 1962, following the Test Ban Treaty and the beginning of detente, was therefore a significant element in the decline of the first new left, cutting it off from a broad political base. But new left influence in the Labour Party had also been achieved through interventions at Labour Party Conferences (the idea of free daily Conference newsheets and commentaries on the debates was an invention of the then-editor of *NLR* and provided the present writer with one of his most memorable early political experiences), and through pamphlets and articles in *NLR* that engaged with Labour's internal debates. The take-up of the Galbraithian themes of private affluence and public squalor by the Labour Party was, for example, influenced by the serious treatment of these issues, as a new mode of analysis of the contradictions of consumer capitalism, by *New Left Review*.[3] The continuing contributions of a number of trade unionists and associated intellectuals (e.g. Norman Willis, Jack Jones, Lawrence Daly, Clive Jenkins, John Hughes, Michael Barratt Brown) also maintained the new left's contact with the trade unions, building on the industrial traditions of the Communist Party even after the departure from it of many key individuals after 1956. Edward Thompson was quite right in his claim that one important role of the *New Reasoner*, and more broadly of the New Left in Britain, was to make it possible for most ex-members of the British Communist Party to remain committed socialists in good faith after they left. Few succumbed to disenchantment and the slide into Cold War postures which had occurred when a previous generation had left the CP.

The Labour Party was seriously affected by the collapse of this early new left. Gaitskellite revisionism, which at least had some serious basis and intellectual commitment in the work of Anthony Crosland, was succeeded by the brilliant but chameleon-like leadership of Harold Wilson, who was a consummate tactician lacking any interest in theoretical analysis or long-term goals. Wilson was able to 'resolve' the argument about the nature of affluent capitalism with rhetorical sparkle and wit, but in a way that lacked analytical or programmatic substance. He evaded the fundamental divisions of class in British society, by calling upon the emergent new technical strata, and by heaping all his invective on the most traditionalist and status-ridden elements of the British elite — the grouse-moor Etonians who now turn out to have been mild radicals by 1980s standards. He appealed to a spirit of modernization, yet failed to sustain a challenge to the major institutional obstacles to economic modernization: that is to say, the power of the financial sector, Britain's lingering imperial role, and the incubus of the sterling area. His anti-Europeanism, though popular with the left, merely put off the necessity of a continental realignment of post-colonial Britain until the British economy was too weak to compete success-fully inside the Common Market.

There was little serious debate about this whole programme, prior to and during 1964, as the Labour Party stood mesmerized by Wilson's astonishing burst of energy and brilliance.[4] Wilson's electoral success was an overpowering argument in itself, after the successive failures of the 1960s. The sterling crisis of 1966, the abandonment of much of Labour's economic programme (the National Plan, the wresting of economic powers from the Treasury), and the degeneration of Wilsonism into a wholly mysti-fying rhetoric of 'strong government' (when the government had shown in 1966 its irrevocable weakness in face of the City and IMF) produced little coherent response from the left. The dispersal of the first new left made it especially difficult to maintain any dialogue between left-wing opponents of compromise within the Labour Party, and oppositional currents outside. Furthermore, the oppor-tunist and pragmatic cast of Wilson's, and later Callaghan's, leader-ship made *any* serious dialogue, on a more-than-tactical level, difficult. The moral attachment of elements of the right to the Labour Party was also weakened by post-Gaitskell pragmatism — a trend which foreshadowed the later defection of the SDP 'gang of four'. Instead of a party whose internal life had been dominated by ideological debate, the Labour Party came to consist for a time of parliamentary factions manoeuvring to gain the ear of a leader whom they hoped, in his illusory depths, was 'really' on their side.

Outside the Labour Party, the 'new left' became a number of separate tendencies. The Trotskyist left, which had been somewhat contained and overshadowed in the period of CND's greatest strength, was able to use its more disciplined organizational methods to grow in the vacuum created by the decline of the more open and populist new left. The mass student mobilization of 1968, the movement against the Vietnam War, and the Anti-Nazi

League, provided a mass context in which the International Marxist Group and the Socialist Workers Party were able to provide some effective leadership, and from which they could draw recruits.

The evolution of Marxist theoretical currents ran in some respects parallel to the organizational development of the Leninist political groupings. The super-theoreticism of the one may have been in contrast to the super-activism of the other, yet they expressed a common antipathy to the more eclectic, moralist and humanist formulations of the earlier 'movement'. Whereas the politics of the early new left had implied some sense of shared membership and dialogue with liberal-democratic politics,[5] the new Marxism was more separatist. Theories of an 'epistemological break' within Marx's work between an earlier humanism and a later scientific materialism, and arguments for a distinctive and adversarial 'Marxist' discourse set in opposition to 'bourgeois' forms of knowledge, were cognate with a rejection of more eclectic, moralist, or implicitly reformist modes of active politics. While these movements brought about a considerable politicization of the universities and the newer professions, and could draw quite large numbers onto the streets at specific moments of crisis, there was no long-term organizational growth. The Communist Party, which was part of these various activist developments, continued its numerical decline despite finding some new space on the more liberal and reformist wing of the new intelligentsia. The Communist University of London, and *Marxism Today* after its conversion into the most lively and interesting political magazine in Britain, kept up the rethinking of Marxism in both theory and practice which had been one main task of the early new left. Its political orientation towards 'Euro-Communism' — the adaptation of Communist Parties to democratic and reformist modes of action, while retaining commitment to long-term socialist goals — was analogous to the earlier new left's attempted revision and updating of left socialist positions. With Eric Hobsbawm's intervention in the 'Forward March of Labour Halted' debate,[6] and the Euro-Communists' advocacy of a 'broad class alliance' strategy for the Labour Party, there has been an eventual drawing together of positions.

Some attempts were made to revive the original unifying conception of a new left theory and practice: the *May Day Manifesto* of 1967, for example, saw Raymond Williams, Edward Thompson and Stuart Hall collaborating with a group of younger writers and activists to formulate and propagate a coherent analysis.[7] The aim of this group was to set new goals for a socialist politics, which would

link the 'traditional' issues of class and poverty with the newer
politics of race, the anti-war movement, communications, and
generational and 'qualitative' issues.

In retrospect, 1967 was not a propitious moment for an initiative
of this kind. Disenchantment with Labour governments in office
produces a falling, not a rising curve of popular involvement, and it
is difficult to bring popular pressure to bear on a government at such
a time. The established Labour left did not have the nerve to bring
its opposition to a point, or even to balance the pressures facing the
government from the right.[8] In such circumstances, opponents of
capitulation, in or out of the party, could only shout impotently
from the sidelines. In any case, the persuasive and still reasonable
tones of the *May Day Manifesto* were drowned a year later in the
angrier and more dramatic international upsurge of 1968, which set
an apocalyptic political agenda, for a time.

In this more militant and expressive political climate, new
demands and tendencies of all sorts burst on to the scene. Maoism
and third worldism, syndicalism, the cause of black power, sexual
liberation, death to the family, communitarianism, and a general
existential liberation were the prevailing ideologies. This also
opened the eyes of the hitherto parochial English once and for all to
events and ideas coming from abroad. 'Paris, London, Rome,
Berlin: We Shall Fight and We Shall Win', went the slogan
(Berkeley should be added to this list). This explosion mobilized a
new political generation, the products of the prosperity and educational expansion of the 1950s and 1960s. It left some radicals of an
earlier generation (especially if they found themselves the teachers
of these turbulent students) somewhat uncomfortable. It projected
some others, who had once thought of themselves as moderate
socialists, all the way over the right, in an outraged reaction that led
both in England and America to the formation of neo-Conservatism
as an intellectual movement.

But the weaknesses of the *May Day Manifesto's* strategy were
more fundamental than can be explained by this historical contingency. It replicated the difficulties of the early new left movement.
These were later repeated in 1980 in the comet-like rise and fall of
the *Beyond the Fragments* grouping, following the publication of
Sheila Rowbotham, Hilary Wainwright and Lynne Segal's
pamphlet of that title which confronted left vanguardism with the
democratic and participatory lessons of the feminist movement.[9]
Later still, the Socialist Society has reproduced some of the same
contradictions. These difficulties are too similar and recurrent not

to be recognized as the contradictions of a particular political model. This is the idea of a multi-issue political 'movement' which, however, lacks an organizational base in an established political party, and even claims to be superior to the 'dead' or bureaucratic routines of machine politics.

Those 'new left' initiatives which chose either a more restricted and specialized field of operation, or a more specific method of work, such as a journal, an annual conference or some other form of regular publication, succeeded much better in maintaining and reproducing themselves than the would-be unifying movements. George Clark's community organizing initiative in Notting Hill — which was inspired by the Committee of 100 and the American civil rights movement and involved the London new left club at a very early stage — did succeed in starting a distinctive method of political work. This became temporarily institutionalized as a radical experimental extension of government, via the Home Office Community Development Projects,[10] which offered a valuable political and intellectual experience and training for numbers of social science graduates politicized in the climate of '1968'. These projects intersected with the development of the Conference of Socialist Economists, and have subsequently provided cadres and working methods for the community-based initiatives of some of the new-style Labour local authorities.

The Institute for Workers' Control is another example of successful concentration of effort, identified with a particular institutional base (the trade unions) and achieving a particular synthesis of intellectual and practical work, around the issue of industrial democracy. This won real political influence, not least through the support of Jack Jones, in the setting-up and recommendations of the Bullock Report on industrial democracy, though sadly it was overtaken by the rise of unemployment and the general turn of British politics to the right after 1976.

Journals committed to intellectual theoretical work — for example, *New Left Review* or the many specialized radical or Marxist journals such as *Radical Philosophy, Radical Science Journal, Critical Social Policy, History Workshop, Red Letters, Ideology and Consciousness* or *Capital and Class* — have also been capable of sustaining very productive activity over a long period. Some of these professional and intellectual communities, notably the Marxist economists and other social scientists around the Conference of Socialist Economists, and the popular historians around *History Workshop*, have been able to establish a forum for wider political discussion, crystallizing dominant issues at particular moments. The new left has had a distinctively protean character for over twenty years. Its radical culture is a network with many separate but interlocking nodes of thought and action: initiatives occur at various points and gain a sometimes large though volatile response. One can identify a whole series of conferences — put on by socialist feminists, *Marxism Today*, *Critical Social Policy*, the Conference of Socialist Economists, *History Workshop*, the Socialist Society, *Beyond the Fragments* — which have attracted attention well beyond their immediate 'constituency', and created a national political focus for a short period. This 'network' structure, while strong and durable as a cultural and intellectual matrix, is not however well adapted to the tasks of political organization.

Early on, the *May Day Manifesto* authors formed a political committee and helped to set up local groups which had some of the characteristics of the earlier left clubs. They tended to be broad, non-sectarian groupings of the more intellectually oriented activists from various movements and parties in a particular area. Some were close to the Labour Party, some became involved in community politics, some were rooted in the universities. But the hopeless dispersal of their energies seemed to prove that, once key members were in other full-time work, and once it had been decided not to develop another journal, the free-floating style of student and post-graduate life was not sufficient for political work on a multi-issue basis. Thus the Manifesto's intellectual fertility ended with its initial statement. The successive failures of this 'new left' conception of a political movement outside the established parties would seem to suggest it defies some basic laws of political organisation.

Political initiative on the left after 1968 rested for several years with the vanguard neo-Trotskyist groups. They achieved some growth during the early 1970s, through the student movement, the 'Victory to the NLF' Vietnam campaign, the Anti-Nazi League, and 'rank and file' trade union activity especially in public sector unions (including professional groups such as teachers and social workers). Their superior discipline, and willingness to tithe their members to pay full-time workers, gave them far greater organizational resources than the looser associations of the earlier new left. In the early seventies, their main efforts were devoted to building a socialist revolutionary movement (and then, in some cases, a party) in opposition to Labour. The move to the left which took place in programmatic terms inside the Labour Party from 1970 to 1974, in the backwash of the 1970 election defeat, thus occurred with a much lesser involvement of the ultra-left than after the second defeat of 1979. However, the cohesion and discipline of the sects were built at the cost of dogmatism, stridency and a damaging tendency to internal fission and explusion. There was a high rate of 'burn-out' of novice members. Other important movements, such as the feminists, experienced sectarian incursion as exploitative and harmful. Big and violent demonstrations did not amount to a political strategy. When it became evident that the sects were not going to succeed in building a revolutionary rival to the Labour Party, some of them, and many more of their ex-members, turned once again to the Labour Party, and the current period of 'entryism' began.

The far left had learned the same lesson as the milder tendencies of the new left: there is little space for independents in English politics, not least because of the massive advantage enjoyed by big parties under the first-past-the-post electoral system. 'One foot in and one foot out' had been replaced by all-out competition and warfare, extending to savage attempts to discredit and undermine Labour's political and trade union leadership. This having failed, the next move was to try to capture the party from inside. This is not, of course, the description of a 'tight-knit' political conspiracy, shifting its tactics as the moment demanded. Political learning and change took place in a wide and continually rejuvenated radical network. Most key individuals remained committed to their own chosen strategy. Shifts in dominant strategies resulted from the gain or loss of influence by key figures or groupings, not for the most part from Machiavellian changes of plan by individuals. The volatile and flexible nature of the extra-party new left (in contrast to the relative rigidity of the Communist Party) provided favourable conditions for such rapid political learning and adaptation to new circumstances.

To assess this strategy of working within the Labour Party, and its prospects, it will be necessary to say more about that party itself.

The Labour Party

If the radical intelligentsia of the New Left has found itself devoid of a firm political foothold for most of its history, the main alternative site of socialist activity, the Labour Party, has been no success story either. As everyone knows, a long-term decline in the proportion of votes cast, dating from 1966, led to the disaster of a 28 per cent national poll in 1983. Even with unemployment above the level of the 1930s, the Conservatives still stand ahead of Labour in the polls. The split with the SDP in 1980, and the consequent division of the anti-Conservative vote, has already conferred enormous advantage on the Thatcherites, Their impregnable Parliamentary position and favourable showing in the polls explain their capacity to persevere with an unsuccessful and costly economic strategy, which meets little serious opposition from Conservative or business ranks. The Labour Party, despite some infusion of new membership in the 1970s, is desperately short of funds. It is able to put far fewer paid organizers in the field than one of its component, and ultimately parasitic, sects, the Militant Tendency. Its professional organization, both in the regions and at Walworth Road, is a by-word of inadequacy. While the new leadership of Neil Kinnock is highly aware of the need to recapture popular support, there is little sign of a coherent strategy for doing so. What has gone wrong, and what, if anything, can be done about it?

The Evolution of Labourism

Criticism of British 'Labourism' and 'parliamentary socialism' has been an important thread in new left writing for more than twenty years. Perry Anderson and Tom Nairn[11] identified the mainly defensive and inward-looking 'corporatism' of the British working-class culture and institutional structure, honeycombing bourgeois society with alternative collectivist institutions that were mainly committed to self-defence and survival, not to the transformation of society in their own image. They attributed these qualities in part to deficiencies in the British bourgeois tradition. The British bourgeoisie had not, they argued, established a militant democratic and republican ideology, or wrested power decisively from the older aristocracy. Instead, it had compromised with the dominant ruling class from the seventeenth century onwards, transforming economic life into first agrarian and then industrial capitalism, but adopting the social and cultural values of the traditional upper class. This ultimately had serious consequences for Britain's economic performance, in the relegation of industrial production to subordinate cultural status, and the preference of ruling-class elites for professional, imperial and other more gentlemanly pursuits. This experience of class accommodation and compromise also inhibited the formation of a radical intelligentsia. Radical intellectuals tended to identify more often with the agrarian and pre-industrial past than with the modern and rationalist future. Their main reference, as Raymond Williams makes clear in his pioneering *Culture and Society*[12] and many subsequent essays on individual social critics, was to ideals of social responsibility and pre-industrial moral integration, not to a spirit of modernity or militant democratic rationalism.

The evolution of the British Labour Party reflected the class-divided nature of the society in which it emerged, and the dominant attitudes of both its working-class and radical middle-class members. Gareth Stedman Jones has described how the Labour Party was built upon a class alliance, between the philanthropic upper-middle-class descendants of Edwardian liberalism, and a deferential working-class movement, organized primarily through trade unions, which were divided from one another by craft or trade. [13] The middle-class component of the Party reflected different ideological traditions. The Fabians, who were initially sceptical of the arguments for a separate working-class party, and placed their main hopes in 'permeating' the Liberals, were modern utilitarians, believing in rational administration in alliance with a strong national (and imperial) State.

A tradition of Non-Conformist liberalism produced an ethical radicalism and socialism, pacifist-inclined, anti-imperialist, and committed to ideas of social justice, compassion, and sometimes equality. Upper-middle-class socialists, for understandable reasons of history and situation, tended to share the wide national regard for the miracle of the British Constitution, and to believe that a parliamentary system which had peacefully produced political democracy might go on to produce social and economic democracy. There were more 'ideological' and Marxist-influenced traditions of thought too, though these had been marginalized during the development of the Labour Party through its deep division with the Communist Party, the defeat and decline of the Independent Labour Party, and the subordination of the trades council movement to the established union bureaucracies.

This 'class alliance' made possible the incorporation of the trade union movement into the war economy, in return for a substantial programme of social reforms both during and after the war. The Labour Party settled after the war for a 'class truce' of full employment, a welfare State, and a predominantly privately owned economy. It gave relatively low priority to the public ownership of viable sectors of private industry after the original nationalization of bankrupt sectors had been accomplished. The Labour Party was firmly controlled by a combination of middle-class politicans, led by the quintessentially upper-middle-class philanthropic figure of Attlee, and trade union bosses such as Bevin and Deakin of the Transport and General Workers Union.

The constitution and procedures of the Labour Party facilitated this structure of control. Trade unions had an overwhelming majority of votes at Party Conference. The convention whereby each union voted as a block — often after the most minimal rank-and file participation, and sometimes virtually at the personal behest of general secretaries — ensured both an overwhelming domination by working-class interests in policy formation, and a rather low level of political participation and content. The prestige attaching to Parliament and its Members gave MPs a freedom of decision which was rarely challenged by their Constituency Parties. (CLPs). Nomination was usually for life, except in case of grave misdemeanour, and accountability was at a low level. Even now, though the CLPs are generally to the left, the balance of opinion in the Parliamentary Labour Party is to the right, though all members are dependent on a CLP for nomination.

The third element of this tripartite structure, the Constituency Party, has until recently had only a subordinate role in the control of the Party. Richard Crossman gave a characteristically candid account of this situation when he said that the Labour Party had a democratic centralist character. In return for doing all the electoral work, members were given the illusion of effective participation in the formation of policy. Power in reality lay with the trade union leadership, who controlled Conference and a majority of seats on the National Executive Committee, and with Members of Parliament whose role in parliament and government was subject to little control. Once in office, Labour ministers also gained much power vis-à-vis ordinary MPs and the party from the British conventions of Cabinet government.

This constitutional structure functioned in a stable way when both the majority of trade union votes and the Parliamentary Labour Party were in the hands of the right wing. Constituency activism was restrained by means of injunctions against organized factionalism and periodic purges conducted by regional and national organizers. In this way, and as a result of its own constitutionalism, the main left opposition of the 1950s, the Tribune group, was trapped in relative impotence. While it could elicit a rapturous response at Annual Conference and its fringe meetings, and return popular left-wingers to the Constituency Section of the NEC, it remained in a minority position so long as the trade unions voted firmly for the right. This equilibrium began to be upset during the 1950s, however, during the years of repeated electoral defeat. The Gaitskellite leadership believed that the 'working class' characteristics of the Labour Party were becoming an electoral encumbrance, and its socialist commitments to public ownership an unpopular anomaly. If Gaitskell and his supporters failed to revise Clause Four of the Constitution, this was less because of opposition from the 'new' and 'old' lefts, than because of trade union loyalty to a traditional 'class' conception of Labour politics. The support for CND of a new Transport and General Workers Union leadership — Frank Cousins having been installed by an accident of succession — then led to Gaitskell's loss of an important Conference vote on unilateral disarmament in 1960. Though this was reversed a year later, the battle gave notice that the old tripartite coalition of trade-union, parliamentary, and constituency power could become bitterly contested.

Wilson appeared to resolve these contradictions for a time, as we have described above, by cleverly blurring both class and political identifications. But the Labour governments of 1964–1970 and 1970–1974 aroused increasing left-wing opposition inside the Labour Party and trade unions. Conference repeatedly voted to condemn Labour government policies, and more seriously, the trade unions came into open collision with Labour Governments over incomes policy and industrial legislation, defeating *In Place of Strife* in 1969 and rejecting, with grave results, the politically unrealistic 5 per cent pay norm in 1978–79.

Stedman Jones has described this process as the breakdown of Labour's earlier class alliance. The erosion of social deference, and rising economic expectations, made trade unionists reluctant to accept the Labour government's promises of deferred gratifications. Elements of the middle class who had somewhat patronisingly supported earlier working-class reforms became resentful of narrowing income differentials and threats to their relative privileges — for example, through the comprehensive reorganization of education and the attack on the grammar school. Class membership and class culture became less powerful influences on political alignment, and were replaced by narrower and more sectional definitions of self-interest. In both the working and the middle class, public sector employees remained more committed to Labour, as the supporter of the public sector, while private sector employees became more receptive to Conservative demands for lower taxation and a more competitive economy.

The 1970 and 1979 defeats provoked resentment and rethinking among Labour Party members, especially among the new social strata who had begun flowing into the Party in the 1970s. The development of new middle-class occupations, the expansion of public sector employment, and the concentration of social problems (and professional workers identified with them) in the inner cities, produced a new echelon of Labour Party activists. They joined Labour Parties which had sometimes become hollow shells — basically small elites of local councillors with very low membership and participation. They either drove out the old working-class leaderships or obliged them to share power with the newcomers. These new members had sometimes had their first experience in politics through the Trotskyist sects, and in the late 1970s several sectarian groupings began deliberately to organize for influence inside the Labour Party. These groups campaigned not so much for the traditional left-wing objective of a red-blooded socialist manifesto, as for a change in the constitution of the party itself. Without this, leftists concluded after the debacle of 1979, no left-wing programme would ever be carried out, even if it were adopted. Constitutionalism within the Labour Party, whose main article of faith had been the importance of Conference resolutions as a means of registering political gains in the Party, had been destroyed by the experience of the Wilson and Callaghan governments, which had ignored Conference.[14]

In 1945, Britain was the most favourably placed of all major nations to achieve an enduring form of democratic socialism. A large majority (70 per cent approximately) of its population were manual workers, mainly employed in traditional industries. It had a unified trade union movement, and a single working-class party which could count on all but a fraction of left-of-centre votes. A Labour government had just been elected with an overwhelming majority, and an enthusiastic mandate to create a just post-war social order. This 'demographic opportunity' for British socialism has now been irrevocably lost, finally wrecked by the failures of the 1964–70 and 1974–79 governments. Labour's traditional occupational constituencies, and the communities which they supported, have significantly declined, while the new occupations which have replaced them do not share the same self-definitions of class, or the same collectivist and egalitarian values. British society has become both sectionalist and more individualist. The outbreak of bitter conflict over Labour's constitution (and the defection of the SDP) is a symptom of the collapse of a whole model of political change. The debate from now on must be about how to construct a more pluralist conception of socialism for Britain, and how to build a party which can bring this about.

The Constitutional Debates

The purpose and meaning of the constitutional reforms of 1980 was to shift power away from the Parliamentary Labour Party, which had lost credibility with the membership after the failure of the 1974–79 governments. Both the constituency parties and the trade unions gained power through this shift in that the 40 percent trade union, 30 per cent CLP and 30 per cent PLP division of votes for leadership elections replaced a system in which *all* votes had been cast by the Parliamentary party. The 30 per cent CLP share was also considerably larger than its proportion of votes on Conference motions or the election of NEC members. This made it clear that the constituency membership was both instigator and main beneficiary of this change. The adoption of mandatory reselection of MPs was a further advance for the constituency parties, which now at last had some sanction they could bring to bear on sitting Members whose votes or contributions displeased them. The NEC control of the Manifesto was also an advance for the left. Even if a majority of the NEC was still elected by the trade unions, it was more open to political pressure from the left than the Parliamentary Party, which was both more conservative and also far more sensitive to the attitudes of voters outside the party. In any case, the left had gained much more influence inside the trade unions, in recent years, as a result of the consolidation of the left's leadership of the TGWU, the rise of public sector unions such as NUPE, and the radicalization of some unions facing serious erosion of their industrial base, such as the mineworkers and more recently the National Union of Railwaymen. The fact that the unions were willing to concede so large a proportion of votes to the constituency parties, and to join them in attempting to constrain the parliamentary leadership, was an indication of how disenchanted with it they had become.

The Social Democrats

The Social Democrats made the constitutional decisions of 1980 their public grounds for leaving the Labour Party, and beginning the formation of the SDP and its Alliance with the Liberal Party. Their critique of the constitutional reforms went much further than a demand for the restoration of the *status quo ante*. They now objected to *any* role by the trade unions in the funding and control of the Labour Party, as well as attacking the unrepresentative role of Labour activists, infiltrators and bogey-men of all kinds. They repudiated the fundamental collectivism and class orientation of the Labour Party, which, as Samuel Beer has pointed out, has been its normative basis since its foundation.[15] Labour's political thinking is majoritarian. Whether in the trade unions' block vote procedure or in the decision of local branch, Parliamentary Party or annual Conference, the idea is that majority votes should bind everyone since they represent the interest of a unified working class. For the same reasons such decisions have the power of mandate over constituency or trade union delegates. When they reach Parliament, these principles conflict with an alternative Burkean constitutional doctrine according to which MPs necessarily have the autonomy to interpret the interests of State as they see fit, without being subject to external mandate. But the majority principle holds to some extent there too, in the idea that a majority of the PLP should have the power to determine policy, and membership of the Shadow or real Cabinet.

The SDP's abandonment of all this resulted from its repudiation of class politics in principle, a position which developed out of the earlier Gaitskellite efforts to banish Labour's 'cloth cap image' and socialist ideology. The SDP adopted instead a more individualist theory of political leadership, enunciated most clearly by Joseph Schumpeter,[16] which holds that leaders should compete in a pluralistic political system for the support of voters, but not be tied by collective mandate to any particular class or interest. The SDP's denial of the significance of class interests for political alignment is implausible as a general theory of capitalist politics. It makes more sense, however, if one recognizes the SDP to be a party seeking to lift itself *above* social classes and to mediate between them, using the 'neutral' structure of the State as its basis of power and legitimation. To this extent, as Stuart Hall suggested soon after the formation of the SDP, David Owen may be said to have 'Bonapartist' inclinations, both personally and in his role in relation to class conflicts.

While any party seems obliged to confer some rights on its ordinary members, the SDP does this with reluctance (remembering the Labour Party), and has succeeded in establishing a far more pronounced relationship of deference between leaders and followers than exists in the Liberal Party. Its 'ideal' form of representation approximates to that of the United States, where national party organizations and their active memberships are weak, and where a ceaseless competition between alternative leaders through the primary system is the main means of candidate and policy selection.

Vanguardism and its Limitations

While the constituency left had some success with its programme of constitutional reforms, the immediate political outcome was a catastrophe. The left in the period immediately after 1979 became blind to the broader political conditions on which it must depend for success. Convinced that it had been betrayed by the leadership — the crimes of the SDP defectors were, to some, only degrees worse than those of the right-wingers who remained — the left focused its main attention on seeking to supplant it or tie its hands for the future. Many on the left shared with the sectarian groups a deluded view of the real attitudes of the British working class, of which socialist and egalitarian values form only one part. There was a millennarian idea abroad that the people would respond if only a strong enough lead were given, regardless of what majorities could actually be shown to believe about such issues as defence, taxation or public ownership. So inward-looking was the left in the earlier phases of this struggle that it failed to realize the damage that would be done to Labour's popular support by the spectacle of such bitter intra-party warfare on television and in the press. The inability or unwillingness of the members of the former Callaghan government to make any critical appraisal of what had gone wrong also assisted the process of disintegration — after the moment of defeat, something might have been saved by some public acceptance of responsibility. While Tony Benn was blamed for voicing criticisms of a government of which he had been a member, more extraordinary was the continued silent acquiescence in Callaghan's incomparable blunders, long after the point when the need for a self-critical balance sheet of the Wilson–Callaghan government had become obvious. By keeping silent, those in the centre lost their power to influence the party.

A major mistake by the left was Tony Benn's decision to run for the deputy leadership, once Michael Foot had been elected leader. This candidacy, in the particular circumstances, contradicted Labour's need to hold the support of a broad electorate. If Denis Healey had won the leadership, Benn would have provided an invigorating and acceptable balance. But his attempt to become deputy to Foot could only signify to the electorate that the left was determined to capture the entire party, there and then. Benn was by no means a natural candidate of the new Labour left, being a late convert from the role of democratic radical from an upper-middle-class background, a well-established route to prominence as a left-of centre MP. There was some opportunist misuse of Benn's personal popularity in encouraging this campaign, which squandered much of his invaluable public appeal; in the longer run his influence might have been greater if an inevitably highly-personalized contest had been avoided at this time. The experience also undermined Foot's position when it was necessary for the left to sustain it — if only, we can now see, to avoid worse electoral damage.

Whereas, after the 1979 election, left vanguardism took the form of inner-party struggle, after the 1983 disaster it has taken the form of industrial struggle, in the miners' strike. Disregard of the NUM's own ballot procedures probably cost its leadership the support of the Nottinghamshire miners, and consequently that of many other trade unionists. It has throughout been the weak point of the miners' appeal for wider solidarity that for the first time in the history of the union they have failed to bring out all their members. While Arthur Scargill's leadership has been aggressive and determined, it has also tended to disregard the sentiments of people not already identified with his own cause. Like the left in the Labour Party after 1979, the NUM's idea seems to have been that militant example could prevail over any odds. The tragedy is that this has probably cost the miners and the working-class movement the less total but more certain victory that was probably available to them after only a short strike. The climb-down of the Coal Board and Government from the original closure proposals, which might conceivably have been achieved would have been preferable to the long-drawn-out defeat that now seems the likeliest outcome. The example of Mrs Thatcher's Falklands War, in which victory was achieved through force of will against the apparent odds, may have been an unfortunate unconscious model for this strike.

The Labour Party had earlier reflected a 'corporatist', deferential and class-divided social structure. Perhaps its post-war alliance of middle-class administrators and organized trade union movement might have succeeded, but for the loss of direction brought about by the Cold War and the narrow election defeat of 1951. If Labour, and not the Conservatives, had been able to administer the post-war improvement in living standards, a 'Swedish solution' might have been possible for Britain.

The Labour Party was, however, very poorly adapted to cope with the social changes associated with 'affluence'. The initiative in defending working-class interests passed from the party, whose main resource from 1940 to 1951 had been the occupancy of government office, to the trade unions. But the autonomy of individual unions, and the state of collectivist competition which prevailed between different groups of workers in the pursuit of earning levels, made any common trade union strategy difficult to evolve. Successive TUC general secretaries have agonized over this problem. For short periods, particular coalitions of unions were able to co-ordinate a common political and industrial strategy with Labour governments — the period of the 'social contract', made possible by the trade union leadership of Jack Jones and Hugh Scanlon, is the most important case. But it was never possible to sustain these agreements for long enough, not least because Labour governments did not succeed in maintaining the stable economic growth on which collective restraint by unions depended. The forces of militant sectionalism were favoured by the fragmented and decentralized British trade union structure (they were also urged on by the far left, which strove to outbid and discredit moderate leaderships in industrial conflict). Labour's organizational and cutural weaknesses were another factor contributing to its failure. It had only the most meagre apparatus for research, policy-formation and electoral organization, and when Wilson declared the aim of making Labour the dominant governing party (to reverse years of Conservative hegemony), this remained a vainglorious rhetoric. In practice, Labour lost contact after 1966 with the emerging 'new constituencies' among the young, women, ethnic minorities, and the nationalists of Scotland and Wales.

The split between 'industrial' and trade union, and individual and local membership, institutionalized the separation of work from politics, confining the unions to a predominantly economistic mode of action (wage-bargaining) and the local parties to mobilization of the vote. Labour's exclusively territorial mode of organization, through ward branches, which was probably intended to restrict the activity of factions and concentrate the minds of members on election work, inhibited the internal life of the party. It was made difficult for party members to get together on the basis of shared interests — for example, in education, health, gender, or ethnicity. Such parcellization was a help rather than a hindrance to the factions (once the NEC stopped proscribing them), since it conferred advantage on active minorities who attended meetings assiduously. Local meetings were often a tedious round of 'resolutions', mostly a substitute for either doing or learning. While the party sought to concentrate its members' minds on election-winning, it neglected the importance of full-time organizers, a large membership, or the raising of adequate funds. The Conservative Party seems paradoxically to encourage greater freedom of association within its local branches (consider the importance of the Young Conservatives as a recruiting agent), even though it imposes many informal restraints on how this freedom may be used.

Perhaps this long crisis of political obsolescence was made worse by the fact that many elements involved in the new left and the single-issue campaigns of the 1960s turned away from the Labour Party. This 'politics of principle' of the radical intelligentsia also helped to cut the Labour Party off from vital new sources of support, leaving it as an unhappy mixture of opportunism and traditionalism.

A Pluralist Labour Party

There is no future for the Labour Party in attempting to reconstitute a trade union and parliamentary duopoly. To this extent, the constitutional reforms of 1980 which attempted to confer greater power on the mass party membership were justified and necessary. What was less satisfactory was the 'substitutionism' which equated an activist minority of the left with the membership of the party as a whole, and that membership with the actual or potential Labour vote. A party should be a transmission mechanism, which allows initiatives by the politically committed and resourceful to mobilize larger numbers. The party is one of the few instruments for raising consciousness which are not grossly subject to the pressure of mass communication, or the daily constraint of occupational circumstance, and it is crucial to any prospect of socialist advance that it should have a leading role. But such transmission can only be effective in a democratic society (where voters do, and should, have a *choice*) if minorities remain accountable and responsive to the attitudes of a larger following. The Labour Party needs procedures to ensure that its programmes and representatives remain in touch with its voters, not misjudge and override their wishes.

The Labour Party has traditionally solved this problem by the expedient but untidy device of giving *de facto* autonomy to MPs (as the representatives of the electorate), while subordinating them to the party membership's decisions on major policies. A preferable alternative would be to involve a larger proportion of the membership in party decisions — and to enlarge the membership itself — so that these more closely reflected the attitudes of Labour voters. The purpose of this is not to 'water down' policy to fit existing opinion. It is to provide a mechanism whereby programmes and positions can be selected and tested for support among a group which is committed to the party but still fairly representative of Labour voters. Power should accrue to activists where they are capable of winning support on issues, not merely as a reward for their tenacity in attending meetings.

A specific mechanism which would serve this purpose is currently under discussion: namely, a mandatory secret ballot of all local party members for candidate selection. While debate on policy and programme should remain deliberative — that is, take place through face-to-face meetings, not by referenda of members — selection of individuals for key offices, especially that of MP, could practically involve all party members, without the requirements of attendance at meetings. The resulting aggregation of individual votes would avoid the numerical distortions of a delegate system; and if the unions issued party cards to locally affiliated members, enabling them to participate individually in votes, this method need not weaken trade union involvement in local candidate selection.

Members of Parliament would thus be required to enjoy the support of a majority of their local party members. Mandatory reselection would be no unreasonable hazard if MPs knew that decisions remained in the hands of a large electorate. Those wishing to gain support would have reason to increase membership — it now often serves them better to restrict it. Open contest between alternative candidates would become normal and educative, instead of exceptional and prone to manipulation and continual accusations of unfairness. It is important to the Labour Party that right-wing as well as left-wing positions should be argued forcefully and publicly, since the total spectrum on which the Party depends clearly stretches to attitudes held on the Labour right and beyond.

The situation of the late 1950s, when fairly reasoned and open ideological debate took place between Croslandites and the left, was healthier than the use of more personalized or devious forms of settling arguments (whether the block vote by the right or minority sectarian caucus by the left). There needs to be space within a party to argue for different political positions. Where a case can be persuasive in this more restricted circle, it may then have a chance of success in changing wider social attitudes. Public demonstrations that party leaders can debate with one another in a comradely and civilized manner are also evidence to the electorate of a party's democratic commitment. It follows that the left should seek opportunity to argue publicly with its ideological opponents, not anathematize them or exclude them from debate.

What is proposed here falls deliberately short of a US type of 'primary' system, where registered voters, not party members, are enfranchized in candidate selection. The American system weakens party organization, since it enables anyone who can amass enough funds and support to address a campaign over the heads of the party to an amorphous electorate. The nomination of party candidates and the choice between candidates of different parties are distinct processes, and the boundary between them should be significant. The former should be open only to party members, with the rights and obligations this implies. A further advantage of membership ballots would be the greater representation of working-class party members, who generally participate less fully in party meetings than the 'new class' of professional and white-collar members.

Elsewhere in this book I argue for a greater emphasis to be given to regional interests in the Labour Party. A more democratic form of candidate selection might well produce greater differentiation by region, since one of the ways in which individuals could build local support would be to represent specific territorial interests. These might also have a distinctive political inflection, given the various political traditions in different areas of the country.

The recent debate on women's and black people's structures in the Labour Party is relevant to a thoroughgoing pluralist conception. The predominantly territorial and trade union principle of organization has clearly inhibited the party's range of representation. Labour should allow the formation and local representation of separate sections for women and ethnic minorities (and other 'sectoral' interest groups too), much as it now does for the Young Socialists, affiliated trade unions and the 'socialist societies' (such as the Socialist Medical or Educational Associations). Institution of the membership ballot would restrict the possibilities of exploiting such 'sectoral' representation for sectarian ends, as has already occurred in the case of the Young Socialists over many years.

The creation of workplace branches could also serve to involve a larger membership through shared life-concerns, and could have the effect of diminishing the separation of industrial and political spheres which has been so harmful to British socialism. Progress towards industrial democracy depends on a more political view being taken of economic and industrial questions, and this would be helped by a more political form of organization in the workplace. If some trade unions vote to disaffiliate from the Labour Party, under Tory legislation requiring ballots on political funds, workplace branches may become additionally valuable in maintaining the political attachment of trade unionists . While some members might participate in a local party through multiple forms of association — branch, sectoral and local — such distortion of the principle of 'one member one vote' would be no more serious than present over-representation through the influence of active delegates. In a larger and more pluralist membership, the role of hyperactive minorities will in any case be constrained by the need to maintain majority support. In candidate ballots, the rule of one member one vote should apply.

The Labour Party will not become a force for democratization and socialist change unless it is able to mobilize and apply greater intellectual resources. One important and long-overdue development has been the successful launch, now on a monthly basis, of *New Socialist*: the Labour Party had previously been as anomalous in the lack of a theoretical journal as in the absence of a daily or Sunday newspaper, and with less excuse. The policy-making apparatus of the party, at both national and local level, has been inferior to that of comparable parties in Western Europe. While the ideas and proposals of the new right have been developed by a variety of business-funded institutes and research agencies, the left has been able to make little capable response to them. The proliferation of sophisticated 'new left' intellectual work in a wide range of social sciences should have made possible the linking of policy to social movements and holistic political analysis. But although there is no longer any reason why programmatic writing need be merely 'piecemeal empiricism', little has been produced of the kind most useful to a political party. The new left's political thinking has tended in its later phases to be largely critical in attitude (often of social democracy) rather than prescriptive, and theoretical rather than applied. Some left critics have been sawing at the branches of the welfare state on which they sat. So Labour's economic policies have been written inadequately by small insider groups of academic consultants, while larger gatherings of socialist intellectuals, in organizations like the Conference of Socialist Economists, have remained marginal to party debate. The policy field in which the party has remained strongest, namely welfare, is the one in which Labour politicans have kept close contact with academics and social movements such as the Child Poverty Action Group.

This pattern is now changing for the better, with the rise of new Labour administrations in the cities, with a rejuvenation of the Fabian Society, and with interventions like the Socialist Society's series of programmatic books (*What Is to Be Done About Health, Law and Order*, etc.). The much-abused Fabians were at least competent and assiduous in their chosen work of equipping politicians with 'blue books' of facts and figures. It should now be possible to conduct policy discussion in a more open and inclusive way than in this mandarin tradition, and yet still ensure that coherent programmes for reform are developed. As a result of various lacks, the Labour Party in office has been forced into dependence on the civil service even for formulation of its own programmatic aims. The more specialized forms of representation proposed above are one remedy for this continuing weakness. But it would also be desirable to increase the resources provided by the State to support certain kinds of party activity, such as research, in proportion to recorded electoral support. This should be seen as a means of democratically redistributing political resources, and as a countervailing force to the money available to the right from business. Trade union funding is not an adequate alternative to this, both because of its quantity, and because of the undue dependence on the trade unions in which it places the Labour Party.

We have described a party structure which, to use Gramsci's terms, has been excessively oriented toward the State rather than to civil society. It is also a formation which has had little conception of the role of 'practical intellectuals', relying instead on a narrow stratum of academics, consultants and officials to provide advice on policy and mass communication. What is proposed, therefore, is to reshape the party on a more pluralistic but also mass basis, and to equip it to intervene over a wider field of social and economic life.

One of the more encouraging developments in the party in recent years had been the rejuvenation of some large parties from the cities and conurbations. This has been the most positive outcome of determined organization by the left among the constituency party membership. Thus, while the popularly oriented and charismatic style of leadership adopted in office has been vital to the success of the GLC, it must not be forgotten that Livingstone and his colleagues' opportunity would never have come if they had not created a political machine which could deliver a Labour Group majority. The Greater London, South Yorkshire, Sheffield and Liverpool City Councils have taken a variety of new policy initiatives (e.g., in the regional enterprise boards for industrial regeneration, and in transport and cultural policies); they have recruited large numbers of research and development workers committed to their basic goals; and they have vigorously defended their key constituencies. Helped politically by the Conservatives' proposal to abolish it, the GLC has become sensitive, after some early excesses, to the plurality of social and cultural interests for which Labour must speak in London in it is to have any chance of lasting success. Some of the metropolitan parties and their leaderships, notably Ken Livingstone and David Blunkett, have astutely recognized the importance of local and national broadcasting in communicating with a mass electorate, and become very skilled in using them. The revitalization of a party, at grassroots, sectoral and administrative levels, need not be at the expense of effective popular presentation. The differences between these regional parties, in political and other ways, are a healthy sign and show the potential of a more diverse and locally rooted kind of political appeal.

A conclusion to be drawn from the above argument is that the separation between the Labour Party and 'single issue' campaigns or activities of the 'new left' intelligentsia must be ended. Significant political influence will not be achieved by action largely cut off from a major party, as a large number of arduous but ill-fated initiatives seem to have confirmed. An English cultural tradition of humanist superiority to the mundane and instrumental world of politics has perhaps been reproduced in the new left intelligentsia's reluctance to take on the burdensome obligations of party membership. On the other side, unless the Labour Party can find a way of making deeper contact with the varied social forces which came to find expression in the 'issue politics' of the 1960s, its days as a major socialist party may be over.

If the Labour Party becomes more tolerant and supportive of certain kinds of membership association — on a sectoral or workplace basis, for example — there is no reason why many activities that now take place in isolation from the party should not take place in future within it. Educational and intellectual forms of work, such as those undertaken by the Socialist Society in the past three years, would be more effective if they connected not only with the amorphous intellectual community which now attends seminars and conferences, but also with the more solid and permanent following of a party branch. Ideas could thus flow in two directions, between the poles of political relevance and practicality provided by the party, and the more free-flowing and objective ways of thinking generated by radical cultural networks. Both local communities and colleges would be appropriate settings in which to develop Socialist Society or similar branches which are also fully part of their local CLPs. Since the Labour Party now tolerates a myriad of actual tough-minded conspiracies in its ranks without much demur, it would be illogical for it to object to such an educational innovation. But if the potential represented by *New Socialist*, the new Fabian groupings or the Socialist Society became more significant in the party, more rational and constructive forms of debate might become more common.

Under a system of proportional representation, there might be scope for an independent party of the left to exercise influence, as the Greens in West Germany have done. In such a case, the predominance of the Labour Party might lessen — which might be a reason for radicals to support electoral reform. But in a plurality system such as Britain currently has, political forces have to find effective expression within large parties, not by competing with them. While this system continues, therefore, socialists can only hope to exercise real influence through Labour as the major working-class party. This is a lesson that the new left has been slow to learn.

The two traditions of the British Labour Party and the new left have separately failed as means of furthering socialism in the past two or three decades. They might have a better chance if they came closer together.

NOTES

1. See the essays by Perry Anderson and Tom Nairn in *Towards Socialism*, eds. P. Anderson and R. Blackburn, London 1965.

2. Anthony Barnett, *Iron Britannia*, London 1983.

3. See especially Stuart Hall, 'The Supply of Demand', in N. Birnbaum, ed., *Out of Apathy*, London 1961.

4. The most prescient comment on the Wilson programme appeared in an article

by Stuart Hall in the journal *People and Politics*, edited by George Clark, in 1964. This journal, *Views*, the *Beyond the Freeze* pamphlet and the *May Day Manifesto* were linked continuations of early new left work.

5. In this respect it resembled the American new left, which had some exemplary influence in England as a result of the civil rights movement and the campaign against the Vietnam War.

6. Eric Hobsbawm's essay is in M. Jacques and F. Mulhern, eds. *The Forward March of Labour Halted?* Verso NLB, London 1981.

7. Raymond Williams, ed., *The May Day Manifesto*, Penguin edition, Harmondsworth 1968.

8. These problems were revealed in the pamphlet *Beyond the Freeze*, which was produced in 1966 by Sean Gervasi and a group linked to *Views* magazine, in response to the Labour Government's negotiations with the IMF. Left Labour MPs, when asked to sign this document, were unhappy about its advocacy of devaluation, since the Government was trying to defend sterling. The policy recommendations were accordingly watered down.

9. Sheila Rowbotham, Lynn Segal, Hilary Wainwright, *Beyond the Fragments*, London 1982.

10. See R. Lees and G. Smith, eds., *Action Research in Community Development*, London 1975.

11. Anderson and Nairn, *op. cit.*, and T. Nairn, 'Anatomy of the Labour Party', reprinted in R. Blackburn, ed., *Revolution and Class Struggle*, NLR Fontana, London 1977.

12. R. Williams, *Culture and Society*, Harmondsworth 1971.

13. G. Stedman Jones, 'Why is the Labour Party in a Mess?', in *Languages of Class*, Cambridge 1983.

14. See Lewis Minkin, *The Labour Party Conference*, Manchester 1980, for the role of Conference during this period.

15. Samuel Beer, *Modern British Politics*, London 1965.

16. J. Schumpeter, *Capitalism, Socialism and Democracy*, London 1977.

3

A Theory of Complex Equality

This chapter is a discussion of the concept of 'complex equality' developed by Michael Walzer in his recent book *Spheres of Justice: A Defence of Pluralism and Equality* (London 1983). Walzer argues for a concept of social justice involving the autonomy of distinct spheres of value. A just society is one in which specific human qualities obtain the respect which is due to them. Injustice occurs where one sphere of values invades another's domain, and particularly where a single dominant one-dimensional system — money under capitalism, political power under tyrannies — invades the autonomy of many spheres. Social justice is understood not only as the respect due to individual human qualities — physical beauty, political courage, filial loyalty — but also to the virtues embodied in different ways of life or social practices. A just society is one in which the virtues of families, political associations, or callings achieve their due expression, and are not subordinated to a single dominant sphere. As values are socially created, a respect for individual differences, and for the autonomy of different social forms, are aspects of the same regard for human diversity.

Walzer's argument is egalitarian as well as pluralist. He contends that the accepted values of contemporary American society already set limits to the power of monetary exchange. Legislative enforcement is given to the claims of political equality, certain welfare entitlements, and civil freedoms, against the otherwise pervasive domain of money. There are some goods that one is forbidden to buy or sell. Walzer thus attempts to justify the case for certain fundamental dimensions of equality in terms of beliefs which are consensually shared in his own (and other) capitalist societies.

Walzer's book is of great importance to contemporary socialist thought because it addresses the sociological facts of diversity and differentiation in modern societies, while retaining a socialist commitment to equality and to its reconciliation with the apparently competing claims of freedom. The more prosperous and seemingly pluralistic society has become in its life-styles, the more difficult it has been for socialists to defend egalitarian ideals against the imputation that they would enforce an unwanted uniformity. Walzer gives a fresh conceptualization to this crucial problem, and offers a way of resolving it that is compatible with the ends of both equality and diversity. I will suggest, however, that his case depends too much on relativist arguments from the particularist values of a given society, and would benefit from a more historical and evolutionary perspective of emerging social claims. He lays undue stress on the dimension of social differentiation, at the expense of a more customary socialist concern with the unequal and contested relationships over time of social classes. In this chapter I will contend that the case for equality needs to foreground the potentialities which arise from changing modes of production and class relations, as well as the diversity of values of existing societies. We have to argue as socialists not only for recognition of differences, but also for some universal equalities.

Nevertheless, the failure to come to terms with the desirable plurality of social forms has been a significant aspect of the crisis of contemporary socialism, and *Spheres of Justice* provides a valuable new approach through which socialists can tackle this theoretical task. Moreover, we should remember that many important changes in the framework of political thought have first been developed in abstract terms, before becoming available to shape practical political argument.

Distributive Justice

Distributive justice has been one of the most contested issues in political philosophy in recent years, and the course of debate has reflected and influenced the deep political shift to the right in Anglo-American politics. Walzer's book seeks to move argument about justice away from the individualist and contractual foundations which it has been given by its most formidable contributors, Robert Nozick and John Rawls.[1] In *Anarchy, State and Utopia* Nozick put forward a stringent concept of individual rights over the disposal of the person and his property which denied most claims of the State to interfere coercively. Nozick's lucidly argued position has been one of the philosophical foundations of the New Right's critique of state intervention in support of goals (such as equality or welfare) which diverge from the outcomes of free market exchange. Walzer's book can be seen in part as a response to the last chapter of *Anarchy, State and Utopia*, called 'A Framework for Utopia', where Nozick gives a list of famous and very different individuals ('Wittgenstein, Elizabeth Taylor, Bertrand Russell . . . . Allen Ginsberg, . . . Picasso, Moses, Einstein, High Hefner, Socrates, Henry Ford . . . you and your parents') and asks whether any utopia could be imagined which would suit all of these. Walzer in effect translates Nozick's vision of different ways of life for individuals into an ideal of a *social* plurality. What is attractive to him are social more than individual differences.

Rawls, for his part, while also starting from a moral presupposition of individual ends, attempted in *A Theory of Justice* to establish norms of social justice by which individual interests could be properly constrained. The ultimate foundation of this position is similar to the universalist individualism of Kant. An ethical position, it is argued, must by definition consider the standpoint of individuals in general, and universal principles are therefore needed to reconcile the claims of different individuals with one another. As is well known, Rawls sets up a hypothetical 'social contract' in which it is assumed that individuals will choose rules not in accordance with their actual situation but in ignorance of the position they would occupy in the outcome of a competitive struggle following an initial starting-point of equality. He deduces from these assumptions the necessity for guaranteed liberties, for equality of opportunity, and for the limiting of social inequalities to those which would benefit the least well-off members of society. The politics of this position, insofar as so abstract an argument generates a specific politics, probably corresponds to advocacy of a welfare state, in which the individualist principles of the market are repressed by interventions that attempt to guarantee fundamental rights, and to ensure that inequalities of income and property function to the advantage of society as a whole. The universalist and humanist character of Rawls's arguments has attracted some socialists, and attempts have been made to extend his list of necessary principles to include political participation, and welfare and other material rights. It is probably in part the absence of a more distinctively socialist analysis of justice which lies behind this attraction, even though Rawls's presuppositions are ultimately liberal rather than socialist in character.

Michael Walzer's book is radically different in its starting-point and method. He argues that goods are socially and culturally created, and are as varied in principle as the forms of social life itself. Though he is wholly unsympathetic to Plato's monistic political conclusions, there is some similarity between Walzer's identification of justice with respect for the values specific to a given social practice, and Plato's derivation of justice from knowledge of the rules of particular callings. But where Plato draws from this analogy a holistic conception of a single hierarchical order of values, Walzer is a radical pluralist and is concerned to assert the necessary distinctiveness and autonomy of different spheres of value.

We can contrast Walzer's position with the individualist and contractarian alternatives by saying that whereas the individual's good is the end of the latter positions (however this is universal-istically defined and limited), Walzer's conception of justice depends upon impersonal and social ideas of value to which in-dividuals are necessarily subordinate, that is to say, which give individual lives their ends and meanings. The world of *Spheres of Justice* consists of differentiated spheres of activity — each deserving and obtaining moral subscription from members — rather than of discrete goods or pleasures whose justification is that individuals want them. A just society, for Walzer, is one in which the autonomy of these different spheres, and the recognition accorded to their own distinctive values, is respected, and not subject to invasion or contamination from other spheres of activity. Walzer is especially opposed to the enforcement over a whole society of the values of a single domain of action and the relations of power that is generates. The main illicit claimants to such unjust hegemony are the power of money, and, somewhat less emphasized but still important in Walzer's view, the power of the state and its bureaucracies.

There is an intrinsic but unstressed connection in Walzer's argument between the concepts *social* and *social-ist*. Whereas con-tractarian arguments at best lead to a kind of egalitarian liberal-ism — a reconciliation of individual ends and happinesses through some universalistic rules of distribution — Walzer asks for neces-sarily *social* definitions of human ends in the first instances. and is implicitly prepared to accept the coercive and indeed unequal rela-tionships within particular spheres of activity which this may imply. He is committed to a concept of membership, with both the rights and obligations this entails. Liberal writers seek to defend the values of freedom through the assertion of individual rights against society and its collectivities. Many socialists, on the other hand, are prepared to accept significant costs arising from the coercive power of the State in order to bring about equality of condition. Walzer seeks to transcend this damaging polarity by arguing for the insulation of one social sphere from another. If there is a plurality of spheres of action, and these are not permitted to invade one another's norms and distributions, then individuals can avoid both tyranny and any general or transferable condition of inferiority. He shares the analysis, though not the politics, of some functionalist writers on inequality [2] for whom any sphere of social values, insofar as it must define qualities of performance, must also create hierarchy. If one respects the values of scholarship, dance, politics, or parenthood, then one must also acknowledge that some will be better than others at these callings. Such forms of social and self-recognition will indeed be a vital part of the social construction and maintenance of these areas of life. The important difference between Walzer and functionalists on this question is his refusal of the idea that there need or should be a single dominating order of values.

Arguments from Political Theory

Walzer's argument is written chiefly in the idiom of political theory. Where contractarian arguments draw chiefly on the 'methodologically individualist' disciplines of psychology and economics, he makes most use of the more holistic discourses of history and anthropology, and, though he does not put it in so many words, sociology. In his defence of his key concept of 'complex equality', he marks out ground which sociologists should be especially willing to take up in developing a more combative response to neo-liberal thought than they have hitherto managed.

Two aspects give Walzer's arguments the distinctive stamp of political theory. First, it has a predominantly normative character and is primarily concerned, as was Walzer's last sustained work, *Just and Unjust Wars,* with questions of justification. His characteristic method is to elaborate a normative concept, such as that of membership or need, and then set out to demonstrate its proper claims and limitations through particular examples, historical or contemporary. Secondly, Walzer takes political membership as his most important universal category. His argument depends on the idea that goods are first socially created and only then, so to speak, available for distribution or disputes about distribution. The boundary of the group is therefore also the boundary of its distributive system, and of the claims that can be made against it. Only if one is defined as a member of a family, or nation, or school, does one have the entitlements to unconditional care, citizenship or educational provision that such membership brings. More universally, only members can share in the characteristically human function of defining and creating social goods. Political citizenship is therefore for Walzer the most fundamental form of membership, and his critique of improper forms of domination, such as those perpetrated by large holders of capital, is based on the contrasting case of political citizenship and the accountable authority which this entails. Although Walzer is generally concerned to stress the particularity of each sphere of justice — which reminds us of Wittgenstein's particularism of 'forms of life' — and thus to refute arguments from universal principles, his discussion of rights to political citizenship comes close to regarding them as a universal prerequisite of justice.

Historical and Sociological Arguments

Walzer is able to demonstrate the social origin of values more tellingly than sociologists usually do, perhaps because of his purposeful focus on normative differences between societies. He contrasts, for instance, the priority given by the ancient Athenians, in their allocation of economic resources, to political participation by citizens, with the emphasis in the medieval Jewish community on the protection of religious and communal identity through schools and academies, and through support of the Jewish poor. Another example he might have given is the priority given to the works of the church in medieval Christian society, the extent of which continues to be made clear to us by its surviving architecture. Material goods have, Walzer asserts, 'a moral and cultural shape . . . The arguments for a minimal state have never recommended themselves to any significant portion of mankind.' The particularism and historical rootedness of Walzer's reasoning enable him to avoid the limiting abstractness that characterizes so much of ethical and normative discourse in politics. For Walzer, the crucial choices are between social forms, not abstract principles. Like some recent writers influenced by Hegel (Charles Taylor and Alasdair MacIntyre, for example[3]), Walzer is more interested in the availability of choices between textured forms of social life than in freedom conceived as the avoidance of specific constraints. If there are social alternatives, individuals can have choices; and if there are no vigorous moral communities to choose, individual freedom is an impoverished state.

Such arguments for the social relatedness of goods and values look to conservative more than liberal philosophical traditions, and demonstrate a line of filiation between organicist and socialist critiques of capitalism which can be seen in the writings of William Morris and R.H.Tawney or, more recently, Raymond Williams and (in his attention to concepts like 'moral economy') Edward Thompson. This organic approach is also a link between Walzer and the classical sociologists. Durkheim was at pains to show that individuality and individualism were the products of a complex and differentiated society, and could not be taken as its point of causal or ethical origin. There was, Durkheim said, a necessarily non-contractual basis to contract, an underlying set of presuppositions of citizenship and law on which individuals depended in order to conduct exchange in peace and security. The sociologists of the late nineteenth century, as Göran Therborn has pointed out, sought to underline the normative basis of social arrangements and the claims for state intervention that they could legitimate, as ways of resisting the solvent and coercive effects of capitalist individualism, and also as an evolutionary alternative to revolutionary Marxism.[4] Walzer's emphasis on the social definition of goods and values has a similarly democratic-socialist objective in relation to contemporary individualism and tyrannical forms of state socialism.

His argument also draws on more contemporary sociological analysis in an attempt to reconcile socialist ideals of equality with the complexity of a modern social order. Sociologists such as Frank Parkin,[5] following Weber, have shown that there are many dimensions of stratification and privilege, and that virtually no group of power-holders or aspirants can be assumed to be innocent of the inclination to monopolize its own advantages. The powers achieved and legitimized through educational or professional qualification, by the possession of capital, by bureaucratic office, or by party membership, all generate inequalities of different kinds. It is hard to conceive that a modern society which wishes to maintain high standards of material life could totally abolish any of these forms of institution — markets, professions, bureaucracies, or parties — and it therefore follows that the consequences of the ensuing forms of inequality will have to be minimized and balanced against one another, rather than wholly transcended. Visions which conceive the abolition of a single dominant form of inequality — such as the replacement of the market by central economic planning — are often blind to the characteristic inequalities of the alternative form. Even arguments for more extensive forms of participatory democracy — for the transparency of social decision-making, as it is sometimes called — often take a simplistic view of what could possibly be 'transparent'. Any modern society has to have innumerable specialisms, many centres of value and decision, and therefore many competing interests, and socialist politics must now take account of these facts. Walzer's concept of 'complex equality' is such an attempt to reconcile the socialist idea of equality with acceptance of a Durkheimian division of labour as an inevitable and beneficial attribute of the modern social order.

The Idea of Complex Equality

Walzer says that his idea of complex equality is an elaboration of arguments first put forward by Pascal. 'We owe different duties to different qualities,' Pascal wrote; 'love is the proper response to charm, fear to strength, and belief to learning.' [6] This was echoed by Marx in his early writings: 'If we assume *man* to be *man*, and his relation to the world to be a human one, then love can be exchanged only for love, trust for trust, and so on. If you wish to enjoy art you must be an artistically educated person; if you wish to exercise influence on other men you must be the sort of person who has a truly stimulating and encouraging effect others. . . If you love unrequitedly, i.e. if your love as love does not call forth love in return, if through the *initial expression* of yourself as a loving person you fail to become a manifestation of yourself as a loving person, to make yourself a loved person, then your love is impotent, it is a misfortune.' [7]

More formally stated, 'complex equality means that no citizen's standing, in one sphere, in regard to one social good, can be undercut by his standing in some other sphere, with regard to some other good.' That is, each distinctive institution should allocate goods in regard to its own appropriate values, and the values of one institution should not be imposed upon others. Thus, health care should be allocated to those in medical need, rather than to those able to pay for it. Access to newspapers or television should depend on the judgements of editors and the choices of readers and viewers, and not on the imperatives of advertising revenue. Attainment of political office should depend on the choices of electors, rather than on financial resources accumulated outside the political sphere, or on cooption by existing monopolists of power. This is an argument about the autonomy of procedures as well as the means of access to powers. Each sphere, Walzer asserts, has its distinctive practices which should be protected from usurpation. Politics, to take a key example, depends on rational deliberation, and on members' sustained commitment and participation, and these are improperly invaded by plebiscitary appeals over the needs of the politically engaged by mass-media exposure of 'personalities'. Walzer cites Japanese schools as a telling counter-instance of a successful insulation of a sphere of activity: they have apparently been able to defend an educational culture of cooperative learning and common practical responsibility against the grain of competitive pressures from the surrounding society.

The implication, then, is that models of good social practice can be found in many existing institutions and social experiences. Walzer seems to be inviting us to celebrate the many forms of social life that we see around us, or that we can know as historically realized forms. He notes, for example, that in many societies holidays have been principally social festivals, not individual time-off, and affirms the social meanings of such shared time. Conversely, he seeks to mobilize these many particular values against the invasion of alien forces from outside. In practice, this is what is most often involved in defending particular institutions such as schools or hospitals or theatres, against public spending cuts for example. Walzer's original contribution is to see that socialism must be the sum of such particular worlds, and not an abstract alternative to them. It is encouraging and unusual to read a socialist who finds a lot to like as well as to dislike in the social forms around him, and regards these as parts of the ecology of a future socialism. Nor is this inconsequential. The political point about 'complex equality' is that it is only through identification with the values of particular callings that individuals may be persuaded to forego the opportunities of individual gain. The spirit of socialism depends on social identifications. It is more likely that these can be mobilized through specific values and relationships, in all their diversity, than on the basis of abstract ethical or even class principles. Typical is Walzer's observation that the family is a kind of welfare state, which guarantees to all its members some modicum of love, friendship, generosity and so on, and which taxes its members for the sake of the guarantee. On the other hand, he is no more than tolerant towards libertarian individualism, which he regards as parasitic on other people's structures.

Pluralism and Socialism

Michael Walzer's book breathes the air of a culture historically committed to pluralism, but it is important to note that he espouses a pluralism of a committed socialist kind. His statement of the defining institutions of a 'decentralized democratic socialism', which include workers' control of companies and factories, is not one to which socialists would take exception. He also seeks to locate the main sources of injustice in his own society, identifying the power of capital and money as the principal forces invasive of other autonomous spheres of value. (Totalitarianism and political monopoly appear as the opposite kind of invasive power, characteristic of the 'actually existing socialisms'.)

Nevertheless, this socialist element is underdeveloped in Walzer's book. He is perhaps anxious to argue his anti-capitalist case very carefully indeed, in order to carry with him as much as possible of his academic readership. Above all, his aim is to demonstrate the social and pluralist character of the values of the good society, against individualists and monists of various kinds, and this has greater emphasis than arguments for an egalitarian definition of justice.

Walzer is particularly concerned to find points of leverage which might have some purchase in present-day experience. Thus he reminds readers of the well-established precedents of arguments against the improper role of money, in simony, prostitution or the sale of political office. He cites a list of 'blocked exchanges' from Arthur Okun's *Equality and Efficiency,* as accepted and necessary limits to the power of money.[8] These include the prohibition (legal or moral) which applies to slavery or the sale of persons, and to commerce in national citizenship, civil and religious freedoms, political rights, certain welfare entitlements, love and friendship. The point of 'blocked exchanges' is that these are existing limitations on the power of money in American society. Even if the barriers are in many cases leaky, the list has the good effect of showing the ground of intrinsic social values which has already been established, or which can be taken up by the left with some consensual support. A positive case is presented for the removal of such major allocation areas as health care from the market sphere, and a crucial point is made about the power of private capital. 'Even within the adversary relations of owners and workers, with unions and grievance procedures in place, owners may still exercise an illegitimate kind of power. They make all sorts of decisions that severely constrain and shape the lives of their employees (and their fellow-citizens too). Might not the enormous capital investment represented by plants, furnaces, machines and assembly lines be better regarded as a political than an economic good?' On the other hand — and this is an important distinction — Walzer sees no reason why particular 'consumer goods' should not be allocated by the market, and argues that the choice thus provided is one of the benefits of a complex society. 'The liveliness of the open market reflects our sense of the great variety of desirable things; and so long as that is our sense, we have no reason not to relish the liveliness . . . . The exchange (of merchandise) is in principle a relation of mutual benefit; and neither the money that the merchant makes, nor the accumulation of things by this or that consumer, poses any threat to complex equality — not if the sphere of money and commodities is properly bounded.' Walzer's concern, here as elsewhere, is with the overstepping of boundaries, not with restricting what has its proper place within them.

On a more critical note, however, Walzer's account underestimates the overwhelming extent to which the powers of capital have invaded all spheres of life. Chances in most spheres of life are determined to a large degree by the inheritance or non-inheritance of wealth. Access to health care, even in societies with socialized medicine, is distorted by inequalities of income and other factors making for unequal take-up. Free public education by no means assures equal opportunity within the educational system. The processes of mass communication and politics are hugely influenced by large-scale capital. Crucial areas of symbolic production (the visual arts, for example) are distorted both by direct commercial colonization, through advertising, and because their goods are treated as objects for speculation and inflation-proof saving, instead of as instrinsic goods. Activities that ought to be principally rewarded by the respect and recognition of a knowledgeable community — such as sports and the performing arts — become means of achieving large fortunes, and thus celebrate not their own values but the more abstract ones of monetary success. At the present time, the powers of capital to invade particular spheres of value seem to be increasing, and various resistances are being defeated or bought up. Even the appearance of footballers with adverts on their shirts, or the staging of company-sponsored theatre productions, ought to offend us as an indication that these activities can no longer stand their ground without paying tribute to overweening corporate power. Walzer's writing lacks sufficient anger on these questions, and he does not stress enough that without fundamental economic equalities his harmony of spheres of justice cannot be attained. There is a need for sustained debates about the possible social architecture of complex equality to which *Spheres of Justice* (and, comparably, Alex Nove's *The Economics of Feasible Socialism*) are important contributions. Walzer's attempt to root diversity of actual social (and historical) forms, and his celebration of social differences as a virtue of a good society, have unexpected and fresh resonances in these generally bleak times for socialist argument. Walzer seeks to remind us of what has already been achieved, of the elements of the good society that exist around us, and suggests that a case for change can be made from the perspective of partially realized goods as well as from the more usual radical standpoint of the deprivations of the oppressed. This argument from plurality has great importance in pointing towards the positive possibilites of a just society. There are, however, problems in Walzer's attempt to give a justification of equality in these terms, and it is to these which I now turn.

Criticisms of Walzer's Relativism

As we have seen, Walzer's discussion of complex equality is directed against all monopolies of value and power — a focus that is itself linked with his particularistic definition of justice as respect for the values of separate spheres of life. Injustice occurs where the values of one sphere invade another, and indeed he suggests that social justice is a concept which has reference only to such questions of boundary and demarcation. A society can thus not be criticized as unjust (whether it is good is a different issue) if it either respects its different spheres of action or maintains a consistency of values across all of them. He suggests that the latter may be the case for the Indian caste system insofar as it does not create any actual plurality of values. Space for argument about injustice, in Walzer's view, is thus only opened up where there is already a plurality of spheres of action and value (the usual case, admittedly) and where their powers begin to invade one another through, for example, the hegemony of capital, state or church. This appears to concede too much to relativist conceptions of value, and to follow functionalist approaches in acknowledging no absolute standards beyond the positively existing norms of a given society. According to this view, a dominant order which successfully suppressed alternative value systems (perhaps a more plausible model than consensus to describe caste society) would thereby suppress or invalidate the grounds by which it could be criticized.

This is clearly an uncomfortable position for Walzer to hold, and elsewhere in his book he seems aware of the need for less relativistic moral foundations. His concept of political citizenship as the model and basis of all spheres of justice (since political decision in the end determines the relations and boundaries of every other sphere) goes some way towards providing these, albeit at the price of a certain inconsistency. On the one hand, Walzer is arguing for a tolerant and pluralistic conception of the social good, through his particularist concept of justice; on the other hand, he needs to establish common minima and limits, without which there can be no equality. His difficulty is to avoid falling back, in making the case for equality, into that very abstract universalism which he seeks to refute. But the relativism by which he avoids this provides little leverage for criticizing the arrangements of unequal societies, unless arguments against them can already be made within their own moral vocabularies. Where a society manifests no explicit conflicts over moral principles, there seem to be no grounds for questioning its inequalities.

One main defect of this position lies in the lack of an explicit historical thesis which could explain the appearance and material possibility of an idea of 'complex equality'. The emergence both of 'complexity' — to which Walzer gives rather more attention — and of 'equality' need to be explained as *historical* facts. But although Walzer provides a wealth of historical detail in his analysis of the idea of pluralism, this is not the same as developing an evolutionary theory that might explain its factual possibility. It may be that such a thesis is implicit in the weight he attaches to the long-term process of differentiation in the development of modern society. But it can hardly be denied that Walzer identifies no historical pattern or meaning in the emergence of egalitarian ideals. The ideal of democracy is there at the beginning in ancient Athens, just as the ideal of community is present among the medieval Jews.

Examples of admirable diversity of social forms are cited in a variety of temporal and spatial locations, from the gift exchange in the Western Pacific to the Sunset Scavenger Company of San Francisco, a workers' cooperative. Walzer has a sense for plurality and diversity as necessary values, and sees that it is both undesirable and impossible to reduce this back to primitive simplicity (except perhaps as one communitarian option in a wider range of social choices). At the same time, he implicitly endorses the division of labour as the dominant process in the making of modern societies. This argument derives in the last resort from the classical economists and sociologists, in their respective individualist and holistic formulations of this process. This thesis of differentiation is one that Walzer shares with functionalist sociologists, but with the difference that comes from his own commitment to equality as well as pluralism.

An Evolutionary Perspective

It is, however, also possible to see the evolution of egalitarian norms as having a positive historical basis. The development of modern society is a story not only of the division of labour but also of successive demands for social rights against various forms of privilege. We can see, following Turner and Marshall, [9] that the first set of modern historical claims was for legal and political equality; the second for minimal economic rights; and the third for more 'qualitative' social and psychological entitlements to such goods as education and an 'unspoiled' or 'civilized' environment. Where Walzer presents his 'blocked exchanges' as a list of moral desiderata resting upon some established consensus, they should surely be seen also as the embodiments of claims to universal rights to the means of life, made in historical succession by the representatives of the bourgeoisie and the industrial working class, and now perhaps by new 'post-industrial' social strata. These different kinds of egalitarian claim (and the movements and institutions to which they gave rise) are not less historical facts than is the diversity of modern social forms. The egalitarian dimension of Walzer's argument may receive a firmer grounding from such a historical approach than from the particularist claims that can be made on behalf of one sphere of justice against its invasion by others, or from a somewhat a priori political universalism. The critique of apparently consensual or hegemonic systems, such as those of caste, may also acquire some leverage by reference to the standard of historical possibility, instead of having to depend upon normative conflicts already actualized (or not) within them. While Walzer's argument currently makes use of Marx's ethical vision, such a historical conception would enable him to link his thesis more closely to the explanatory structure of Marx's work. Finally, if the claims of both equality and differentiation are formulated in historical and sociological terms, it will be possible to avoid the arbitrary coupling of a textured historical argument for differentiation with an abstract universalist argument for equality.

Types of Equality and Inequality

The weakness of Walzer's theoretical and historical arguments for equality, compared with his sophisticated defence of pluralism, leads him to an overcondensed concept of 'complex equality'. One should note that there are two variables contained in this compound concept which can be varied independently of each other. Thus there are four theoretical possibilities, and not two: simple equality, simple inequality, complex equality, and complex inequality. Walzer's most salient contrast is between complex inequality, his preferred form, and simple inequality or tyranny, which is his main negative term. This contrast involves a simultaneous alternation of both terms of the compound concept. Simple equality is recognized as a theoretical possibility, but is rejected as impossible since the means of enforcing it via a monopoly of power in the hands of the state will generate inequalities of another kind. (Again it is notable that Walzer's preoccupation with political theory leads to an emphasis on state forms rather than modes of production as the key limiting condition.) The fourth possibility of complex *in*equality is tackled less explicity in Walzer's argument, which provides us with insufficient criteria for distinguishing between equal and unequal forms of complex society. Indeed, this lack of separate and specific attention to the dimensions of inequality requires him to place so much weight on the invasion of boundary as sole criterion of injustice, that its specificity is achieved at the price of limiting its value as a measure of the social good. Walzer's choice of a notion of equality (complex equality) rather than justice as his ultimate value-concept may also indicate the limitation of his definition of justice. For this may be too relativist to allow the moral discriminations between alternative societies that he as a socialist might want to make.

Walzer's rejection of 'simple equality' as a possibility shows traces of a similar argument of Frank Parkin's to which he refers. In

Marxism and Class Theory: a Bourgeois Critique (op.cit.), Parkin characterizes all claims on goods as either exclusionary (intended to exclude those not already in possession) or usurpationary (intended to supplant those in possession). He leaves no space for an idea of universal rights, or goods which are to be shared equally, even though these have been the main form of demand, and historical achievement, of both bourgeois and working-class movements. While Parkin offers salutary insights into the usurpationary potential of subordinate class claims (e.g., the replacement of monopolies of capital ownership with monopolies of party power), his conceptual exclusion of a *sharing* of power and goods which is neither exclusionary nor usurpationary is harmful to any notion of equality, and gives his book its distinctively cynical tone. For his part, Walzer is openly committed to equality, yet his two-pronged argument in terms of separate spheres of justice and a concept of political rights suggests a somewhat undue sensitivity to the dangers of egalitarian claims and demands per se, especially where these are linked explicitly with social classes. The dismal lessons learned from 'actually existing socialisms' by Parkin and many others may have had a deeper influence on Walzer than he realizes, and led him to abandon some lines of argument which remain necessary to any egalitarian philosophy.

Arguments for Equality and Differentiation

If we give proper emphasis to the separate operative variables of equality and differentiation in the construction of the idea of 'complex equality', can we find a more satisfactory way of generating Walzer's own preferred socialist conclusion from his philosophical premises? The key may lie in distinguishing those domains of value which should be ruled chiefly by the norm of equality, from those in which the claims of differentiation, with its necessary but contained inequalities, should hold sway. The former are of two kinds. On the one hand, there are those spheres which necessarily have the power of determining or invading others. Walzer's argument enables us to identify politics as a sphere in which a measure of equal rights (universal suffrage and freedom of speech and association) should obtain even though specific inequalities of political capacity, reputation and power will emerge from these level foundations. Ownership of the large-scale means of production is a similar case which, in Walzer's terms, can be regarded as political power because of its effects on all men's lives, or which, in more Marxist idiom, is a causal foundation of all other spheres. Choice between relatively equal individual ownership of the means of production, and participatory shares in some form of collective ownership, is not however prescribed by this principle: these alternatives could give rise to different forms of just society. The second category of good which should be allocated on an egalitarian basis is that which is the precondition of individual access to other goods such as health, education, and some basic share in the wealth of society. These coincide with areas of 'blocked exchange' under welfare capitalism, which in these ways recognizes or has been constrained to recognize such ascribed universal rights. While the substantive prescriptions of this argument are similar to Walzer's, it is based not merely on a model of harmonious equilibrium of non-invasive spheres, but on an attempt to establish a framework of legislated equalities within which differentiated spheres of action can find their appropriate space.

The four possibilities generated by Walzer's concept of complex equality can be illustrated by a diagram:

	Equality	Inequality
one dimension (simple)	A 'primitive communism' (self-contradictory in Walzer's view)	B tyranny of single order of power/values
many dimensions (complex)	D many separate value systems, but with discrete non-overlapping hierarchies	C many separate value systems, but some hierarchies (usually derived from capital or a monopoly of political power) determine other distributions

The problem for socialists in complex liberal societies is to achieve a shift from quadrant C to D. The risk is that of a degenerative move instead to quadrant B.

An equality of political and large-scale economic powers is the classical socialist solution. Achieving a *balance* of political and economic centres of power, through a 'mixed economy', is the preferred remedy of social democrats. Walzer's position, though cautiously argued, is a 'market socialism' version of the former.

The Sphere of Place

Walzer identifies a number of institutions and statuses which are crucial to the provision of basic social identity. These include national membership, political citizenship, and kinship — and in addition the rights which are or should be guaranteed by the welfare state (employment, health, education, minimum living standards) afford access to other spheres of justice. Within the framework of this argument, I would point to one other sphere which should be recognised and furthered as a primary source of membership — the institutions of place and neighbourhood. The vitality of local institutions and cultures, even in a differentiated society, is critical for forms of social recognition that are within reach of all citizens, and not just present in the alienated form of national media celebrities.

The first experiences which citizens have of many spheres of value are bound to be in immediate localities, and it is on a platform of local memberships — of schools, theatres, or basketball teams — that involvement in wider national fields of activity should be built. Membership in the activities of a neighbourhood thus has the same importance for a wide variety of forms of life as does national membership as a precondition for all of them. The recent developments of community sports and arts (sports centres seem to be multiplying and thriving in Britain as are no other new fields of social provision), the moves by socialist councils to decentralize control over the administration of services, local involvement in schools, political movements, and self-help groups — all these are roots of a differentiated life. National competitions in these various spheres should be merely the tips of icebergs whose less visible base lies in the towns and villages. When citizens gain identity and status by participation in a field of activity, the greater accomplishments of the most talented can serve as a celebration of what is commonly valued, and not merely envied as a form of escape. The public symbolism of the mass marathon races in London and New York is in this way an encouraging development. It is a mistake to think that in advanced and prosperous societies local relatedness will or should become less important. The denudation of meaning from merely local settings of activity — whether they be local schools, or colleges, or theatres — in favour of national or international 'centres of excellence' is another kind of invasion and alienation from outside, usually backed by monetary values and professional interests.

Meaning is given by participation in activity — by the gift and exchange of time and labour, whether in parenting, politics, or theatre — and for the majority of people this can only conceivably be in a restricted circle known from place of residence or work. Membership in a national activity elite is by definition a 'positional good' that cannot be available to everyone, even on the largest assumptions concerning mobility and travel and electronic communication. (I am leaving aside the social advantages of preserving a large measure of stability of residence and settlement, against these trends.) By supporting local identities, in principle and in policy, socialists can encourage the development of values, differences and choices, at the point at which they immediately matter to most people. Perhaps, given the vigorous local cultures of the United States, Michael Walzer assumed this neighbourly dimension to be self-evident. But it is by no means so in the over-centralised society of Britain. Socialists in advanced societies are now in danger of speaking for declining or residual clases and sectors, rather than for those which are growing in number and influence. They face arguments formulated in terms of the material interests of the majority against which it is hard to mobilize countervailing coalitions. *Spheres of Justice* suggests to me that we might do better to shift the ground of these arguments away from interests and towards goals and values, rather than to meet them on their own individualist and aggregative terms. We should build our conception of socialism from the experience of callings, of art, of localities, of kinship or particular fraternities — all of which are endangered by both tyranny and the rule of capital. We should want socialism to enable men and women to do what they often already try to do, but without the reduction of ends to the one-dimensionality of money.

These considerations may provide some philosophical coherence for the qualitative and environmental politics, in the broadest sense of the latter term, which makes sense in a society now technically capable, in the West, of material abundance. The New Right learned in the seventies to think through the implications of the left's politics of cumulative claims and demands, and defined a crisis of 'overload' and 'excessive expectations' which set the agenda for the current period of reaction. [10] *Spheres of Justice* can be seen as a counter-appropriation which accepts the necessity of a constraining social value-system, yet claims the field of embodied moral goals for the democratic left against the neo-liberalism that is now its main adversary. It offers an important opportunity to a socialist theory of justice.

NOTES

1. R. Nozick, *Anarchy, State and Utopia*, Oxford 1975; J. Rawls, *A Theory of Justice*, Oxford 1973. Walzer tells us that Nozick presented his ideas in a course at Harvard in 1970, the other half of which was given by Walzer.

2. Some of the major articles in the functionalist debate on equality and inequality are reprinted in R. Bendix and S.M. Lipset, eds., *Class, Status and Power*, Glencoe, Ill. 1966.

3. C. Taylor, *Hegel*, Cambridge 1975; A. MacIntyre, *After Virtue*, London 1981

4. See G. Therborn, *Science, Class and Society*, NLB London 1976, for a discussion of this point.

5. See F. Parkin, *Marxism and Class Theory: A Bourgeois Critique*, London 1979.

6. B. Pascal, *The Pensees*, trans. J.M. Cohen, Harmondsworth 1961, p. 96 (no. 244).

7. K. Marx, 'Economic and Philosophical Manuscripts', in *Early Writings*, NLR Pelican, Harmondsworth 1975, p.379.

8. See A. Okun, *Equality and Efficiency*, New York 1975.

9. R.H. Turner, 'The Theme of Contemporary Social Movements', *British Journal of Sociology*, vol. XX no. 4; T.H. Marshall, 'Citizenship and Social Class', in *Class, Citizenship and Social Development*, New York 1973.

10. Among the influential statements of this neo-Conservative view are Daniel Bell, *The Cultural Contradictions of Capitalism*, ed. J. Keane, London 1979; Irving Kristol, *Two Cheers for Capitalism*, New York 1978; and Samuel Brittan, *The Economic Consequences of Democracy*, London 1976. These issues are discussed from a more left-wing point of view by Jurgen Habermas, *Legitimation Crisis*, London 1976, and Claus Offe, *Contradictions of the Welfare State*, Cambridge, Mass. 1984.

4

Power to the Regions

The large disparities in levels of employment and wealth between regions and nations in Britain, especially between 'North' and 'South', and the polarization of voting between left and right which these have increasingly given rise to, have yet to generate a coherent political response on the left. The outmanoeuvring and defeat of the Nationalists in the devolution debates in the 1970s seemed to have killed the national question as a political issue. The Thatcher government has been a militantly centralizing force, and has been able to recover its whole political position through the acting out of the extraordinary fantasy of English national recovery in the Falklands adventure. While there are signs of some revival of nationalist support in Scotland, and of a renewed interest in regional and national questions within the labour movement, this falls far short of a strategy which gives proper weight to territorial inequality and division within the British Isles. This article argues the case for such a 'territorial strategy' for the left in Britain. It will present the advantages of regionalism, and peripheral nationalism, in terms of their possible consequences for the balance of class forces, and the opportunities they may provide to increase the influence of the working class and its allies.

Labour's Tradition

The advantages of regional devolution have been debated in one form or another for the last two decades in British politics (and before the War by G.D.H. Cole). Redressing the disadvantages of the regions was part of the Wilsonian 'modernization' programme for the Labour government elected in 1964. Regional disparities of income and employment had of course been preoccupations of

96

governments since the 1930s. The Labour Party was particularly sensitive to the problems of the relatively deprived regions of the North, South Wales and Scotland, from which so much of its support has always come. Labour's programme of 'technological modernization' was also rooted in some kind of critique of Britain's hereditary and ascriptive class system, with its bias towards rentier incomes and the financial sector, and its subordination of the interests of productive industry. This critique reflected the outlook and interests of rising segments of the middle class,[1] frustrated by upper-class recruitment to and monopoly of top positions, as much as it advanced working-class interests. Wilson's well-projected northern origins made him an effective critic of social exclusiveness, for which, in this early period, he was able to mobilize support from working-class people too, who were glad to see 'them' for once roundly and wittily denounced. The inclusion of a regional dimension in Labour's National Plan was therefore a natural step, and should have been a means of enhancing the influence of those committed to industrial growth in the regions, both local capital and trade unions, against the national financial sector and international economic pressures. But the regional planning agencies established as part of the National Plan were given little power at this time, and never became central to Labour's strategy of economic reconstruction.[2] In any case, this strategy rapidly collapsed.

Regional economic disparities remained a preoccupation of all governments of the post-war consensus, prior to Thatcher's, for reasons of national as well as local economic interest. It was held that the economy 'overheated' through shortages of skilled labour and consequent wage-led inflation whenever full employment was achieved in the most prosperous areas of the Midlands and the South-East. Consequently, high levels of unemployment in other regions could be viewed as 'merely' waste. Resources could theoretically be brought into production in these areas without inflationary consequences anywhere else, and some measure of economic support could be justified as in effect self-financing. A whole panoply of regulatory devices, both positive and negative, was therefore deployed to try to redress regional economic disparities. These included controls on industrial location, subsidies to private investment and direct investment by the state, regional employment premiums and policies to improve transport and communications. The Thatcher government has abandoned most of these.

The need for reforms to rationalize the apparatus of government was a developing preoccupation during the 1960s and 1970s and was another aspect of the programme of managerialist modernization which provided a dominant agenda for governments in this period. The reorganizations of local government, the health service, and social services, were among the major changes effected; one might also see the comprehensive reorganization of secondary education as part of the same general programme for setting up larger, more universalist and professionalized structures. During this debate, there were some persuasive advocacies of regional government, mostly from the social democratic and 'managerialist' wing of the Labour Party. John Mackintosh's *The Devolution of Power* (1968), Derek Senior's Dissenting Memorandum to the Redcliffe-Maud Report on Local Government (1971), and Lord Crowther Hunt and Alan Peacock's Memorandum of Dissent from the Kilbrandon Report on Devolution (1973) were the most important statements of position.[3] These argued the case for regional devolution, on grounds of its consistency with the proposed powers for Scotland and Wales, and the desirability of reversing the centralization of the British state apparatus and civil service (whose potential has been further revealed under Thatcher and Heseltine). Derek Senior's proposal for city-regions also sought to resolve the harmful administrative division between borough and county, town and country, which has been so powerful an instrument for the long-term defence of Tory interests against Labour municipal policies, and has confounded any potential regional challenges to metropolitan policy. But while intellectually these writers were able to present a powerful case, its political influence remained small. No connection was made between the economic plight of the regions, of which Labour goverments were well aware, and the Westminster-dominated system of government, which gave them so little political leverage. Perhaps as a result, the relationship between state expenditure in the regions and their relative need has been neither consistent nor close.[4] Labour's own political apparatus was highly centralized, the result of a history of fear of grassroots activity, infiltration and extra-parliamentary militancy which has similarly stifled the local trades councils. The party's slender bureaucracy of regional organizers for many years had as one of its main preoccupations to monitor the provinces for signs of heresy and rebellion, and to step in and 'dissolve' errant parties. So weak a structure was in no state to welcome the new currents of nationalist feeling when they emerged in Scotland and Wales, and to turn them into a socialist resource. The Labour Party has always had great difficulty in creating any apparatus of its own which does not correspond directly to the functions dictated by the existing parliamentary constitution, which is indeed fetishized to this day. [5]

Municipal political interest did, on the other hand, have some persisting weight in Labour's policies towards the state. Labour's efforts at local government reform, modified by the Conservatives after the 1970 election defeat, attempted to achieve some strengthening of the powers of its big city bases against those of the Tory counties. But the reform of local government, already diluted by the Tories in the interests of the shires in 1972, has proved quite insufficient to arrest the decline of local government in face of the financial and political powers of the centralized state which have been used so determinedly against them by the Thatcher government. While there has been an important influx of new energies and ideas into municipal socialism in the past years (for example, through the establishment of industrial development agencies in the GLC, the West Midlands and Sheffield, and the attempt to institute popular and radical transport policies in South Yorkshire and Greater London), it is clear that a hostile central government can now deploy overwhelming juridical and financial resources against socialist city governments.

If industrial decline in backward English regions, and the arguments for a more rationalized and decentralized structure of government, were one element in the debate about regional devolution in the 1960s and 1970s, its real political force came from a different quarter — the threat to the British state posed by Scottish and Welsh nationalism. These currents made their first major impact in disillusion with the same Labour government which was toying in the early 1960s with these half-hearted regionalist notions: the first Plaid Cymru election victory was at Carmarthen in 1966, the first Scottish Nationalist victory at Hamilton in 1967. The Labour Party, especially in areas where it was directly threatened by nationalist support (Scotland), or indirectly threatened, as it thought, by competition for the largesse of the British state (the North East), reacted with hostility to the emergence of what might in other circumstances have been perceived as potential allies against the metropolitan state, and southern Tory domination.

Consequently, the arguments, reinforced by the rise of nationalism, for generalizing the claims of regional identity and autonomy to the English regions as well as Scotland and Wales fell on deaf ears in the English labour movement. English regional

Labour parties are in any case vestigial structures without the roots in patronage and local power which characterize municipal parties. Leading British politicians characteristically do not emerge from a local base, as do their counterparts in the USA, France, West Germany or Italy, but are mostly metropolitan carpet-baggers who settle on a constituency and make it their own after, rather than before, adoption as its parliamentary candidate. (This may now be changing with the emergence of David Blunkett and Ken Livingstone in a national political role.) So nationalism was perceived largely as a threat to the hegemony of the British Parliament, and to the tenure of power of the Labour and Conservative Parties. Those with access to power in Whitehall showed little interest in conceding it to political forces based elsewhere.

The devolution debate seemed to many in England during the last two Labour governments to be merely a wearisome distraction, a slow wearing down by attrition of the nationalist movements. In fact it had fateful consequences, diverting the attentions of the government from more important matters, and perhaps unwittingly preparing the ground for the Thatcherite reassertion of the power of the metropolitan (and imperial) State. Where subordinate classes have been divided and in conflict with one another (as over immigration and ethnic divisions, among the Protestants and Catholics of Northern Ireland, and in the majority of the British labour movement's response to peripheral nationalism), the beneficiaries have been the regressive elements of the bourgeoisie represented by Thatcherism, who are most traditionally identified with the English state.

The heartland of Thatcherism in 1979 was after all the South-East and West Midlands: polarization in the electoral geography of Britain, between North and South, has never been more marked. Thatcherism spoke loudly to English identity, against immigrants and against class, criminal, terrorist and military threats to the nation. The Falklands crisis has now shown the potential strength of old imperial sentiments, reminding us of a history many on the left had preferred to forget. Characteristically, this patriotic feeling was reported to be less rampant in Scotland and Wales. So far, regional nationalist threats to the British state have worked to the advantage of the right, through the inability of the left to bring these challenges together in any coherent programme for the reconstruction of the state. The neglect of potential territorial bases for organizing support (Labour's election campaigns are distinctively national in organization and presentation) distinguishes the British left from more locally rooted formations elsewhere (France, W. Germany, Italy, the USA).

The local response to nationalism by the left has inevitably been conditioned by the social characteristics of the nationalist leadership in Scotland and Wales. Representing in large part the local professional class and small capital, this leadership, especially in Scotland, has been often anti-socialist. For this reason, local hostility to petty-bourgeois and often regressive social forces has masked for many working-class leaderships, especially in the Labour Party, the potential advantages of a wider geography of regional class alliances on a United Kingdom scale. The most socialist elements in the Labour Party have characteristically, in both their 'old left' and 'new left' variants, taken too centralist a view of the potentiality of the British state. The old left has been parliamentarist and constitutionalist (Michael Foot's *Observer* articles in the summer of 1982 restated this view in unregenerate form), holding that working-class representation could achieve socialist changes through the agency of a 'neutral' state apparatus, whose centralisation would be a means of carrying through reforms on a universal basis. While the 'new left' in the Labour Party clearly perceives that this state apparatus is not benign or neutral, and must first be transformed before other reforms are possible, here there is an undue preoccupation with what the central state apparatus, once in working-class hands, *could* do, even if it took a less naive attitude to its present dispositions.

These perspectives lead to an over-reliance on narrowly working-class institutions (which are often themselves politically weak, and sometimes working-class mainly in name) and a neglect of the other bases of organic support which a socialist party now needs. The long neglect of the dimensions of gender, race, community and cultural activity in the Labour Party is consistent with a lack of appreciation of local and geographical dimensions, of the necessity to make alliances with other class strata in particular regions to meet the overwhelming power of the metropolitan bourgeoisie. This blindness resulted in a failure to find any common ground with the social forces represented by Scottish and Welsh nationalism, if not with their political leaderships. On more specific terrains (the defence of jobs in a particular town, the work of the Scottish and Welsh Development Agencies) these local imperatives are more often recognized, and possible conjunctions of interest between local capital and labour recognized and acted upon. But it has not yet been seen to be necessary to translate this necessary flexibility in class strategy to a national place.

The SDP and Decentralization

The case for regional devolution surfaced again in 1982 with the publication of a Social Democratic Party Green Paper, *Decentralizing Government*, which recommended the establishment of elected regional authorities and the reconstitution of the House of Lords on a basis of regional representation, in some ways analogous to the American Senate or the West Germany Bundesrat. This paper not surprisingly took up many of the arguments expounded by former Labour advocates of devolution such as J.P. MacKintosh. Its case is presented largely in administrative terms, in relation to liberal democratic principles of accountability, wider participation in decision-making, and efficiency. Like earlier advocates, the SDP Decentralization Group draws attention to the enormous accretion of bureaucratic power to central government in recent years, through regional department offices, appointed bodies such as the Health and Water Authorities (many of whose powers were originally taken from elected local government), and ever-tighter financial control of local councils. From the point of view of liberal principles and more accountable administration, these arguments are well made and many socialists might support them as such, given an alternative of centralized state bureaucracy.

Neither the SDP Green Paper nor the earlier supporters of regional devolution in England address themselves to the possible implications of this change in state forms for the relative powers of class interests in Britain. On the assumption that party politics is largely about the advancement of class interests, this is a dimension that needs to be made explicit. It is characteristic of Social Democrat thinking that it represses this level of politics, seeking to present a specific class interest in the universalist terms of ethical principles and efficiency.

One may conjecture that the SDP focus on decentralization continues the earlier managerial interests of the Labour 'modernizers' in seeking forms of administration which are more amenable to rational professionalized control, more responsive to the needs and interests of those they administer, and thus better able to secure consensus and social harmony. In the 1960s and 1970s, major reorganizations of local government, social services, and the National Health Service were substantially influenced by the 'system theories' of corporate management, imported into the public sector from the most sophisticated thinking of the private corporate sector. [6] These theories of corporate planning, while slow to change the actual practices of public bureaucracies, can be seen to be congruent with the interests of new strata of graduate managers and planners, seeking legitimation of their power through more 'scientific' managerial techniques.

But the SDP–Liberal Alliance also brings to its attitudes to government the perspective of outsiders who have an interest in creating new centres of power to offset their relative exclusion from the old ones. An emphasis on legal procedures, participation and decentralization also serves the more specific aptitudes of this credential-holding middle-class stratum, and is adapted to its own distinctive resources in the contest for power. Possessing cultural rather than material capital, it is potentially the most effective operator of participatory procedures. Characteristic institutions of this stratum are the Consumers Association, the pre-school play group movement, parent-teachers' associations, and certain kinds of association for conservation, environmental improvement, or collective 'gentrification'. These social movements of the educated middle class are means of organizing access to benefits from the means of consumption, both individual and collective. Extension of rights of participation in administration, *and* its professionalization through the expansion of paid expert roles for both administrators and politicians, are means of extending the influence of the representatives of this social stratum. The more participatory politics of the United States (far more elective offices, community control of schools, a tradition of community-and issue-rather than class-based mobilization) is a model for British Social Democrats, and Liberals of the newer sort, and the USA also favours those with the greater participatory resources and skills. This seems to be the 'hidden agenda' of the SDP's commitment to decentralization, just as a corresponding emphasis on parliamentary forms reflected the occupational and cultural advantages of earlier generations of European liberals whose typical callings were journalism and the law.

The SDP's regional proposals may also reflect its current position as only an outside challenger for political power, and the Alliance's interest in achieving a secure regional base. The Alliance is further preoccupied with gaining some power of veto over the decisions of the class forces on either side of it, seeing its most feasible (or at least minimal) role as to limit the 'extremism' of left and right. The Green Paper's proposal for a Second Chamber elected from regional constituencies (representing the proposed regions equally, regardless of their unequal populations) seems designed to secure such a veto power, in the same way that proportional representation is designed to make centre parties indispensable to any governing majority. This particular proposal, for equal representation of regions of grossly unequal size in the Second Chamber, is the most pointedly self-interested in the SDP document. Its intended effect seems likely to be that of shoring up the influence of the strongest Alliance regions (the peripheral areas of traditional Liberal strength) against that of the Tory South-East and Labour North. Socialists do not share the SDP's interest in a centrist veto, and while the proposal for a regionally elected Second Chamber should be seriously considered (it is much more likely to win support than the simple abolition of the Lords), the principle of representation in proportion to population should be firmly upheld.

Whatever the SDP's specific perspectives and interests, it does not follow that there may not also be some advantage to the left in the proposed restructuring of the state. For one thing, the disproportionate power conferred on the electoral winner in the 'first past the post' system has in the past four years been exercised effectively by a strong government of the right, with little of the resistance from 'civil society' which a left government similarly elected on a minority vote would have met. It can no longer be assumed that untrammelled power from parliamentary majorities is a resource only for the left. What has to be balanced, in discussions about regional devolution or proportional representation, is the effects which these changes might have in strengthening the political centre, against the possible benefits to the left of a more widely representative and open political structure, in which minorities and parties of the Left would be more able to achieve representation in regional or national assemblies. It may be that a more pluralistic structure of class and cultural allegiances in Britain today would be better reflected in a correspondingly more pluralist electoral system, than through the unrepresentative and dinosaurian machinery of the Labour Party.

This indeed seems to be one of the few areas of radical change that might be opened up by the SDP 'break', and such opportunities, in a society as immobile and conservative as Britain's, should not be spurned without careful consideration. It would be myopic to repeat the sad experience of the devolution debate, when a chance to weaken the grip of the dominant classes was ignored through traditionalist Labour Party and 'constitutional' reflexes. Labour's natural inclination in discussions of decentralization is to favour its municipal strongholds; a recent Labour proposal to devolve the powers of the Water Authorities on to local authorities suggests that this preference continues. The prospects for a new kind of socialist city authority under a Labour central government need to be carefully weighed in this debate, as an alternative to regional power. But the experience of the socialist metropolitan counties does not suggest that they are now ideally structured. What is remarkable about the Greater London and South Yorkshire councils is the size of their political achievement with such limited powers and revenues. The lesson that should be drawn from the government's attempt to abolish them, and from the opposition to it that has been successfully mobilized, is that authorities at this level should have a broader spectrum of functions, not be replaced exactly in their existing form. This probably also means that they should have a broader territorial jurisdiction — becoming gen- uinely regional rather than metropolitan authorities.

Labour may also now be wise to take account of its relative weakness, and no longer assume that it is an inevitable 'alternative government' able to treat all other political formations, left and centre, as enemies to be ignored or crushed. Labour too, as a potential minority party, may have an interest in acquiring some powerful regional bases, to provide a source of patronage and power to sustain its strength when it is not in national office. Without the experience of such power, parties tend to drift into sectarianism, other-worldliness, and impossibilist programmes. Occupancy of local (or regional) office provides training for party cadres, patronage for its apparatus, the opportunity to sustain support for democratic cultural forms, and a record of success in office which the party can use in its national campaigns. A sig- nificant analogy is that of post-war Italy, where the Italian Communist Party has made effective use of regional political bases (in Emilia-Romagna and Umbria, for example) while so far ex- cluded from national political office. Doubts about the prospects of central state power in Britain in the near future (leaving aside any misgivings about the likelihood of the Labour Party using it effectively) might sensibly lead the left to look into the potential advantages of power in regional and peripheral-national authorities.

From this point of view, the most significant fact about the SDP proposal is that it has been put on the table, and makes more feasible a public debate on these questions. However, the mixed response it received at the SDP Conference in the autumn of 1982 made it clear that no progress can be made without the mobilization of support in the regions themselves for a real measure of devolution. The preference of many Social Democrats and Liberals for local rather than regional government power indicates in fact a difference of class interests in alignments on this issue. One might suggest that local government autonomy is most closely adapted to the democratic control of the means of collective consumption, but concentrates power insufficiently to assert control of the means of production or capital. It thus reproduces the essential strength and weakness of social democratic politics. Nevertheless, although regional government is less 'decentralizing' and democratic in its implications (and this is a serious problem), it could concentrate powers sufficient to make coordinated planning and substantial capital investment possible. Regional government ought therefore to make sense to those committed to socialization of the means of production (if only to deal with regional economic disasters) and to managerial strata committed to more rational forms of planning in general.

The attitude of most socialists to the Social Democrats is understandably one of unmitigated hostility. Enmity towards former allies (however antagonistic was the former alliance) tends to be all the greater because of former ties, and because of the bitterness which preceded separation. For these reasons even tactical co-operation with the SDP over a specific issue such as regional devolution is difficult to contemplate. But from the point of view of political realism and the sanguine appreciation of class interests, there could be wider benefits, in certain circumstances, from a parallel commitment on the regional issue. If Labour failed to achieve majority support on its own, the question of its relationship with the political centre would have to be evaluated issue by issue, and if there were commonalities of interest on substantive questions, it would be sensible to recognize them. The defeat of Thatcherism and the discrediting of the politics of the right is the highest priority at the present time, and while the left will wish to inflect this debate in the most socialist direction that is possible, it may have to recognize that the centre parties are a lesser evil which may need to be treated accordingly to stave off a worse one.

The Labour Party has hitherto consisted of an alliance of segments of the salaried, rationalizing middle class, and the working-class movement, as Gareth Stedman Jones recently re-minded us.[7] The move to the right in British politics is in large part the result of the failure and collapse of this 'modernizing middle class', and the formation of the SDP was one response by representatives of this class to this failure. It was, perhaps still is, possible to imagine that this Social Democratic middle-class leadership will recompose a large fraction of the electorate, including many working class voters. The counter-attack within the Labour Party by the forces of the 'moderate left', with the support of the trade unions, during and following the succession of Kinnock to the leadership, has, however, brought some limited recovery, and makes the situation very fluid. What is certain is that any left strategy must now reckon with a plurality of class interests, and the difficulty of achieving power only on the basis of Labour's traditional constituency. This has also been the lesson of the electoral successes achieved by other European socialist parties in recent years, and of the rise of the 'green' tendencies in West Germany and elsewhere. The internal structure of the Labour Party is not adapted to this situation, and a greater openness and plurality of representation needs to be created either within, through internal reform, or without, through proportional representation and the wider political competition that might make possible. It is argued here that a more vigorous regional and territorial dimension to socialist politics would widen the political reach of the left, and that the campaign for more regional power would focus these struggles in their necessarily locally-varied forms. It is here, as in the issues of electoral reform, that a possible coincidence of interest with various parties of the centre, both Nationalist and Alliance, might arise, both in debate about regionalism and nationalism and in some regional administrations that might (as in Italy) eventually arise.

Forms of Regional Government

The proposal advanced by the SDP Decentralization Group, and by Labour advocates such as MacKintosh before them, is for the establishment of nine or eleven regional authorities in England, together with elected national authorities in Scotland and Wales. Various detailed suggestions have been made regarding the size and boundaries of these authorities, and this is not the place to discuss these in detail. The electoral implications of a choice of boundaries for each region are clearly crucial, for example, and would need careful study. MacKintosh's point of departure was the 1964 Labour government's economic planning regions, which were as follows:

Region (or Nation)	Population (1967) (millions)	Administrative centre
Scotland	5.2	Edinburgh
Wales	2.7	Cardiff
Northern	3.3	Newcastle
Yorkshire & Humberside	4.8	Leeds
North West	6.7	Manchester
West Midlands	5.0	Birmingham
East Midlands	3.3	Nottingham
East Anglia	1.6	(London in 1965)
South West	3.6	Bristol
South East (incl. London)	17.1	London

The main modification he proposed was the creation of three regions from the last two listed, called South West (based on Plymouth and including Devon, Cornwall, half Somerset and Dorset), South East (still a very large region including London and most of the surrounding Home Counties area), and South Central (including Bristol, Southampton, Portsmouth and Oxford).

The SDP group has proposed two further regions (making eleven English regions), one of these in the South West area of traditional Liberal strength, and one in the Thames area. This is significant given the accompanying SDP proposal for a Second Chamber in which regions would have equal weight. There are also variations in regard to the East and North Midlands, and a convincing alternative proposal for London and the South East which would treat Greater London as a region on its own (with a population of 7 million) and redistribute the surrounding Home Counties to separate regions.

The treatment of London and the South East is obviously a difficulty. To give this region the boundaries suggested by patterns of communication and economic coherence creates a region far more populous than the rest, and thus likely to reproduce the metropolitan dominance which regionalization is intended to counter. On the other hand, it is difficult to construct coherent regional authorities out of the South Eastern counties exclusive of Greater London. The best solution in this case might be to maintain the existing geographical extent of the GLC's jurisdiction, and en- large its functions, while creating a separate South Eastern Counties authority. This would avoid an excessively large and dominant metropolitan authority, and might also be more acceptable politically to the other parties (since a South Eastern authority would escape Labour control). Other problems concern Scotland and Wales, which might best, as Crowther Hunt proposed, have some regional divisions within larger national authorities. [8]

The powers proposed for the regions by MacKintosh, Crowther Hunt and the SDP group were primarily to be taken from national government, and from the appointed authorities like those responsible for health and water. MacKintosh's list was extensive, and included:

Regional Planning (including major communications)
Highways; Regional Transport
Housing (large scale redevelopment, overspill, new towns)
Agriculture; Forestry; Fishing
Countryside Amenities
Police; Fire Services
Water Supplies (and river pollution, flood control, main drainage)
Education (higher, further, in some cases secondary)
Refuse Disposal
Support for the Arts
Hospitals (and Preventive Medicine, General Practitioner and Welfare Services)
General Competence (to do anything not prohibited by law which might be in the interests of the electors).

In addition, Crowther Hunt gave particular importance to regional economic development functions. The powers to develop Regional Enterprise Boards, economic development agencies, and investment banks would be one of the most important priorities for socialists.

Local government would clearly be profoundly affected by regional reform. MacKintosh suggested that the regional authorities should be allowed to create their own appropriate form of local government. The SDP group argues that one existing tier of local government would have to be abolished. It attaches greater priority than MacKintosh to the restoration of local government powers, proposing that these be exercised through funds allocated by regional authorities, rather than in a direct relationship with central government. The financial basis for these arrangements is clearly crucial: it is the dependence of local government on Whitehall grants which has provided the main lever of Thatcherite control. MacKintosh proposed a per capita and needs-related grant to regional government, together with a small local income tax. Regional authorities would be able to determine their own priorities of expenditure within this allocaiton. Crowther Hunt added that regional authorities should be able to finance additional expenditure within set limits, to allow some scope for reflationary economic policies within the regions without undue jeopardy to national counter-inflationary policies. The SDP proposal is to reduce the share of grant-related local government expenditure by the diversion of the proceeds of one third of income tax to the local authorities. There is an ambivalence within the SDP position between the aims of strengthening regional and local government, and their financial proposals seem designed to favour the latter more than the former. Socialists on the other hand should have an interest in creating regional authorities strong enough to exercise substantial economic powers, and to become agencies of public ownership in their own right.

The objective of establishing regional authorities with political strength might be best met by having a cabinet rather than a local government committee system, as MacKintosh proposed. This is likely to produce more visible leaderships than are usually achieved in local government (the cases of Ken Livingstone and David Blunkett being exceptional) and thus to assist the mobilization of political support behind their programmes. The experience of the Thatcher government shows this to be quite crucial. It would be similarly imperative for elected councillors or at least executive members to be paid. For socialists, strengthening the capacities and powers of elected politicians in this way should be one benefit from this reform. It might be realistic to recognize that such a change should be accompanied by the adoption both of proportional representation, and by a measure of state subsidy to political parties. It is hard to imagine working-class parties being able to operate effectively at this additional level at their present level of resources and a new level of government is likely to need the legitimacy it would obtain from being more fairly representative of public opinion.

There are parallels between the present emphasis of the Labour Left on a strategy of democratization — for example, in the demands for abolition of the House of Lords, for the accountability of the police, for locally determined public transport policies — and the potential objectives of elected regional government. Appointed executive bodies now control Health, Water, the Universities, Manpower Services and Industrial Training, and the Police. A strategy for bringing all of these under elected regional control would seem to have more prospect of success then separate campaigns to achieve democratic control of these services.

Regionalization also offers advantages so far as socialist economic strategy is concerned. A renewal of commitment to public ownership was an advance of Labour policy in the 1970s —

democratic control of capital is surely the fundamental principle of socialist policy. But the unpopularity of centralized forms of nationalization, and the weakness of Labour governments in bargaining with private corporations, must be taken into account in any realistic strategy. A stronger statutory basis for regional enterprise boards may open a way towards more popular interventionist programmes, especially as in some regions the priority to be given to creating employment will be locally unanswerable. Socialists in Scotland and Wales have forcefully indicated how they would wish to use such powers, and one objective of these reforms is to secure the necessary autonomy for Scotland and Wales.

Experience in Italy, in the regions controlled by Communist governments or Communist-led majority coalitions has been that some cooperation from small private capital can be won by working-class-controlled authorities that are committed to regional economic goals, and that are in any case the permanent, efficient and legitimate administrations of their locality. One object of regional government should be to achieve class coalitions in which capital's local interests oblige it to cooperate in socialist economic programmes. In some regions, trade unions and the Labour Party would be in a much weaker position than in others: there would be no uniformity in the bargaining relationships established, just as there has been wide variation in Italy. But in a situation in which national political power for a government of the working class may be currently unattainable, in any real terms, there may nevertheless be opportunity to achieve some stronger regional hegemonies. The working class has often been disunited and disorganized by the emotions of nationalism — the Falklands factor — and even by the posing of the 'integrity of the nation' as an issue in the devolution debate. There should be an opposing strategy, which mobilizes provincial interests and the attachments to specific localities as a countervailing pressure to the power of the market.

There is some question of whether 'regional identities' any longer exist as significant political potentialities, aside from the nationalisms of Scotland and Wales. Certainly there has been a marked decline of regional inputs into national political life. At different periods these have been from Free Trade Manchester, Social Imperialist Birmingham, Red Clydeside, and the mining communities of South Wales. Consumerism and mass communications have had their effects in dissolving regional particularity and consciousness. This metropolitan domination seems on the whole now to be a conservative force, sucking initiative and ability out of the provinces and absorbing it in the large-scale operations of modern capital, which include the cultural institutions of broadcasting, the national press, and the subsidised national theatre companies. The opportunity to stimulate local and regional culture, and to develop deversity of education and cultural provision,[9] should be one advantage of regional government, enabling socialists in some places to attempt on a larger scale what has been falteringly attempted through municipal programmes. Socialist historians might be able to make some contribution to such cultural regeneration. It may be more feasible to argue on a regional basis for democratic control and open access to the mass media, than it appears to be on a national basis, where socialists have achieved little against the ideological defences of liberalism and the market. Of course, much 'regionalism' will be parochial and even conservative; this is already the case with part of the nationalist movements, as socialists who support them make clear. But society is too complex to expect or insist on uniform patterns of culture, and the diversity which increased regional autonomy might make possible should be accepted as beneficial, and as providing a more open environment in which socialists can assert their own positions.

The case for a stronger regional and territorial dimension to the politics of the left is argued here not merely in terms of desirable policies for the reform of government. What is proposed is essentially a programme of mobilization, which might enable discontents and political hopes to be expressed in a more meaningful and locally rooted way. While there have to be tangible common objectives for such territorially based campaigns (the transfer of significant powers from irresponsible state agencies and departments, and the acquisition of substantial economic and planning powers over the private sector are critical), the campaigns in different regions must generate their own identity and objectives if they are to have any effect. Arguments for public investment programmes would be more persuasive if they were linked to regional economic interests than they have been as a general 'alternative economic strategy'. An element of American-style competition between regions (States in the USA) for central government funding of capital projects (e.g. a Severn Barrage, the Channel Tunnel, railway electrification, thermal insulation of all housing and private housing in a region) might win more support for them, especially where they would generate local employment. The centralism of the British Parliament has undermined the powers of MPs and their parties to defend their local interests. Regional disparities in income and employment levels, though lessening in recent years, may be in part an outcome of this. Since public investment schemes must be an important element of any serious programme to reduce unemployment, a strengthening of the political means to achieve these is important to economic strategy also.

The Greater London and South Yorkshire councils have demonstrated the potential of what are in effect regionally based councils to mobilize more interest and support than local government has achieved in Britain for many years, and their public transport policies illustrate distinctive socialist goals for regional government. These examples need to be broadened into a much wider regional strategy. If different parties and elements of the left were able to cooperate in developing 'alternative regional plans', they might be able to create some more representative and broad-based participation in a campaign for a new politics that could defeat Thatcherism.

NOTES

1. This literature of 'modernization' was reviewed and criticized by Perry Anderson in his influential 'Origins of the Present Crisis', *New Left Review* 23, 1964. While the stratum of scientific and technical workers to whom Wilson's 'technological' rhetoric was addressed were often working in new industries located in the Midlands and South East, the broad 'industrial' emphasis of this strategy linked these interests with the older provincial bases of British manufacturing.

2. J.P. MacKintosh, *The Devolution of Power*, Harmondsworth 1968, considered the fate of these agencies. Regional economic policy is also discussed in S. Holland, *The Regional Problem*, London 1976, and H. Armstrong and J. Taylor, *Regional Economic Policy*, London 1978.

3. Further guidance to the literature on this topic can be obtained from E. Craven, ed., *Regional Devolution and Social Policy*, London 1975. The Buchanan Report, *Traffic in Towns*, was among the other important documents of this period which recommended regional planning.

4. See table 1 of the SDP Green Paper *Decentralising Government, 1982.*

5. *The consequences of this 'constitutionalism' for the left in Britain have been an important theme of a number of writers associated with New Left Review*, including Tom Nairn, 'Anatomy of the Labour Party', reprinted in R. Blackburn, ed., *Revolution and Class Struggle*, NLR Fontana, London 1977.

6. This development was discussed by Cynthia Cockburn in *The Local State*, London 1978.

7. In an article in *New Socialist*, No. 3, Jan.-Feb. 1982.

8. A major omission from the above list is Northern Ireland which, though manifestly an intractable problem all on its own, would have to be considered in any proposal for national or regional self-government. The next chapter of this book is devoted to the whole question of Northern Irish political structures.

9. In chapter nine I argue a case for the regional control of institutions of post-18 education. Chapter seven, *A Statutory Right to Work*, also suggests that regional authorities should have significant responsibilities for employment creation.

5

Self-Determination and Repartition in Northern Ireland

I should say at the outset that I am an outsider to this problem. Never having visited and much less lived in Northern Irelnd or the Republic, I do not have that everyday familiarity with the history and contemporary reality of its politics that comes from personal experience and relationship. This is without doubt a serious disqualification, and one that has caused me to feel a lack of fitness to write about it for many years. I hope readers will make allowances for this as they note the inevitable errors and misconstructions in what follows.[1]

Nevertheless, at least since the Ulster Workers' Strike of 1974 and the subsequent collapse of the experiment in 'power-sharing', I have had a consistent view of the problem. This was essentially that the conflict, as defined by virtually all its participants, was incapable of solution, and was doomed, short of a repartition of Northern Ireland, to continue interminably with deeply harmful effects on all those who were exposed to its influence.[2]

Northern Ireland has seemed an outstanding example of an issue in which, on all sides, preconceptions and ideological definitions have been able comfortably to take precedence over facts. Thus, to take some examples, British governments have wished away the political problems of the Provisional IRA's real strength by pejoratively defining its members as 'terrorists' and 'criminals', on the assumption that if they were perceived as such they would be amenable to the remedies that do usually bring success against mere criminality. Supporters of the Republican movement, on the other hand, in their definition of the problem as one of 'British Imperialism', have chosen to neglect the actual existence and allegiances of the Protestant community in Northern Ireland. They have appeared not to recognize that in the real world the achievement of 'Troops Out' would mean a civil war in which Protestants would start a good deal better placed than Catholics in point of both arms and organization. Socialists have been less guilty of a politics of wish-fulfilment, the dreams of a secular working-class revolution in all Ireland having been so obviously battered by recent experience. Attempts to grapple with the contradictory implications of nationalism for a socialist perspective, and with the actual stage of development of capitalism and imperialism in contemporary Ireland, represent some of the more significant engagements with the unhappy world of facts.[3]

With hindsight, it is possible to see the struggle for reforms in the late 1960s and early 1970s as an attempt to 'modernize' Northern Ireland, to assimilate it to the model of advanced capitalist development then in process in both mainland Britain and the Republic. The 'civil rights' projects of 1968 were a notably 'modern' movement, influenced in form by the new radicalism of American blacks and West European students, and universalistic rather than sectarian or nationalist in their aims. In an effort to accommodate these protests, British governments sought to substitute an impersonal and bureaucratic form of administration for one based on patronage and sectarian monopoly — and indeed some progress was made in reducing discrimination in the areas of housing allocation and employment. Governments also tried to divert the Northern Irish from their communal and sectarian preoccupations by exposing them to the benefits of welfare capitalism. This was supported by an analysis that the main source of political 'backwardness' in the province was relative deprivation, in both the public and the private sphere. The hope was that if economic development could increase jobs and incomes, and if the social services and housing system could be made more just, both communities might become diverted from their unhealthy 'tribal' preoccupation with each other, and find greater reason, in the case of the Catholics, for appreciating the beneficence of the British State compared with the inferior providing-power of the Republic.

The evidence of practical indifference on the part of the Southern population to events in the North supported the view that in the long run a highly politicized nationalism could be abated above all by the experience of relative affluence: improvements in the economy and living standards of the Republic in this period seemed to go hand in hand with the erosion of the strength of old nationalist sentiments. What British governments, and their modernizing allies in the North, seemed to be hoping for was the development of privatization and political apathy in place of the powerful communal passions which uniquely reigned in this benighted part of the realm. It was a recipe that (at one time) seemed to have worked quite well on the mainland to defuse the ideological and class passions of an earlier period.

The failure to 'bring off' this economic and social miracle just before its more general disintegration in the rest of the United Kingdom has important explanations in the history and geography of Ireland, to which we will return. But it should be noted that its immediate agent, in 1974, in the failure to confront and defeat the Ulster Workers' Strike, was the Wilson Government. The lack of resolve of Labour Governments in the 1960s and 1970s, in the face of structural obstacles to their own 'modernization' project for British society, made a decisive contribution to our present political plight. Other nettles not grasped by these governments were the grip of the United States over Britain's international alignments, the preponderant influence of the City over economic policy, and, some would say, the barriers posed by the syndicalist wage-bargaining power of the trade unions to an expansionary economic strategy. There are surprising similarities between the recent trajectory of Northern Ireland and that of the rest of the UK: in both the failure of a modernization programme launched by a government of the Centre has initiated a period of regression and re-polarization. Shortly after the politics of consensus broke down in Northern Ireland, it suffered a similar fate on the mainland. There is a further ironic parallel in the critical destructive role of the Ulster Workers' Strike in 1974, considering the eventual fate of the British governments of 1964, 1970 and 1974. Northern Ireland, while usually regarded as an aberration from the norms of British politics, a particularly obstinate legacy of past mistakes, from this perspective turns out to be only an extreme symptom of the national condition.

There are more specific parallels. The leading role assigned to the armed forces and the police in Northern Ireland is consistent with the general priority accorded to the means of violence and law-enforcement by the Thatcher Government: Northern Ireland appears to function as a laboratory and training ground for counter-insurgency operations. The same complicated amalgam of arguments from national self-respect and democratic rights that proved so potent in justifying the armed defence of the Falklands is also the presupposition of all-party consensus on Northern Ireland. Because in each case there are conflicting claims to consider (those of the Argentinians and the Falkland Islanders, those of both communities in Northern Ireland), it has been difficult to define either issue in terms of self-government or imperialism, and the left has won little popular support for more pacific positions. The strength of Thatcherism on these matter has been its ability to incorporate apparently 'democratic' principles within its assertions of national interest, the armed State presenting itself as the defender of majority rights and civil peace.

In Northern Ireland, religious and national confrontation has taken the place of more conventional preoccupations, in modern capitalist societies, with economic ends. But on the mainland too, it may be realistic to regard the Thatcherite programme more as an anachronistic and deluded moral fundamentalism — in this case of social strata disadvantaged by the arrangements and necessary compromises of advanced capitalism — than as a rational strategy for common economic advance. The Northern Ireland conflict would then appear less as a peculiar anachronism than as a virulent case of the 'British disease', and of the precedence this gives to various forms of inherited status over the more rationalistic and open relations of social class. The attempted 'modernization' of Northern Ireland followed twenty years of affluence in Britain and regression and stasis in Northern Ireland initiated the reaction of the Thatcher years. It will certainly take a major renewal in the politics of the mainland, and a determined and rigorous commitment to a more open and rational social order, to bring any new progress to the province.

Though the demise of the power-sharing administration in 1974 triggered the collapse of the reform project in Northern Ireland, it is unlikely that any combination of political determination and economic resources could have succeeded in making the present six-county area viable. The demography of Northern Ireland is itself maximally unfavourable to peace and harmony. If the Catholic and Protestant populations were nearer to numerical parity, then the case for an equitable distribution of political power would be consistent with majoritarian principles and procedures. As it is, the Catholic population is much too large a proportion of the total to be discounted, but too small to support an arithmetical case for equity, or to lead to the close balance of electoral forces which would produce this, for example through the agency of a balancing centre party.

Equally important are the wider national aspirations of the two communities and their deep-rooted conflicts. There is a curious symmetry between the Protestants' insistence on loyalty to a State to which in practice they have not been in the least loyal, and the Republican movement's commitment to a united Ireland despite its lack of sympathy for the actual government and social order of the Republic. To gain legitimacy among Catholics, 'power sharing' required not only some equity in the internal division of power and resources, but also acknowledgement of the 'Irish dimension' — that is, the ultimate unity of all Ireland. Half-way houses are hard to find here, since from the Protestant point of view any acknowledgement of the legitimacy of a united Ireland is a step towards acceptance of their own minority status. Only a renewed confederation of Britain and the Irish Republic could square that circle (even that, within the broader identity of the European Community, was not beyond some post-nationalist imaginations). But such a solution has never seemed very practical politics.

The conflicts, over both domestic administration and national affiliation *are* irreconcilable under present conditions, and there can be few who believe that the search for compromises and a modus vivendi between the two communities can now possibly succeed. On the one hand, as Eamonn McCann has put it: 'The Provos will not be beaten while there is no generally accepted political solution. And there will be no generally accepted solution while the Provos remain unbeaten.' On the other, the Protestants of Ulster have shown from the struggle over Home Rule to the Ulster Workers' Strike the force of their aversion to the Catholic South, and to any risk of subordination within a United Ireland. With the growing influence of Ian Paisley in Protestant Politics, and the greater political legitimacy of Sinn Fein and the Provisionals since the 1983 hunger strikes, polarization is more severe than at any time since the beginning of the Troubles.

No solution appears to lie in the endorsement of the entrenched positions of either sectarian nationalism. As a matter of political and para-military reality, both Protestant and Catholic communities have the physical and moral resources to defend their boundaries regardless of the decisions of the British Government. Moreover, given the current complexion of British politics and the debility of the left within it, it seems altogether unlikely that a British government, having failed even to impose power-sharing on the Protestants of the North, could or would now force them into a united Ireland. Thus the fundamentalist claims of the two opposed nationalisms, and the compromises sought by middle-class liberals, capitalist modernizers, and British governments since 1968, seem alike incapable of realization.

As in the instructive parallel case of the Falkland Islands, it should be noted that there are real moral complexities as well as intransigent political factors operating to impede a solution. The moral complexity arises from the partial justice of the claims of both communities to live under governments of their own choosing. The justice of the claims of the long-oppressed and subordinated Catholics of the North needs no elaboration here. There can be no justification for a form of government which denies the Catholic population both its preferred national identity, and the rights and powers of self-rule. Arguments based on the existence of a 'majority' of Protestants in the North can hardly stand up in the light of the 1922 Partition, the pressing weight of the history of Ireland and its relations with England, and the actual preferences of the Catholics of the North. Yet the wishes of Northern Ireland Protestants not to be subordinated to a Catholic majority also have some symmetrical legitimacy,regardless of the greater sympathy one might have for the claims of the community which has been historically subordinated and ill-treated. Rights of self-government should not be subject to forfeit as a result of such a history, nor can they be accorded simply on the basis of moral sympathies. The imperial origins of the Protestant settlement cannot have much weight today in deciding the territorial rights of a population originally settled three hundred years ago. Nor is the assertion that the Northern Irish State is merely a dependency of British imperialism unproblematic, given the negative economic and political value of the province to the United Kingdom today, and the evident hope of many British governments since 1968 that the Protestants would accept some dilution both of their own power and of Britain's undivided sovereignty over the North. The main interest of British governments today, both objectively and subjectively, is no longer to perpetuate British rule over Northern Ireland, but to stabilize the area under some form of parliamentary and broadly capitalist regime.

The fact is that claims of self-determination are virtually 'undecidable' in such a situation, in which a majority in one part of the country becomes a minority in the territory as a whole. What follows is the need to separate the claims of each community to self-government from their claims to exercise government over each other. I shall argue that this separation, endorsing the claims to 'self-determination' of Protestant *and* Catholic communities but neither of their claims to subordinate the other, is the essential basis for making any progress with the problem.

The claims of self-determination for both communities are, of course, uniquely difficult to realize in Northern Ireland. Protestants and Catholics do not live in clearly demarcated and self-contained parts of the territory — if they did, Partition would not have taken the terrible form we saw in 1922, ot it would have been easier to modify in later years. Unlike Canada, Belgium or even, Cyprus, where two communities largely live in separate spaces, Northern Ireland exhibits a combination of local communal segregation and broader-scale territorial intermixture. The pattern of settlement is like a mosaic: the separate pieces have become more homogeneous during the troubles as both Protestants and Catholics have fled from exposed or mixed areas to the safety of more uniform ones, but the pieces are also relatively small and interspersed with one another. There are predominant concentrations of Catholic and Protestant populations in different areas of the six counties — the Catholic population is largest in the west and south, and in West Belfast; the Protestants are concentrated in the east-central area, including Belfast where they comprise more than three-quarters of the population. Nevertheless, according to a report based on 1971 Census figures, Catholics are in a majority of more than 70 per cent in only two out of twenty-six district councils. Even the most drastic re-partition of mainly Catholic areas contiguous to the Republic would leave nearly half the Catholic population of 576,000 (approx.) in a mainly Protestant province, and would place 200,000 out of 954,000 (approx.) Protestants in predominantly Catholic territory. While the 1981 Census results are likely to demonstrate further significant population movements, and an increased homogeneity within each segment of the mosaic, it is unlikely to have redistributed the population substantially by *region* — the change that could do most to further a resolution of the sectarian conflict.

This pattern of population distribution is of much more than administrative importance. It gives a quite distinctive sociological character to the conflict within Northern Ireland, furthering a particular form of domination by Protestant over Catholic, and reinforcing and reproducing the historic antagonisms of the two communities. Any proposals for resolving such a deep-seated historical problem as this must depend on some model of analysis which allows the identification of potentially critical causal variables. The argument of this chapter attaches particular importance to the 'sociological' fact of this pattern of locally homogeneous, mixed, but not integrated settlement. Its particular effect has been to enforce the saliency of the social category and moral boundary of

'Catholic' and 'Protestant' for each community. Neither side possesses an unchallenged physical territorial space, in which a taken-for-granted and quotidian sense of identity could develop, leaving time for other internal social differentiations to be elaborated. In the absence of such a 'given', *social* space has had to be continually asserted and marked out — hence the never-ending process of sectarian demarcation and discrimination which inhabitants and observers of Northern Ireland describe. Names — both christian names and surnames — are Protestant or Catholic. Streets and estates are Protestant or Catholic territory. Intermarriage between religions is frowned upon, and unusual. There are various contested ways of referring to Northern Ireland itself — as 'Ulster', or 'the Six Counties', or 'the Province', or 'the North of Ireland' — depending on communal or national identification. And there are the endless processions and marches, so distinctive a feature of Northern Irish life, in which the social identity that cannot just be assumed is affirmed by insult and by confrontation with 'the other', which gives each community its raison d'être.

Each community has its history, its music, its days of celebration and mourning. The evocations of the Battle of the Boyne — so absurd to most English people, who are slightly embarrassed by public celebrations of anything more momentous than a Cup Final victory — have their meaning in the affirmation of the ever-threatened existence of a sectarian community. This street ritual serves also to mark out ownership and exclusion of physical space, not given the comfortable distance of a foreign frontier. The Apprentice Boys' March round the walls of Derry each July, and its ritual humuliation of the Catholic territory below the walls, is the most well-known example of such territorial assertion.

The emphasis in the rituals of Northern Ireland on public mourning for deaths suffered for the sectarian cause can also be explained by the intense preoccupation of each of these communities with their relationship to the other. The commemoration of the final sacrifice, giving a public meaning to death now rare in the more privatized and secularized society of the mainland, is a claim on the allegiance of the living, and also a celebration of the faithfulness of the dead. Even the notorious punishments meted out to traitors and suspected informers — tarrings and featherings, knee-cappings and the rest — have a specific ritual force in this culture of shame, involving affirmation of the obligations of membership as well as more utilitarian considerations of deterrence. Mere association with British soldiers, and not just the provision of tangible assistance, is a reason for punishment. The social affirmations and rejections of these events, for example, the deaths by hunger strike of Bobby Sands and his comrades have proved a much more powerful social force than any at the disposal of reform-minded governments in London or Belfast.

Violence and the threat of violence do, of course, have a particularly important effect on the maintenance of communal identity, and the spatial pattern of settlement undoubtedly lends itself to a pervasive and unpredictable potential for violence in many areas of the North. The close conjunction of areas of friendly and hostile territory provides both a secure base for the organization of para-military action, and potential for it within easy access. While the overwhelming possession of the official means of violence by members of one community — through the RUC — or by the British army is an additional and separate factor making for armed confrontation, it is hard to envisage any long-term pacification while communities are inter-located as they are. The threat of injury or death to members of one's own community is of course the most potent possible mode of reinforcement of collective identity, and para-military forces are able to claim support as defenders and avengers of their communities.

One sociologist, Douglas Young,[4] writing about this situation in 1973 after two years' research in Northern Ireland, went so far as to argue that the state of conflict was self-equilibrating, providing a social identity and moral satisfactions for its participants far more potent than anything else available. He suggested that while there were no apparent formal rules of conflict resolution, there were nevertheless homeostatic tendencies which led each side to limit the damage it did to the other, maintaining communal antagonism and thus the position of leaderships committed to its conduct at a steady yet stable level. Viewed from this perspective, the British army of occupation has a most convenient function, since no injuries to its members (who are mostly outsiders) are likely to jeopardize the stable tension needed to maintain the status quo.

Young argued that in Northern Ireland sectarian conflict was an end in itself, such that the process of mutual self-definition by each side in terms of the hated, despised or feared qualities of the other had come to dominate the formation of values and social identity in each community. Socialists have often pointed out how the stratifying or oppositional principle of social class has been displaced by that of religion in Northern Ireland, but more private and differentiated identities are also squeezed by the continuous communal pressure. This situation of 'social feud' enables us to understand the 'utopianism' and futility of the claims of each opposed nationalism, both of which, if enacted, would lead to a civil war that no one in fact wants or could benefit from. The institution of the feud can be highly stable even where opposed sides appear to work ceaselessly for each other's destruction. From this point of view, the intolerance of compromise, the ease with which its advocates have been repeatedly forced to the margin, and the lack of interest in any solutions that might be *workable*, are again consistent with a pattern of pathological confrontation. It is not to deny a history of callousness towards the Catholic population, and of its humiliation and subordination by the Protestants, to point out the self-destructiveness of Irish nationalist strategy, whose stated programme seems to point in reality towards a pogrom against its own people. I would not wish to minimize the experiences of a people subjected to military occupation, or the brutalized habits of a soldiery in such a situation, but it is important to insist on the inconsistencies of a propaganda campaign which judges British military behaviour by the standards of a peaceful civil society, while simultaneously claiming the licences and rights of military men-at-arms for its own combatants. The entire failure to consider the possibility of separated jurisdiction for the two communities might in this context be described as a 'symptomatic absence'. These sectarian communities, as they are currently constituted, need the existence of the other. How could Ulster Protestantism maintain its archaic fervour if it were not for the threat of Rome? How much priority would most Catholics give to the cause of a United Ireland if they were no longer subject to Protestant power and humiliation? (Possibly about as much priority as is now given by the population of the Republic.) One can of course identify many sources of 'secondary gain' in this conflict, among local leaderships, both civil and armed, of different persuasions. One does not imagine even that James Prior was sent to Belfast in the hope that he would achieve a triumph of compromise and mediation. The value of the province as a laboratory for British armed forces and police procedures has often been pointed out. But such secondary interests in the status quo themselves only gain their possibility from the existence of a self-reproducing social structure. To 'blame' particular combatants in this struggle for its interminable perpetuation is to risk falling into the manichean habits of thought which have so long obstructed any real process of change.

Self-determination for both Catholics and Protestants, within separate states if this is what each community would choose, seems the appropriate resolution of an undecidable conflict of 'majority' and 'minority' rights. But the knot of this problem has of course been tied extremely tight, and there is no easy formula for loosening it. The pattern of intercalated settlement that maintains sectarian antipathy also makes a solution by territorial separation and boundary difficult to achieve. Essential to this argument, however, is the view that if there could be a boundary — a more conventional kind of frontier — then communal conflict would become less oppressive. At the level of the phenomenology of everyday life, the salience of 'the other', felt not least through the experience of terror, would be considerably diminished, and space would begin to open up for other differentiations and discriminations. A political and economic order could evolve in which religious affiliation would no longer determine power and authority. Catholics and Protestants would each provide leaderships in their own terrain. Security would become a more ordinary problem, since the management of law and order would no longer be superimposed on communal conflict, and policing and military force would no longer, for the Catholic population, be in the hands of aliens to their community (whether Protestant or British). Conflict between provinces or states, across a frontier, is likely to be less pervasive and more limited in scope. For states habitually seek a monopoly of physical violence within their area of jurisdiction, and in the absence of a chronic pattern of communal antagonism and conflicting nationalisms it is likely that successor States would acquire more of these conventional powers.

A mere redrawing of frontiers would go only a little way towards achieving this pattern of uniform national identities within distinct territorial boundaries. A recent study of the feasibility of repartition, given the existing population distribution, has estimated that the most favourable redefinition of boundaries, which would involve separating the predominantly Catholic areas of the West and South from the existing territory of Northern Ireland, would still leave a very substantial number and proportion of Catholics under Protestant hegemony in the remaining part. Thus, a repartition which ceded the largest feasible area of contiguous territory would change a distribution of population which is now about 62 per cent Protestant and 38 per cent Catholic to one which would be 74 per cent Protestant and 26 per cent Catholic. In particular the large Catholic population of West Belfast explains why a relatively simple territorial realignment would not achieve the desired effects. [5]

If this solution is to be considered further, therefore, it seems necessary to contemplate the physical movement and redistribution of part of the Catholic and Protestant population, so that a pattern of local concentration and territory-wide dispersal could evolve into a more concentrated form of settlement. This idea of moving populations has seemed, understandably perhaps, 'unthinkable' during the years of the Troubles so far. But it is my view that the present impasse in Northern Ireland is so profound, and its costs especially to the people of the North so great, that it is appropriate to consider these questions of location, upsetting as they may be to people who will regard their own claim to their birthplace and home as called into question. Permanent civil conflict — virtually latent or suppressed civil war — with its attendant evils of terrorization, brutalization and impoverishment is not the kind of state to which one should become resigned, as policy-makers in Britain seem to have done. A strategy which over a reasonable length of time might resolve this historic problem on a permanent basis is surely worth consideration.

As all parties to the conflict have always realized, the British Government's definition of the problem is itself an important factor in determining the expectations and behaviour of participants. We should recognize and admit that Northern Ireland as now constituted is unviable, and that the claims of its two communities are, and seem likely to remain, fundamentally incompatible with one another. It is neither possible nor desirable to suppress the demands of these communities by force. Compromise within Northern Ireland has proved impossible to achieve. Therefore the British Government should declare its intention to seek a solution which respects the rights of self-determination of both communities, by means of a redefinition of boundaries and by the facilitation of movements of people to constitute communities which lack a significant 'minority problem' of either denomination. Given the constitution of nationally and religiously homogeneous communities, it should be the intention to provide each with a choice, by referendum and/or election, of national affiliation. A Protestant province could choose independence, or remain associated with the United Kingdom. A Catholic province could also choose independence, membership of the Irish Republic, or some form of association with both British and Irish States. The commitment of the British Government should be to allow a choice of preferred modes of government for each community, but to allow neither any jurisdiction over the choices of the other.

It would be possible to outline, at an early stage, the likely approximate boundaries of the regions or states, taking into account existing population distributions, sensible frontiers, and a division of land which is equitable in regard to resources and to the need to create two viable economies. Since Northern Ireland is currently economically dominated by Belfast and has a pattern of communications centred on that city, it would be necessary to undertake substantial infrastructural investment, in the period preparatory to re-partition, to ensure that a territory which excluded Belfast was nevertheless economically viable for its inhabitants. The long history of discrimination in industrial investment between 'Catholic' and 'Protestant' areas would again require deliberate redress, which might be easier once the veto of Protestant power within a unitary state was overcome. Substantial economic assistance might be sought and obtained from the EEC and the United States in pursuit of such a long-term resolution of the problem of Northern Ireland. The active involvement of the Irish Republic, with funding support from the EEC and the USA, might make possible the construction of a viable economy for a 'Catholic' region in or out of the Republic which would not be feasible without initial external support. One would expect that the British Government would also direct economic assistance towards the inauguration of a Catholic province, even if this were to choose absorption in the Irish Republic, as part of its obligation to its citizens. The difficulties in the way of a peaceful resettlement and redrawing of boundaries are so great that substantial investments would be in any case needed, so that people would have promise of a better material life to justify what would in some instances be a serious loss regarding their sense of 'home' and their historic territorial rights.

It seems that Derry, in such a re-partition, would be wholly part of the Catholic territory. Belfast, unavoidably it seems, has to be Protestant, despite the great difficulties posed by the large Catholic population which would, over a period of years, have to move or accept a permanent subordinate status in the UK or in a mainly Protestant State. 'Berlin' solutions of a divided city, with different sovereignties over different segments, do not seem promising.

The British Government could assist in a process of relocation not only by indicating its long-term intentions, and by appropriately planned investment, but also by intervention in the housing market. It could purchase land and houses at an advantageous price from members of either community seeking to relocate themselves as part of this programme. It could then re-sell land and property, on favourable terms, to incoming populations. It could aim to foster a spirit of collective exchange and mutual help rather than one of 'scorched earth', by ensuring that it would be to householders' advantage to leave their own and common space in good repair. Similar inducements could be offered to the holders of council tenancies, in terms of equivalent rights and financial assistance. The existing distribution of population is such that substantial numbers both of Catholics and Protestants would be involved in movement, and this sharing of loss and gain by both communities would provide an important element of equity.

Once separate states or jurisdictions were established, it seems likely that any remaining minority communities would face stringent demands for their loyalty and conformity. Protestants in Catholic Ireland might thus be subject to 'Catholic laws' (from which they are now protected by the secularism and religious indifference of the British State). Catholics might find themselves subject to something more like 'Stormont' government than has existed in recent years. Such a prospect might have the effect of a negative sanction, encouraging population movement once the intention to define new boundaries at the end of a stated period had been declared.

Such a programme of communal separation and repartition might be allotted a substantial period — even ten years might not be too much — for the necessary economic and political preparations. Although a solution which requires physical movement of significant numbers of people is abnormal and intrinsically undesirable, it seems less so than the indefinite persistence of the present situation in Northern Ireland. It should also be pointed out that very large numbers of citizens of that region have already moved their homes in the course of the Troubles — possibly no fewer than would be involved in the transfers here considered. In any case, while a British government might indicate its future proposals for redefining sovereignty in the province, and the principles and approximate geographical lines of repartition it envisages, it would be left to individual citizens to determine, in the conditions prevailing and anticipated, where they wished to live. No doubt significant minorities would, for one reason or another, place retention of their existing homes above any other consideration.

A proposal along these lines involves real losses for both nationalisms, and it is in this sense a compromise of a different type from those previously discussed. Given the dynamics of this conflict, any compromise which promised to resolve it would meet with resistance, for fear of the empty social space which would then have to be faced. A concept of 'national divorce' suggests itself. Those whose political programme for Northern Ireland depends on the active use of armed force seem ill-placed to criticize this admittedly radical proposal on grounds of humanitarianism and human rights, though this will assuredly not stop them from doing so. It is only the possibility that the British Government could take some autonomous step towards resolving the problem which makes this solution conceivable without a civil war. Those in Britain who have at times speculated about the salutary effects which a threat to withdraw from Northern Ireland might have on the conflict have had some awareness of the role that British intervention has played, among other things, as a kind of coping stone to the whole structure.

This is all a far cry from envisaging a socialist future for any part of Ireland. It is, however, likely that the displacing of sectarian conflict as the predominant issue of Northern Irish politics would lead to more open class division in both Protestant and Catholic communities, and might in time open the way to the emergence of a more universalistic, rational and class-based political community. More specifically, the solidarity already seen among Protestant industrial workers might come to be deployed against, and not in alliance with, the dominant Protestant bourgeoisie, and a Catholic working class habituated to relatively high standards of secular liberties and welfare legislation might seek to transfer these expectations to a Republican setting. Both of these factors would lessen the enthusiasm of British and Irish Governments for re-partition, though such threats are probably too long-term and indeterminate to weight very heavily in anyone's calculations.

There are wider benefits to political development in Britain which might follow from a settlement of the Northern Irish problem. The process of increased militarization and civil surveillance set in train by the security campaign in Northern Ireland would be arrested, and it would again become easier to defend civil liberties throughout the United Kingdom. The resolution of this aspect of the British 'national problem' might also open the way to some general dismantling of the more coercive and centralizing aspects of the British national state, making it more feasible to arrange appropriate measures of regional and national self-government within the remainder of the British Isles. Certainly any serious consideration of greater regional or national autonomy in Britain now rapidly comes up against the problem of extending any proposed devolution to the Northern Ireland case. It is difficult to assess the more diffuse cultural and social effects of such an intractable armed struggle, especially given the tendency in mainland Britain to distance the events of Northern Ireland. But it seems likely that the effects of continued terrorism even in areas normally remote from it are to reinforce authoritarian, irrational and paranoid states of mind, and generally to reduce confidence in the possibilities of rational and peaceful change. It is hard to imagine a more optimistic and progressive climate in British politics while the Northern Ireland situation remains in its present intractable and shameful state. These are additional grounds for encouraging the most open discussion of alternative options and arguments and for breaking the official consensus which seems to envisage no more than a long-term containment of the situation.

Finally, I believe that if re-partition is not discussed, planned and introduced in the ordered and peaceful way that is proposed, it may well happen eventually by violence. While one could envisage this as the result of 'Civil War', should the British Government tire of the situation and withdraw its forces, another scenario is that a British government of the right gives effective licence to the Protestant community to achieve such an outcome by main force, on some provocation or other. The worsening economic situation and changing demography of Northern Ireland (Catholics are increasing as a proportion of the population) seem likely to intensify the crisis as time goes by.

It is because such an eventual catastrophic outcome seems inscribed in the present conflict that it seems justifiable to me to propose the unusual and intrinsically unwelcome solution that has been described here.

NOTES

1. An earlier version of this chapter was first given as a talk to a summer school of the Socialist Society in 1983. I am grateful to Francis Mulhern and Michael Walzer for their detailed comments — neither has any responsibility for the argument of the article.

2. The near-assassination of Mrs Thatcher and most of her Government on 6 October 1984 is only the latest and most dramatic impingement of the problems of Northern Ireland on the political life of Britain. Surely this must make it obvious to everyone that the situation cannot be allowed to drift on for a further period of years.

3. See Tom Nairn, *The Break-up of Britain*, NLB, London 1977, p. Bew, P.

Gibbon, H. Patterson, *The State in Northern Ireland*, Manchester 1979; L. O'Dowd, B. Rolston, M. Tomlinson, *Northern Ireland: Between Civil Rights and Civil War*, CSE Books, 1980.

4. Douglas Young's paper, 'Northern Ireland: a Case for the Non-Obsolescence of the Concept of Honour', drew on the ideas of Georg Simmel on conflict as a stable form of social relation. The paper is unfortunately unpublished.

5. This appeared as a chapter by Paul Compton, 'The Demographic Background', in David Watt, ed., *The Constitution of Northern Ireland: Problems and Prospects*, Royal Institute of International Affairs, 1981. It concluded that repartition was unfeasible without considerable population exchange.

6

Political Arguments for Proportional Representation

There can hardly be much doubt about the extremity of the crisis now facing the Labour movement so far as its electoral prospects are concerned. The long-term electoral decline presciently brought to the attention of the left in Eric Hobsbawm's *The Forward March of Labour Halted*, [1] and further detailed in the recent *Politics of Thatcherism* collection, [2] arrived at a still more critical point in the 1983 General Election. Labour now survives as the overwhelmingly dominant opposition party in Parliament only thanks to an electoral system which translates a 28 per cent share of the national vote into a 33 per cent share of Parliamentary seats, and which conversely gives Labour's main rivals, the Alliance Parties, a 4 per cent share of Parliamentary seats from a 26 per cent share of the vote. Furthermore, Ivor Crewe, Doreen Massey and others have documented the precise geography of this decline, whose most salient features are the destruction of Labour as a majority party in the south of England (except for inner London), the loss of majority support among skilled manual workers and of preponderant support even among trade unionists, and the increasing dependence of Labour on demographically and occupationally declining sectors of the population. [3]

Several of the factors which contribute most to the propensity to vote Labour (trade union membership, council tenancies, public sector employment) are themselves vulnerable to Conservative strategies which, in addition to more intrinsically ideological ends, are designed to destroy Labour's electoral base — for example, private house ownership, privatization, and unemployment insofar as this weakens trade union organisation. Less obvious factors which have influenced the electoral geography of Britain are long-term trends towards urban and industrial dispersal, and the migration of populations away from large industrial centres to smaller towns especially in the south of the country. These trends, encouraged by employers, by government locational policies, and by policies and funding decisions which have favoured the counties over the cities, have had the effect of dissolving working-class identifications at both workplace and place of residence. The reduction in the average workforce size at a given plant is probably more important in diminishing class consciousness and solidarity than the converse but less visible trend, from the workers' point of view, of increases in the size of companies. The Boundary Commission's recommendations prior to the election, which already made Labour's task significantly more difficult, were a result of these demographic changes. Not only did they directly 'lose' the Labour Party approximately eighteen seats; they also reduced the number of 'marginal' seats as a proportion of the total, thus increasing the difficulty of ever regaining a Parliamentary majority.

In this chapter I want to discuss the implications of Labour's share of the 1983 poll, and the long and almost continuous decline which led up to it, for future socialist electoral strategy. I shall argue that it is now necessary to examine the implications of the present 'first past the post' electoral system, and the possible forms of 'proportional representation' which are alternatives to it, for the prospects of Labour and other existing or putative left-wing parties in Britain. As a matter of principle, it is neither defensible nor feasible to make the hope of socialism depend upon the exploitation of an unfair electoral system. But to put the matter for the moment simply in terms of party advantage, a system which has been for over fifty years highly favourable in its operations to the Labour Party (and also to the Conservatives), and has been disadvantageous to third parties where their support is not regionally concentrated (as with the Northern Irish parties or the Scottish Nationalists), now threatens to doom Labour to permanent exclusion from office.

Labour formerly had the advantages of an overwhelming division of votes between two parties, and also of the local concentration of its vote as a consequence of class divisions and their reflection in the population balance of constituencies. 'Third parties' (until recently mainly the Liberals) had the disadvantage of a share of the vote that was too small to produce many seats, given its even distribution across classes and therefore between constituencies.[4] But as the Labour (and Conservative) share of the vote has declined, and the Liberal and now Alliance vote has increased, this plurality or first-past-the post system, while still giving Labour more than its due share of seats, has also entailed that the division of the non-

Conservative vote in many constituencies yields an overwhelming Conservative majority in Parliament out of all proportion to the party's minority electoral support. The Alliance's targeting of Labour rather than Tory votes in the 1983 election (the result of a tactical victory of the SDP, and especially David Owen, over the Liberals in determining the shape of the Alliance campaign) exaggerated this effect. If the Alliance had set out to win more of its vote from the Tories, and had encouraged tactical voting against them even where Labour would have benefited, a 'hung' Parliament might have resulted. But even this outcome, which could be imagined as a consequence of a reduced Tory and an improved Labour vote in the next election, would fall short of the aim of a Labour victory, not to mention a sustained tenure of power which, as Mrs Thatcher well understands, is the prerequisite for substantial structural change in society. It is now very difficult to imagine how any such victory could be achieved, given the scale of increase in Labour's proportion of the vote that would be needed, the very low base from which Labour now starts in the south of the country, and the unlikelihood that the competition of the Alliance will simply melt away. The Liberals and the SPD have effective political leaderships, and their share of the poll makes it easy for them to rebut the earlier Labour argument that a vote for a third party was a wasted vote. They will now with equal plausibility be able to say this of Labour in many constituencies. Electoral outcomes are, of course, difficult to forecast. The greater volatility of political allegiance in recent years could lead to a sudden upswing in support for Labour, as it has done for the Alliance. One could envisage the Alliance functioning as an unwitting conveyor belt, taking new votes from the Tories and passing its old ones to Labour, in an election in which the predominant movement was against Thatcherism. These uncertainties require us to be very cautious in deciding what electoral strategy might be most effective. Nevertheless, already in 1983 a record swing would have been needed for Labour to have formed a majority government, and it is hard to be sanguine about the prospects today.

The most probable outcome of electoral contests under the existing rules seems to be a successful divide-and-rule operation by the Conservatives. So long as two Opposition parties or groupings divide the non-Conservative vote, Tories can continue to win elections on several per cent *less* of the vote than they secured in April 1983. This pattern in 1983 worked against the Labour Party more strongly than against the Alliance, since Labour voters proved more willing to vote 'tactically' for the most strongly placed non-Tory candidate. Thus the Labour vote collapsed in many areas of Alliance strength in southern England, while large Alliance votes sapped Labour majorities in inner-city areas, for example in London. The effect of such a destructive competition between Labour and the Alliance parties could be a long-term shift in the balance of political and class power in favour of the Right, not only assuring Conservative electoral predominance but undermining the strength of the more moderate forces in the Conservative Party who have previously been able to insist on the electoral necessity of 'trimming towards the centre'. The serious political consequences of such a loss of a party's monopoly over the representation of the left can be seen from comparative examples. On the one side, the strength of Swedish social democracy derives in large part from the contrast between its more-or-less unified representation of the left and the competition of three smaller parties for the votes of the centre and right. Conversely, the weakness of the left in France and Italy after the war (and in Italy still) stemmed from the division between Communist and non-Communist parties, and the difficulties put in the way of their cooperation. Only the renewal of the Socialist Party, and its rise to a dominant position on the left, has changed this situation in France. The historical advantage enjoyed by the Labour Party in Britain — a two party system in which it had no effective competition for representation of the forces left of centre — seems now in the process of disappearance.

The prospect that the Labour–Alliance electoral division will result in one or more further Thatcherite victories is bad enough. But there is a still worse scenario to consider: namely, that the electoral system which in the 1920s and 1930s helped Labour to replace the Liberals as the main Opposition party, will from now on exercise its main biasing effect in favour of the Liberal–SDP Alliance and against the Labour Party, thus producing, over a period of one or two further elections, a two-party system in which the Liberal–SDP Alliance is the second major party. Since the present Conservative leadership seems aggressively committed to the extirpation of socialist politics as a real option for Britain, it must be supposed that it will give such help as it can to this historic project, where it does not endanger its own hold on power to do so. One example of such an intervention is the current attack on links between the trade unions and the Labour Party, which is designed to enforce new balloting mechanisms and arrangements for 'contracting out' of political funding. It now seems clear that such moves will find some support within the trade union movement, where there has been a re-emergence of vocal support for non-political unionism and for a line of seeking to extract such benefits as can be got from talking with Mr Tebbitt. While this tendency has been put into abeyance by the government's banning of unions at GCHQ Cheltenham, and by the miners' strike, this tendency will re-emerge not least in those unions which fail to retain the support of their members for Labour Party affiliation when compulsory ballots take place. Published data on the voting behaviour and political attitudes show that such moves may be able to win significant support among trades union members.

It seems clear that the decline in the share of the vote won by the Labour Party in recent elections reflects deep changes in class structure and consciousness in Britain, and not only political failures by Labour both in and out of office. No account of this process has been entirely satisfactory. Early versions of the 'embourgeoisement' thesis were refuted both by the evidence of continuing inequalities produced by mainly socialist researchers, [5] and by Labour's success in winning electoral support in the 1960s and 1970s which removed some of the political interest in this view. Sociologists such as Lockwood and Goldthorpe were able to demonstrate that earlier class cultures were being replaced not by a unified 'middle-class' ideology and life-style but by a greater sectionalism or 'instrumental collectivism'.[6] A more differentiated range of occupational and other interest groups emerged which were more assertive than earlier class formations in pursuit of their interests. White-collar and professional workers began to adopt more militant strategies to defend their interests, and 'collective consumers' in sectors such as housing, social security, the environment, and education also became mobilized and vociferous.[7] The outcome of these developments can be best described as a process of fragmentation of the class structure, and a weakening of normative or ethical constraints on sectionalist demands of various kinds.

This process has been furthered by the post-war experience of greater prosperity and attendant high aspirations, as well as by successful political mobilization around a wide range of demands which the State has been pressed to meet by legislative action or economic provision. The development of direct action and pressure-group politics of all kinds, originally conceived by the left as a new wave of radicalization, has in fact led to an increased assertiveness in the pursuit of collective ends by interest groups of both right and left. One can cite many examples of colonization of the State by right-wing or propertied interests, to set against the victorious confrontations in the 1970s of such groups as the miners. The success of the National Farmers Union in securing the deployment of subsidies to farmers and landowners,[8] the support won for the forces of law and order or defence and the favourable treatment given to owner occupation and increasingly to private medicine are some instances. The rise of a politics of the radical right — through 'moral reform campaigns' against abortion, pornography, and egalitarian educational policies, with the support of extensive business-funded political research, and even with an illicit 'physical force' dimension provided in certain areas by neo-fascist groups — followed and imitated the earlier development of self-active politics by the left. The pressure on government brought about by this greater assertiveness from all quarters led to influential definitions of a general 'legitimation crisis'.[9] In Britain, the catchword of 'inflation', which provides a condensed metaphor for all these problems,[10] has been appropriated by the Thatcherites, even though the Right has contributed its full share of 'inflationary' demands and, if one considers the budgets for defence and policing, continues to do so.

Political ideologies which were formerly able to organize a broad spectrum of support on both right and left appear to have decayed, giving rise to a lessened attachment to the two major political parties, and a much-noted volatility of electoral support. Margaret Thatcher has not, for example, achieved the proportion of the vote won by Edward Heath in 1970, let alone MacMillan in the 1950s. On the Labour side, as Gareth Stedman Jones has pointed out, the decay was a class coalition of middle-class progressivism and working-class corporatism. This depended on a style of leadership in trade unions and local councils which came under attack as an unacceptable form of bureaucrats' or bosses' rule in the 1960s. It also depended on the acceptance by a working-class Labour electorate and party membership of an upper-middle-class leadership formed by minority liberal traditions of conscience and social responsibility for the worse-off. This description seems clearly to fit the leaderships of Attlee and Gaitskell (the perceptive Wilson was already an adaptation to a more fluid social climate). Benn still has some of the attributes of a patrician radical leader of this kind, although his politics are of course very different.[11]

For many years much historical confidence was placed in the benign workings of this 'class alliance'. The Fabian faith in the 'inevitability of gradualism' was based on a confidence that the forces of Labour and its middle-class allies represented a rising class formation, or at least the unfolding in consciousness and self-recognition of a formation that was already mostly working-class in its objective social position. Social demography seemed to be on the side of the angels: data showing that 70 per cent of the population in the 1950s could be classified as manual workers gave confidence that an electoral majority should be possible for socialism, if only the various impediments to political enlightenment could be cast away. The explanation of the failures of British Labourism by *New Left Review* authors in the 1960s involved the view that the objective demographic conditions had long existed in Britain for a majority for socialism, and that the deficient factor lay in the 'subjective' sphere of consciousness and ideology.

On the Conservative side, ideological 'cement' was provided by a more traditional spirit of social deference which served to mobilize substantial working-class support behind predominantly upper-class leaderships. Perhaps more important, it enabled consensus-minded party managers to maintain control over their own following, by issuing injunctions of deference towards leaders that excluded it from any effective influence on policy. This conciliation of the trade unions, decolonization, and the build-up of the State sector, were allowed to proceed without much resistance from the Tory ranks, until the more conflict-ridden period of the Heath leadership.

The internal difficulties of the Labour Party in recent years, and its problems in finding an adequate response to its electoral slide, are connected to the fragmentation of its class, and in the broadest sense ideological, base. The move to the left after 1979, and the ensuing bitter disputes and defection of the SDP, should not be seen only as a political response to the catastrophic outcome of the 1974–79 governments. It also reflected growing differences within Labour's social constituencies, and the emergence to positions of power of the representatives of new social forces. The take-over of inner-city Constituency Parties by new (albeit in some respects fundamentalist) formations was due to the concentrated deprivation and poverty in such areas, which are characterized by high levels of unemployment, large ethnic minority populations, and acute problems and conflicts over state services in such sectors as housing, policing, and education and training. Inner-city areas also have a significant educated middle-class population which, being mainly young, faces its own employment crisis as State expenditure contracts, and is also strongly identified with the interests of the clients of public services. This has formed the basis for a new 'class alliance' between middle-class functionaries much less privileged than their Fabian predecessors and a working class or sub-working class with much weaker networks of family, neighbourhood and class organization than the earlier industrial working-class communities.

More traditional sectors of Labour support — the occupational communities of the older industrial areas, the skilled working class, and white-collar and professional workers still in employment in more prosperous areas — have been difficult to carry along with these newer 'constituencies', and the differences of interest are reflected in conflicts within the trade unions, within the Labour Party, and between the Labour Party and competing parties. Council house sales and the general encouragement of house-ownership are an example of an issue which divides Labour's potential supporters. Whereas in areas of deprivation party members and those they represent have an overriding interest in the improvement of council house stocks, those with higher incomes and in better-off neighbourhoods may have a material interest in obtaining access to the privilege long accorded to middle-class owner-occupiers. In a similar way, a commitment to large-scale state spending may look different in areas where there is no other conceivable source of investment and jobs, and in those areas of southern Britain where new industries and services are still being established through the market and where State spending is equated with higher tax burdens.

This new political formation has adopted more assertive strategies for advancing its interests than the respectable and somewhat cosy arrangements of Labour traditionalism. Lacking the 'constitutionalism' of earlier elites, which perhaps served the purpose of conferring respectability and office-worthiness on working-class leaders, these new leaderships have sought to use administrative machinery (especially in local government) in more openly political ways. They have also at times been less inhibited in the use of industrial sanctions, as with the 'winter of discontent' public service strikes. These mainly metropolitan areas have also been hospitable to various forms of cultural and moral non-conformity — radical arts, feminist and gay groups, etc. — and this has been another significant component of the 'new politics' and its attempt to adapt local government services to the needs it expresses. This pattern, in which rather segmented and differentiated social constituencies actively seek representation and a share of political resources, is in some respects more familiar in American city politics. A different line of fracture was revealed during the devolution debate, between regional and peripheral nationalist interests and a 'parliamentarist' and provincial Labour identification with the central State. Given Neil Kinnock's earlier opposition to devolution in Wales, this conflict may well re-emerge as an important factor in the future.

This process of social fragmentation is at the root not only of Labour's disabling internal divisions, but also of its major loss of support to the Conservative right and to the Liberal–Social Democrat Alliance. In the case of certain crucial segments (the skilled working class, and other layers in the south of Britain), Labour has lost its dominant electoral position among strata which remain absolutely crucial to its prospects.It is clear that it will be no easy task to construct even that degree of public unity and workable compromise that is a precondition of any electoral improvement. Mere aggregation of sectional demands from separate 'constituencies' (women, blacks, trade unionists, etc.) does not produce a coherent programme or ideology, but an actual synthesis so far seems beyond anyone's understanding. If it is true that the substantive support, in terms of material interest, for 'left policies' is confined to certain class groups, then it seems unlikely to say the least that 'the more left the better' would by itself prove a successful recipe for revival. On the other hand, it is crucial to recognize that such left programmes do coincide with real if localized interests, and are not merely the product of factional conspiracy and machination. It is important, especially for those committed to the relevance of class analysis for socialist politics, to examine critically the appeal of the various possible components of party policy to different class fractions.

In this situation, it seems wildly optimistic to imagine that Labour can in short order recapture the lost segments of its support. The metropolitan inner cities and the areas of declining industry no more look like the basis of a winning electoral coalition in Britain than they do in the United States, yet these are the necessary core of Labour's support and cannot be abandoned without precipitating a complete collapse and capitulation to the Alliance. The overwhelming present strength of Thatcherism rests on disabling social as well as political divisions between these subordinate class formations. It is against this bleak prospect that the case for a commitment to electoral reform needs to be examined.

The main effect of a commitment to PR would be to make possible a de facto truce between the Labour Party and the SDP–Liberal Alliance, in place of the present war-to-the-death from which the Labour Party, having most to lose has so far been the major loser. A further important result could be to recompose the balance of power within the Alliance to the advantage of the Liberals and the disadvantage of the SDP, Labour's main competitor in urban areas. A commitment (or at least openness) to PR by the Labour Party would in itself be a major factor making for the reconstruction of an anti-Thatcher alliance, in place of the anti-socialist collusion between Tories and the Alliance which has dominated recent British politics.

Most discussion of the likely political effects of electoral reform concerns itself with hypothetical effects on parliamentary representation of an election held under PR procedures. It is plausibly suggested that this would give centre parties a pivotal role out of proportion to their electoral strength: on the positive side this might make a government of the Right, like Mrs Thatcher's, difficult to sustain; but on the negative side, it would similarly preclude the formation of radical socialist governments, except in the unlikely circumstance that Labour wins an absolute majority of votes and seats. To confer such a veto power on renegades from the Labour Party would be a bitter pill for socialists to swallow.

These issues have to be faced, but there is a prior stage which is perhaps equally important, and in which the political forces are perhaps stacked more favourably to the left. Proportional Representation has to be legislated by Parliament before any elections can take place under its rules. While Labour's prospects of forming a majority government in the next General Election now seem poor, the Alliance's are even worse; with a more even spread of votes across social classes and thus electoral constituencies, it needs far more votes than Labour to achieve an equivalent number of seats. It seems thus that the Alliance is not likely to achieve PR (on which its access to power in the short run depends) without the support of the Labour Party. (The current leadership of the Tory Party, as the main beneficiary of the present arrangements, is now totally hostile to reform.

The effect of this tactical situation could be that if Labour were committed to support the introduction of PR in the next Parliament, the Alliance would have an 'objective interest' in seeing the Labour Party returned to government. The interest of the Liberals would be especially convergent with Labour's, since they are strongest for the most part in constituencies and areas of the country where Labour is weakest. The real interest of the Liberals (and to a lesser extent the

SDP) would therefore be to give Labour the clearest run possible in its strongest area, and to achieve some corresponding concession from Labour in its own areas of greatest strength. If Labour were committed to PR, and the Tories were not, a repetition of the result of the 1983 election would merely prevent the implementation of the reform most crucial to the Alliance's prospects. One would expect politicians, faced with this strategic situation, to draw appropriate conclusions, and to modify their tactics accordingly.

There might be two principal consequences of such a 'truce'. So far as electoral competition is concerned, one might expect either an agreement not to stand candidates against Labour in certain crucial seats, or much more probably a de facto agreement to fight only token campaigns. In these circumstances a Liberal advance to a secure though still minority position would depend far more on Labour's success than on the SDP's. A 'squeeze' on the SDP would therefore be likely from both Labour and Liberal quarters, hardly an unwelcome prospect to Labour Party members. One might also expect some tacit re-drawing of ideological lines to give broader support to a de facto compact of the anti-Thatcherite parties on constitutional reform. The Labour and Alliance formations would have incentive to find areas of agreement, and to reconstruct the outlines of a new class alliance against the right. In the absence of a mobilizing rhetoric against the right, agreement on PR could seem merely opportunistic, and might be dangerously vulnerable to Tory attack.

Other obstacles to an anti-Thatcher alliance would also be removed by a Labour commitment to electoral reform. With the prospect of PR, interests of the centre would feel less vulnerable to exploitation by the left of a factitious parliamentary majority. And the imperative necessity to destroy the Labour Party as a condition of political survival would also disappear if there were a commitment to a more fairly representative electoral system.

Labour's bargaining position in the period preparatory to such reform might well be quite strong. It might agree to legislate PR only for the General Election that would take place after the expiry of a normal term of Parliament. If it were electorally successful, in these conditions of 'mitigated competition', it would have opportunity to restore its share of the vote as the major left-of-centre party. While it might thereafter have to accept coalition government or reliance on minor party support, this would be consistent with its actual electoral results over many years.

A PR initiative by Labour might be carried through in such a way as to put very severe and perhaps fatal strains on the SDP–Liberal Alliance, and might succeed in altogether removing the threat to Labour from the SDP. Since Labour has more power than the SDP to secure a fair share of parliamentary respresentation for the Liberal Party (fair in relation to the proportion of votes cast), it has a considerable bargaining advantage if it should decide to use it. The Liberals represent a constituency which may be regarded as complementary rather than competitive with Labour's. Its core support is in peripheral areas, and is drawn from the older and newer sections of the middle class identified with the 'small is beautiful' causes of independent businesses, professional independence, civil liberties, local democracy, and regional and national devolution. The SDP's core cadre, on the other hand, is the modern counterpart of the middle-class managerialist element of Labour's original class alliance. Whereas the Liberal membership has a secularized, Nonconformist ethical outlook and does not on the whole aspire strongly to governmental power, the SDP cadre consists of ex-MPs and their 'yuppy' (young upwardly-mobile professional) followers, who are strongly cathected on to the idea of power. There is much greater bitterness inside the SDP than in the Liberal Party towards the Labour Party, which they hold responsible for driving them into the political wilderness. The record of such ex-socialist formations in other countries (e.g. Italy, Australia) is that they remain profoundly hostile to the mainstream Labour parties from which they have split. Reconciliation with the SDP, even given the great political advantages it might have to both sides, seems therefore an unlikely option. Alliance with the Liberals, on the other hand, was negotiated by the Callaghan Government (by Michael Foot, it seems), and though the record of this coalition is not one which many would wish to repeat, the Liberals do not bear the main responsibility for its failure. There is evidence, from the nuclear debate and from the positions taken up by some more radical Liberal politicians, that the Liberal Party's following shares certain positions with Labour, and that agreement might be possible on some areas of policy. This would appear to be a less unpopular and difficult line to pursue in the Labour Party than the idea of any arrangement with the SDP.

A multi-party system seems in any case a more appropriate reflection of a fragmented class and territorial structure than the old two-party system which has long since ceased to be able to contain, either in electoral or in programmatic terms, these plural constituencies. One consequence of such a multi-party structure might be to make debates about specific issues and programmes of greater importance than more diffuse 'ideological' preferences, and thus to make political choices more explicit and rational in character. The argument for the acceptance of the necessity of coalitions and compromises based on agreed programmes in these conditions does not depend on the preference for 'continuity' or 'moderation' usually expressed by advocates of PR.

There is no reason why, in such a competition, Labour should not be able to win support for its programmes (for example, non-nuclear defence, overthrowing the power of the City and rentier interests over economic policy, support for social welfare, regional devolution, enhanced State investment and workers' rights) and to force appropriate compromises on the other parties involved. A situation in which Labour is able to compete for support with rival parties (the proportional share of the vote becoming a vital index of strength, as it now is in Italian politics), but avoids the costs of a war to the death with them, seems likely to make more possible the resumption of a 'forward march' for progressive social forces in this country.

This strategy might also bring effective pressure to bear on the Conservatives to moderate their policies, in as much as it led to a significant electoral threat. One reason for the domination of the Tory Party by its right has been the extreme structural debility of the opposition since the SDP defected with 8 to 10 per cent of the former Labour vote. It is an unwelcome paradox that the course outlined above might do more to force 'conciliatory' job-creation and public investment policies than militant modes of resistance for which no sanctions, excepting urban riot, now seem to exist. If Labour were once able to form a government, it would seem astonishing altruism to introduce an electoral reform which would reduce its share of seats. There is an element of risk — after all, it is possible that Labour could win a majority without such a commitment. But judging one's actual strength is critical to political conflict, and the assessment made here is that while the Alliance and Labour seek each other's destruction, the Right will rule.

There are technical issues to be considered in regard to the most preferable form of proportional representation. But as the main political effects argued for here depend upon a closer equation between the proportion of votes cast for parties, and their representation in parliament, the differences between alternative methods are perhaps secondary so long as they secure this end. The various options available have been lucidly presented in Vernon

Bogdanor's recent book *The People and the Party System*,[13] though with recommendations (for a Single Transferable Vote system) whose purpose may not be shared by many socialist readers. Bogdanor distinguishes alternative systems by the criterion of whether they offer voters a choice between individual candidates (Single Transferable Vote, Regional List systems), or only between parties which have themselves chosen the candidates (Party List Systems). He also identifies a number of hybrids, such as the West German system (where electors have two votes to enable them to elect half the candidates by constituency and the other half by party list to secure proportionality), and the Additional Member System, recommended in 1976 by the Commission on Electoral Reform established by the Hansard Society. The latter is in fact an adaptation of the West German system to British conventions of 'constituency representation', such that three quarters of candidates would be elected by constituency, and the remaining quarter from lists of 'best losers' by region.

One paradox of the present British system is that it has a rhetoric of constituency representation by individual member, and a reality of voting by party preference. It should be important to socialists to strengthen — and internally democratize — the functions of parties in formulating and debating coherent programmes, and in providing a means of informed participation in political debate. A system such as the Single Transferable Vote, which might encourage a personalized 'notable politics' (as the expensive machinery of American primary and presidential politics seems to do) against the organizing role of parties, should therefore be opposed. It seems most likely that a compromise system, such as the West German or Additional Member system, would be the most desirable and feasible, preserving an element of constituency representation while also maintaining at least the existing role of parties.

Any system of proportional representation is likely to give advantages to small or new parties, compared with the operation of the plurality system. Even the five per cent minimum threshold of votes needed to secure representation has not prevented the electoral breakthrough of the Greens in West Germany. This provides an important potential counter to the 'centripetal' tendencies of Proportional Representation, created by the pivotal role which it sometimes confers on centre parties.

Such systems have obvious attractions for the various sections of the left in Britain, which could seek representation with less risk of inadvertently helping the right. If the above analysis of an increasingly fragmented class structure is correct, there are electoral advantages in a system which would allow more flexible and differentiated representation to forces left of centre.The argument in this chapter has been based on rather gloomy assumptions about Labour's chances in coming elections. There may be inclinations to 'wait and see', at best preserving this option (with preliminary steps such as the Commission on Electoral Reform recommended by Ken Livingstone) until the outcome of the next election is known. But delay and equivocation would be a mistake. The argument for democratization of the electoral system offers a means of isolating the Thatcherites, of standing as principled advocates of democracy, and of drawing advantage from an existing electoral strength which may not be available to Labour, if it does not adapt to new conditions, for many more years.

NOTES

1. In M. Jacques and F. Mulhern, eds., *The Forward March of Labour Halted?*, Verso NLB, London 1981.

2. M. Jacques and S. Hall, eds., *The Politics of Thatcherism*, London 1982.

3. D. Massey, 'The Contours of Victory . . . Dimensions of Defeat', *Marxism Today*, July 1983. Ivor Crewe, et al., 'Partisan De-alignment in Britain 1964–74; is Britain's Two-Party System Really about to Crumble?' *Electoral Studies*, I, 1982. I. Crewe, 'The Labour Party and the Electorate,' in D. Kavanagh, ed., *The Politics of the Labour Party*, London 1982.

4. If the Liberals' share of the vote came from specific social classes, rather than being evenly spread across them, they would win more seats because of the distinctive class composition of many constituencies (working-class in the inner cities, middle-class in the outer suburbs, and so on).

5. There is a very extensive literature on social inequalities in Britain. For more recent accounts, see P. Townsend, *Poverty in the United Kingdon*, Harmondsworth 1979; J. Westergaard and H. Resler, *Class in a Capitalist Society; A Study of Contemporary Britain*, Harmondsworth 1976.

6. J.H. Goldthorpe and D. Lockwood et al., *The Affluent Worker*, 3 vols., Cambridge 1968-9. For a summary statement of their theoretical argument, see 'Afluence and the British Class Structure', *Sociological Review*, Vol. 11, No.2, 1963.

7. The importance of collective consumption for voting behaviour is explored in P. Dunleavy, 'The Urban Basis of Political Alignment: Social Class, Domestic Property Ownership, and State Intervention in Consumption Processes', *British Journal of Political Science*, Vol. 9, No. 3, July 1979. See also 'The Political Implications of Sectoral Cleavages and the Growth of State Employment,' *Political Studies*, Vol. 28, 1 - 2, 1980

8. For an unexpected critique of the farming lobby by a Conservative MP, see R. Body, *Agriculture: the Triumph and the Shame*, London 1982.

9. For an account of the debate about the alleged 'ungovernability' of Britain see A.H. Birch, 'Overload, Ungovernability and Delegitimation: The Theories and the

British Case', *British Journal of Political Science*, No. 14, part 2, April 1984. The first influential statements of this thesis were M. Crozier, S. Huntingdon, and J. Watanuki, *The Crisis of Democracy*, New York 1975, and A. King, 'Overload: Problems of Governing in the 1970s', *Political Studies*, vol. 20, no. 3, 1975. See also S. Brittan, *The Economic Consequences of Democracy*, London 1977.

10. F. Hirsch and J.H. Goldthorpe, eds., *The Political Economy of Inflation*, London 1978.

11. See Raphael Samuel's perceptive article on 'Benn: 'Past and Present', *New Statesman*, 28 September 1984.

12. V. Bogdanor, *The People and the Party System*, Cambridge 1981.

7

A Statutory Right to Work

It was widely believed after the second World War in Britain that the 'right to work' had been generally won; the greatest economic evil of the pre-war years seemed to have been overcome through reforms.[1] Yet now, again, unemployment has returned in a seemingly permanent form and there appears to be neither the understanding nor the will to confront the problem effectively. Among professional economists, there has been an influential revival of pre-Keynesian, neo-classical perspectives which have sought to reconceptualize unemployment as 'voluntary' and as the product of rigidities in the labour market and of disincentives to work created by the welfare system.[2] This position has provided the theoretical basis for the Thatcher and Reagan programmes, which are premissed on the belief that the Keynesian arrangements of the post-war period, far from abolishing unemployment, as was thought, in fact had merely caused inflation and made worse the recession that has 'inevitably' followed it. Nor has the problem of unemployment yet had the priority that one might have expected from economists of the left.[3] Neo-Keynesian policy debates have continued through the recent period to concentrate instead on the advocacy of incomes policy as a means of controlling inflation, on the balance of payments problem, or on the system of international credit. These had been the fundamental preoccupations of economic policy-makers within both the Labour Party and the Social Democratic Party. While such forms of restored Keynesianism would, unquestionably, mark an improvement over the policies of the radical right, it seems doubtful whether conventional demand-management remedies alone could succeed in restoring the full employment levels of the 1950s and 1960s.

Since I am a sociologist rather than an economist, the approach to the problem of unemployment in this chapter will be unavoidably naive in technical economic terms. Without detailed quantification, the following argument proposes a kind of 'middle-range' theory, starting from the value-premiss that the right to employment is a central attribute of citizenship, and grounding this in a historical perspective of the struggle for 'social rights'. Specific institutional changes are proposed by which this right might be made effective. This level of programmatic thinking, which imagines the effects of a specific structural reform on the whole economic system, seems to me essential to the development of socialist strategy in the coming period. The practical reason of the left must be bold enough to explore the outer limits of the possible, and hopefully this initial argument for a campaign based on the demand for a right to work will be taken up and criticized by those more qualified than myself to test its technical implications.

Liberal democracies such as Britain accord many rights to their citizens, and the development of 'social democracy' has been widely understood as the extension of these rights from a negative and largely political definition into a system of positive social and economic entitlements. The liberal definition of rights originally concerned itself with the 'negative freedom' not to be interfered with by other citizens and especially the state — Locke's rights to life, liberty and possessions. This definition corresponded with the emergence of agrarian capitalism and chiefly formulated the rights of property-owners. Subsequently, universal rights to political participation were won through extensions in the franchise as the state's importance in determining the conditions of life of social classes became understood and contested. The 'welfare state', established through the need to achieve mass mobilization and consensus in wartime, and through working-class pressure, enlarged these rights into increasing social and economic entitlements, in the broader concept of citizenship described in T.H. Marshall's seminal article[4] of the post-war reconstruction period. As a result of these changes, rights to education for children up to the age of sixteen (and subject to certain limiting conditions beyond), rights to health care, and rights to a minimum level of subsistence through entitlements to social security and supplementary benefit, are among the social and economic rights which British nationality and residence (itself newly restricted through immigration laws) entitle citizens to. These rights of the citizen have, as their necessary obverse, obligations upon the state to fulfil them in specified ways, and they are enforceable (though with some practical difficulty) at law.

The idea of full employment as a 'social right' is contemporary with the development of other provisions of the welfare state, deriving from Beveridge and Keynes's proposals for the management of welfare capitalism, and from the organized popular pressures which gave weight to these during and after the Second World War. But while it was widely believed that full employment or the right to a job was the keystone to the whole edifice of welfare (Beveridge thought that welfare provision should be confined to those not able to work), this was never thought of as an individual, legal entitlement in the same way that the other social rights were conceived. Full employment was to be achieved not by guaranteeing a job to each separate individual (in the same way that local education authorities are obliged to find school places for each child), but by measures affecting the aggregate of employment in the economy as a whole, which would then create the conditions in which individuals *could* find jobs. Keynes's theories of demand management and the practical success of post-war governments in maintaining unprecedented levels of full employment (with some regional disparities) for twenty years made this seem a feasible way of fulfilling this 'right to work', and the difference between this and other rights of citizenship in regard to their form of implementation did not attract attention.

In fact, the contrast between the legally enforceable rights to certain kinds of social and welfare provision, and the absence of any enforceable right of the individual to work, represents a major division within the fabric of welfare capitalism between the sector dominated by the market and by economic contract, and the sector regulated by the state through the universal provision of various services or income entitlement.[5] 'Work' is not conceived primarily as a 'benefit' to the individual to be claimed by him or her like an entitlement to income, but is provided in the first instance in the interests of employers. The supply of labour and its levels of payment are determined by the mutual interest of employer and worker, and not by consideration of need or principle, in the theory and practice of the market. As Edward Thompson has shown, this was one of the most bitterly contested principles of the capitalist economy. The success of a market economy depends on its mechanism for allocating resources in an efficient way, and labour is one of its major resources (according to Marx, the only ultimate source of value). It thus appears to be in the interest of the working of the economy as a whole, and thus a common interest, that labour should be deployed in ways advantageous to employers and not deployed where it is not advantageous to them. While these laws are followed most closely at the present time in the market sector, where profit and loss measure efficiency or inefficiency in the allocation of resources, they are also often followed as a matter of policy in the non-trading parts of the state sector. Here too, workers are employed, at least in principle, at the lowest cost and measures are sought (pupil-teacher ratios, patient-doctor ratios, bed-occupancy rates etc.) which enable them to be deployed in the most efficient way.

Keynesian reforms sought to preserve this principle of allocating labour in accordance with the needs of the market while creating a *de facto* right to work by manipulating the aggregate demand for labour so that it balanced the supply. But it now appears that this system of providing full employment through a market regulated by budgetary management has irretrievably broken down, not only in Britain but throughout the capitalist world. There is now no 'full employment' and thus no 'right to work', and little or no prospect of these being restored. While political parties in Britain offer various prescriptions for reducing unemployment and creating more jobs, none has a programme for restoring the full-employment position of the post-war period, and all now refrain from declaring 'full employment' to be a feasible objective. Many analysts in fact forecast that the situation will become worse, not better; the capital investment needed to improve Britain's competitive position in manufacturing industry (if it takes place) may well destroy more jobs than it creates. The problem of a long-run increase in unemployment is in fact becoming recognized as a general problem of advanced economies, and this further discourages particular governments from believing they can solve it on their own. Particularly crucial in the gestation of the problem on an international scale has been the pursuit of deflationary policies by so many capitalist governments, and also the effective displacement especially of unskilled labour in advanced countries by investment in newly industrializing counties. Another factor may be the saturation of markets in the advanced countries with the consumer products of the last wave of expansion (consumer durables, motor cars, etc.), and the failure to create sufficiently extensive consumer demand in the developing world to offset this. But while one can envisage this trend to higher unemployment being arrested by a move towards expansionist economic policies, especially if this takes place on an international scale, it is hard to imagine that any change in these external market conditions will resore full employment as it was known immediately after the war. Indeed, the absence of any significant proponents in Britain of such an optimistic view tells its own ominous story. In these circumstances, the prospects for full employment in Britain, one of the weakest of the advanced economies, are bleak indeed.

It has perhaps to be accepted that the phase of capitalist development in which 'Keynesian' techniques of budgetary management could ensure full employment has passed. This is not to say that Keynesian approaches to the economy are not preferable to monetarist ones; they give a different priority to employment and output over the avoidance of inflation and returns to rentier capital, and are associated with commitments to real rather than formal conditions of citizenship. Especially this would be the case if they were supplemented in a weak economy such as Britain's by the additional instruments of direct control over the balance of trade, as the Cambridge neo-Keynesians of Wynne Godley's group have advocated. It is also true that 'Keynesian' measures would be more effectively deployed on an international (or even a European) scale than by a single state in isolation. But the problem seems to go deeper than the rejection of Keynesian measures, and few analysts appear to imagine that full employment would be restored in the West even if these measures were now generally introduced. Different theorizations and different forms of intervention in market economies are now needed if the goal of full employment or jobs for all is again to be made an attainable one.

In this chapter I want to suggest that the mode of addressing the problem of the right to work needs to be radically altered. Instead of the level of employment being treated as a dependent variable — the contingent outcome of various macro-economic management techniques — I shall argue that it should become a limiting planned condition for the operation of mixed economies that there should be a job available for each individual who chooses to work. Faced with a long-term increase in unemployment on the present catastrophic scale, it would be possible to argue for a more thoroughgoing transformation of capitalist economies into wholly planned or socially owned systems. But my argument here adopts a different approach, taking as a point of departure the problem of unemployment (which of course has many other ramifications), and outlining only that degree of intervention in the market economy which would establish a right of work for all.

There are many precedents for such specific and local interventions into the workings of the market economy. Until a few years ago, most people thought that 'full employment' was already the result of such an intervention, following the teachings of Keynes. But in addition, these economies are able to function while their governments determine that no one should work below a certain age, that all between certain ages should go to school, and that all needing medical treatment (more or less) receive it. The entire state welfare system represents a compromise between the allocations of the free market and the application of universal and uniform rules of provision following public decisions. There is no reason to assume that this boundary between the domain of the market and the domain of collective decision has been fixed for all time, or that new limiting conditions to the operations of the market cannot be set when evident need and popular demand justify it. It is possible to plan parts of market systems without planning all of them (just as conversely some Eastern European economies and now China are attempting to introduce markets into planned economies without introducing large-scale private ownership, and without abolishing a basic framework of planning). It is a matter of working out the implications for the rest of the economic and social system of deciding to achieve by planning what can now be achieved by no other method, namely a universal right to work.

What will be proposed is that the 'right to work' should become a right which can be claimed by each individual and enforced through the law like other social rights. A proposal which makes the right to work universal and legally enforceable offers a fundamental re-orientation to this problem, and will get us away from the cautious bidding of political parties to reduce the unemployment total by this or that unsatisfactory figure, implausible enough even in prospect without allowing for the attrition which experience of government would undoubtedly bring. The point of the proposal is that it makes the provision of employment, like the provision of health care, education or political rights, an absolute obligation of government, and no longer a contingent aim dependent on trade-offs with various other economic objectives. Many specific mechanisms to reduce unemployment have already been initiated in mixed economies — employment subsidies, industrial training and work-experience schemes, job-creation programmes — but these have everywhere been conceived as temporary and ad hoc programmes.

Only so far as young people are concerned, where short-term training and work experience programmes are evolving into more permanent schemes, have these been conceived in principle in comprehensive terms. It is the essence of this proposal that the state would take responsibility, through these and other measures, for finding work for all these whom the 'free' employment market was not able to place.

A proposal to institutionalize a universal 'right to work' may have the merit of connecting with beliefs which enjoy wide support and not only on the political left. It is obvious that the absence of work involves a massive waste for society in the products and services not made or provided. It represents a loss for each individual deprived of work, and with the existing levels of unemployment in Britain there can be few without first-hand acquaintance with many people beset by this catastrophic experience. Reciprocity of giving and receiving is a natural social condition,[6] and there is a need to contribute to the well-being of others as well as to be cared for by them. It is part of the common-sense meaning of the idea of work, and not only a result of its organization through the market, that 'work' involves a contribution to the welfare of others. (One of the conditions which the definition of work as a right would have to meet is to make this element of contribution real; work, unlike education, health care or income-maintenance cannot be provided merely as a benefit to its recipient.) For these reasons, what is being proposed may be less utopian than some may initially think. It may be that the support that can be won for a specific transformation in the capitalist economy, in response to a major and obvious dysfunction such as unemployment, will be much greater than socialists can now achieve for more ambitious but abstract programmes. The discourse of rights and citizenship may also have more resonance among British people as a language of political reform than any other that is available. That certainly seems to be the leading precedent for major reforms in this society, in which systematic political ideas of any kind have few supporters. Certainly it is urgent that there should be a much more fundamental discussion about the retreat from full employment and about the possible ways of recovering this lost political ground. There seems to be a fatalistic and defeatist consensus among politicians and opinion-formers of left and centre at the present time that the problem is insoluble, and that it would only raise false expectations to propose solutions. It is this demoralized climate of public opinion that has to be challenged.

The proposal to socialize the labour market to a degree sufficient to provide a universal right to work competes with the market theory which is now being tested to destruction on the British economy. This alternative theory is open to fundamental moral as well as theoretical objection, especially for the overriding priority it accords to the principle of reward according to desert rather than need in the allocation of resources. Market theorists defend themselves against (justified) accusations of heartlessness by postulating, in defence of actual unemployment, a 'natural' level of unemployment which public policy can make worse but never, in the long run, better. Part of the revisionary exercise of Chicago economics in the last few years has been to argue that post-war full employment was in fact merely an untenable short-run defiance of these laws, rather than the managed long-run equilibrium at a level of full employment, but only about the acceptance as 'natural' of whatever level of unemployment turns out to remain once its prescriptions are followed. (It is in reality arguing for the necessity of a substantial 'reserve army of labour'.). Meanwhile the prescriptions in countless Institute of Economic Affairs pamphlets are for attacks on trade-union powers as a prime source of reigidity in the labour market (a less attended problem is the rigidity caused by defensiveness and fear in the working population), and for the restoration of markets in as many public services (such as health and education) or public owned industries (oil, telecommunications) as possible. It seems improbable, from the evidence so far, that this programme could ever restore the British economy to general prosperity.

A particular problem for this laissex-faire model, which looks back to the nineteenth century for its model of successful operation, is provided by the welfare system itself. I shall contend that the intention of the welfare system, of insulating the dependent and unemployed population from the harsh consequences of the labour market, is to some degree effective and that this undermines the classical impact of unemployment — of the reserve army of labour — in making possible the profitable redeployment of capital. To this extent, the right's hosility to the welfare system has a rational basis. Its case is often presented in false and simplistic terms, as an assertion that present levels of unemployment can be explained by the unemployed preferring to remain idle at existing levels of social security benefit instead of taking available jobs. Evidence on actual levels of unemployment and on the attitudes of the unemployed show this to be in general a false claim. There are manifestly many more millions seeking work than there are currently jobs available. Nevertheless there may be more indirect mechanisms which have some of the same effects.[7]

The 'reserve army' of the unemployed can exercise its full coercive force on the conditions and wages of employed labour only when it faces even more adverse conditions of existence than is now the case. In nineteenth-century circumstances, when the unemployed faced starvation or the workhouse (and when trade unions encountered much greater difficulty in defending the interests of the employed), the downward pressures on wage levels and employees' powers exercised by unemployment were incomparably greater than in present conditions. While the unemployed are (even poorly) supported by a social security system and the employed are protected by strong trade unions, the outcome of unemployment appears to be the creation of a boundary between the occupational communities of the employed and the unemployed. Sociological evidence suggests in fact segregated patterns of social relationship and a kind of passive and resigned adjustment to unemployment, with increased depression and illness. This may explain why it is that while there has been some slow-down in the rate of wage inflation in conjuction with the rise of unemployment, there has not been a collapse of wage-rates. Rather, what is more striking is the insultation of the employed population from the effects of unemployment. Standards of living of the majority in work have by and large been maintained, while the unemployed have been plunged into poverty and have had to bear the main economic burden of the recession. While this has helped to restrict the unpopularity of the government, it has severely limited also the competitive 'benefits' of unemployment which are its main result according to free market theory. Were it the case that workers and their families were faced with actual starvation or incarceration as a result of job-loss, the opportunities for employers to reduce wages, to strike-break, and to attack the position of those in work, would surely have been considerably greater than they now are. Governments of course fear that the desperation which further reductions in subsistence standards for the unemployed would bring might be mobilized against them, and not against trade unions or those in work. The risks of unrest give many interests an incentive to prefer to maintain passivity, at the cost of providing a measure of subsistence, to the full rigours of the market. Nevertheless, this strategy has deprived capital of much significant benefit from unemployment to offset the losses of declining demand.

It is not only the institutions of the welfare state that work against the operation of the harsh market model favoured by the Thatcherities, but also the climate of moral assumptions now established over two whole generations. In the powerfully individualist ideological climate of the nineteenth century it was possible to enforce the view that poverty and unemployment were the fault of the individual alone and not the responsibility of society. But while the Government and its supporters have made strenuous attempts to attach blame to the unemployed (via campaigns against 'scroungers', 'fiddlers' and so on), it is widely recognized that unemployment is not primarily the fault of the unemployed. Perhaps corresponding to the large-scale nature of modern economic organization, and certainly to the extended role of government in social life, is a deep level of recognition of the social rather than individual origin of these problems. And in a society in which universalist moral claims to fairness and justice have become entrenched, it becomes politically difficult to propose the punishment of the unemployed for the indirect benefit of others: market ideology just does not command this level of popular assent. There are therefore strong pressures, sustained by a small but significant number of Conservatives,[8] to maintain the value of social security benefits, and the Government has been limited in its ability to use their drastic reduction as a means of indirect assault on general wage levels.

The Government's public expenditure strategy has been another casualty of the interaction of the welfare system with rising unemployment. Savings in local government spending and in nationalized industry investment (mainly on capital budgets) have been offset by lost revenues from taxation and increased payments in unemployment and social security benefits — a direct result of unemployment. Hopes of substantial reductions of interest rates, through lessened government demands for borrowing, were also aborted, until far into the recession. The Government has succeeded in increasing the proportion of national income spent by the state, when one of its principal objectives was to reduce it.

So all in all, it seems that the monetarist policies pursued by the Thatcher Government have been a serious failure in its own terms. The costs of deflation in lost productive capacity, reduced investment and lost profits have been far greater than its benefits to British industrial capital. A further period of Thatcherism would no doubt see further attempts to restore competitiveness through attacks on the welfare system and trade-union powers; these are logical enough from a neo-liberal standpoint. But the dysfunctions of this process (reduced demand and the disincentive to invest) seem greater than its positive effects. More capital seems to have been dismantled or to have migrated out of Britain than has been generated from increased exploitation. There seems to be an increasing and cumulative difficulty, the longer the present programme proceeds, of competing on an open market basis with the advanced countries of Western Europe and Japan, and with the industrializing low-wage economies of Latin America and South-East Asia. In a fully competitive system without the intervention of the state it seems likely that the British economy will merely continue in its decline.

This failure of monetarism ought to be opening up space for different solutions to the problems of the economy. One aspect of the above argument is particularly relevant. The 'statutory right to work' is intended to transfer the resources of the state from maintaining citizens out of work, to maintaining them (the population of working age, that is) in work. Moreover, the cooperation of trade unions with an expansionist economic strategy may be easier to secure in exchange for the substantial addition to workers' rights that would be involved in a statutory right to a job. Where Thatcherism has attacked the postwar foundations of a guaranteed income and trade-union rights, the proposal for a statutory right to work seeks to build on them, as positive contributions rather than impediments to economic success.

The proposal for a statutory right to work incorporates a number of assumptions. A key value-premiss is that a realizable right to work would be an important extension of citizenship and equality; so important that if it cannot any longer be guaranteed by the techniques of macro-economic management, it should be secured by other forms of political intervention. What economists call the 'non-pecuniary' benefits of work, both to the individual and to society (e.g., the sense of meaning, reciprocity and social recognition) are given weight in assigning such priority to the right to work. It is, secondly, now recognized that material productive powers today make possible (and perhaps necessary) a simultaneous reduction in the total volume of work required:[9]. A guaranteed right to work is not seen as an alternative or competitor to this view, but its complement: it will be a disaster if the 'decline of work' is accomplished by throwing more and more of the population into redundancy and pauperism. It is, thirdly, recognized that there is an unavoidable distortion in considering this proposal separately from a wider programme of economic expansion and reconstruction, which would in any case involve the large-scale and deliberate creation of jobs. Some measure of artifical isolation of the 'statutory right' proposal from the wider economic context seems unavoidable for reasons of presentation; it is not possible for me to present it as part of a total economic plan. Finally, and for similar reasons of analytical simplicity, the case for a statutory right to work — to an actual job — is argued in ways intended to be compatible with many of the existing characteristics of the labour market.

The contractual basis of the private labour market, and the quasi-contractual basis of the public labour market, could be as far as possible preserved, while the agencies concerned with implementing a universal right to work confined themselves to 'last resort' or 'residual' functions. Such a measure of socialization of the labour market will seem to some unduly minimalist. It should be pointed out, however, that it is on a contractual labour market that the functions of trade unions and collective bargaining now depend; most measures of socialization and planning in this area (such as incomes policies) are already resisted by the trade unions, and their support is unlikely to be forthcoming for any broader regulation of the labour market than is proposed here. Further, there are reasons for giving emphasis to the re-emergence of mass unemployment as a decisive issue for capitalist economies, and for regarding the argument about it as being as critical as in the debates of the Thirties. A universal access to work at a fair income is conceived as the moral basis of economic citzenship, capable of winning more universal support than any other normative principle at this time. These are grounds for attempting to explore the minimum conditions by which this might be achieved. The conferring upon work of the status of an enforceable right would be a considerable gain even if it only restored ground that had been thought already won(until a few years ago) by other means. It was resistance to the indirect consequences of full employment (a widening agenda of popular demands, pressure for increased intervention by the state, and so on) which led to the revival of the neo-liberal right, and reconquering this lost territory would not be without benefits for economic and cultural democracy.

Socialists in recent years have been more preoccupied with enhanced democratic control of capital than with ideas of socialization of the labour market. A larger planning role for the state, public ownership, industrial democracy, democratic control of pension funds and other worker-owned capital, and an extended frontier of trade-union bargaining have been various means of seeking greater employee or public control of capital. Meanwhile it has seemed in the interests of labour, or at least of its trade-union institutions, to defend the labour market against regulation and instead to support collective bargaining as the main agency of working-class power. These movements to obtain more democratic control of capital have been recently in retreat in Britain. Far from repudiating these aims, the measures proposed here would provide a source of support for those wishing to see capital made democratically accountable and may help to reverse this adverse political tide. But it is argued, against recent left-wing consensus, that the labour market can no longer be left to 'collective bargaining' to defend the interests of labour. It is doubtful, in fact, if egalitarian aims have generally been served by these methods, aside from the contradictoriness of favouring planning of two main factors of production but not of the third. The restoration of full employment must depend on the enhanced role of the state and on the imposition of new minimal principles of operation for the economy by planned means. The implications of this degree of 'socialization' of the labour market simply have to be faced up to, to avoid worse harm.

As things now stand, there is a fundamental irrationality in the market mechanism, in the displacing of the costs of unemployment from firms in the market sector, which seem to 'benefit' from job loss, to the welfare system, which bears its costs. The costs and benefits to the individual employer of a decision to employ a worker are quite different from its social costs. The higher the levels of state expenditure the greater is the disparity between the private and social costs of unemployment, and the greater the external diseconomies of redundancy. If employers had individually to pay the costs of maintaining their own displaced workers (instead of merely paying generally for them through high taxation and interest rates), the diseconomies of maintaining large populations without work would be more evident to them. Where it leaves resources of labour and capital idle, the market sector continues to consume from the state while contributing nothing to it.

In recent years, the relationship between the state and the market sectors has been influentially defined by the neo-liberals of the Right as a parasitic one, in which a greedy public sector spends resources produced by the private sector, which is thus subjected to a crippling burden of taxation and high interest rates. This argument has wilfully neglected to notice that the boundary between the public and private sectors is different from that between the planned and market sectors, and that the welfare system contributes to wealth as well as consuming it, through its planned and non-traded services. State enterprises such as British Telecom and Britoil are also able to earn surpluses and make a net contribution to national wealth. The state sector can achieve increases in the real product of its planned services through increases in efficiency or through improved techniques, for example in teaching or health care. As a result of these ideological omissions and distortions, this critical view of state spending as a 'burden' on the private sector has widely been accepted as a reason for reducing state expenditure and as the model on which the Thatcher Government's policies are based.

This model offers a biased account of the respective contributions of private and public sectors to the national wealth at the best of times. But in a market economy predisposed to create unemployment (through the international migration of capital to low-wage regions, and technological displacement of labour) the balance of advantage between 'planned' and 'market' operations in the economy shifts decisively towards planning. Even while it leaves large potential resources of capital and labour unused, and thus reduces its contribution to state funding through taxation, the capitalist sector nevertheless continues to depend on the state to maintain and reproduce those resources of labour and capital. So, for example, the state sustains increasing deficits on underused railway lines, coal mines, and steelworks, and has to pay for health, education and social security (needed for the reproduction of labour) from a diminished tax-base. As the private sector continues to decline in response to reduction in demand for its product, the neo-liberal right demands yet further reductions in the burden of welfare and state spending. Yet pursuing these measures brings about a further downward spiral, whose effect is to inflict irrecoverable losses on the economy, and to degrade civilized standards of life, even undermining the conditions of liberal democracy itself. This road may lead to the imposition of 'law and order' by armed force, and to authoritarian government, if these deprivations eventually lead to revolt.[10] There is no reason to believe that the natural low point of this recessionary cycle for the United Kingdon has been anywhere near reached. It is for this reason that more extensive planning rather than a more perfect market is appropriate to the condition of an economy which already has a major state sector.

It was against an earlier version of this situation that Keynes insisted in the 1930s, as an enlightened supporter of capitalism, that the minimum condition for the successful operation of market economies was that they made full use of their resources of labour and capital. Capitalism, he correctly thought, had to devise that measure of planning which would ensure full employment and therefore a minimum acceptable share in society's resources for all. His critique of the unregulated market system has lost none of its relevance, but what is in doubt is whether the limited kinds of intervention he proposed can now ensure full employment in the long run. In fully planned socialist economies, or planned market economies in conditions of full war mobilization, these conditions are secured as an aspect of more total planning of resources, including labour. (There are drawbacks too, but it is hard to imagine, if a 'wartime mobilization' was again called for in Britain, that unemployment would not disappear as rapidly as it did in 1940.) But in these proposals I want to test out whether specific forms of socialization can be devised to meet these objectives, short of a system of comprehensive economic planning. For, at this point, there is likely to be wider support for economic reforms specifically related to unemployment than for a more general socialist economy. In any case, it needs to be demonstrated what forms of intervention may and may not be feasible, even in a socialized economy. An economy which has abolished large-scale private ownership of capital (a defining objective of socialism) may still have reason to make use of market mechanisms to ensure an efficient allocation of its productive resources.[11]

The essence of this proposal is that those unable to find work through the existing mechanisms of the labour market would be able to register with a specified state agency and become its employees. Let us call this the Statutory or Regional Labour Board. This agency would have the obligation to find or provide work for all such persons and would be expected to maintain those arrangements which would enable it to meet such a demand. This is not dissimilar to the way in which a local education authority is required to maintain enough school places to meet the requirements of eligible children, or in which a health authority makes provision available. The agency, whose possible forms will be discussed in a moment, might have three major means for the provision of work — all corresponding to piecemeal measures already employed by the British and other governments for job-creation.[12] First, the state could offer subsidies to private employers to take on additional workers. Secondly, it could provide subsidies to other public-sector employers for the same purpose. Thirdly, jobs could be directly created by schemes initiated or funded through the Board. The workers concerned would in all cases be paid the rate normally appropriate for the job as negotiated by trade unions or wage councils or set in the corresponding free market. This proposal for a universal right to work is not to be equated with schemes deliberately designed to undercut normal wage rates. On the other hand, the normal obligations of workers to perform tasks responsibly and efficiently would also apply and employment would be conditional upon these obligations being met.

Especially from the standpoint of countering likely attacks from the Right, it is important to specify some of the economic justifications for the provision of state subsidies for job creation, and the scale on which these might be justified in terms of net economic benefit to society as a whole. The key argument is that the state would act rationally were it to reimburse the employers of hitherto unemployed workers up to the full cost to it of their maintenance out of employment. There would be no economic loss to the state if the equivalent maintenance costs were paid in respect of an employed worker rather than for an unemployed person. Any subsidy less than the full cost to the state of maintaining an unemployed person will conversely lead to a net benefit. The payments which it is relevant to consider are not only direct payments in unemployment and supplementary benefit which form the most obvious basis for calculating 'economic' subsidy levels, but also that portion of state expenditures normally paid for in taxation and national insurance by employed workers, which the unemployed do not pay. While state expenditure in supporting employment in the market sector (it is immaterial from this point of view whether firms are publicly or privately owned, where they are required to operate at a surplus) do not exceed expenditures made and revenues foregone in relation to the unemployed, they would seem to be *economically* justified. The Treasury's Economic Progress Report for February 1981 calculated this figure of the total cost to the state of an averaged unemployed worker from the private sector at £3,400 per annum, but much higher figures have also been suggested. If we further assume that firms in receipt of such subsidies behave rationally in terms of market theory and employ workers only where their marginal product equals their marginal cost to the employer (net of subsidies, etc), then it follows that the employment of such 'subsidized' workers is no less advantageous than not employing them. Given lower subsidies, or higher marginal outputs, or taking into account non-pecuniary and indirect benefits to the workers and society (less illness, for example), there will be a net social benefit from the arrangement.

This argument is presented above as a justification of subsidies to employers in the market sector, as one prong of a broader employment-entitlement strategy. There would be problems in ensuring that such subsidy arrangements did not disrupt the operations of the market in labour, and ingenuity would be needed to insulate the labour market as a whole from its possible dysfunctions. We will assume for present purposes that it is economically desirable that the labour market *should* allocate resources efficiently, and that such considerations cannot wholly be abandoned in favour of non-economic considerations. We also assume that a market sector — indeed a private sector — of some scale continues in existence while this proposal is implemented. While this proposal does have implications of a major kind for the balance of planned and market, public and private sectors (in favour of the relative growth of the public sector), it would be beyond the scope of the present discussion to propose the abolition of the private sector and the labour market as a precondition for it. For these reasons the argument assumes an attempt to implement a statutory right to work within a capitalist economy and accepts the conditions that this will unavoidably impose. Clearly much institutional ingenuity will be needed to make this feasible, and it is important to distinguish the particular devices proposed below, which will no doubt be capable of much improvement, from these general principles.

Steps would have to be taken to limit the potential distortions of this procedure. If firms can engage some workers at subsidized wage rates, why would they choose to engage any others at non-subsidized rates, for instance? One such limitation could be effected by the regional implementation of such a programme, such that the level of funding available for the implementation of the statutory right to work was proportional to the level of unemployment in that particular region. This would avoid one of the major problems of labour market policy since the War, which is that measures of reflation intended to reduce unemployment in relatively depressed areas produce labour scarcity in more prosperous areas long before universal full employment is reached. The funding to ensure that labour is fully employed should be locally and regionally directed, and not confused with a general reflationary package.

If geographical structuring is one means of controlling the unintended effects of this employment programme, a temporal structuring would be another. The level of subsidy available (let us suppose to employers operating in the market, whether private, public or cooperative) would be related to the level of unemployment in a region at a given point of time, and the permissable subsidy would be periodically (annually?) re-determined as this level fluctuated. There should therefore be a tendency for the subsidy to be self-cancelling, in the sense that as its multiplier effects led to general economic expansion and the taking-on of non-subsidized labour, so the future level of unemployment on which the next determination of funding would be based would be lower.

An additional limitation might be that firms would be able to take on only a fixed proportion of their workforce from this Statutory Board in any given year (this proportion being set in relation to regional unemployment levels). This would equalize the advantage of subsidy to firms in a given region and avoid another kind of distortion. Another limitation might be that firms could only employ workers from the Statutory Board for one year at a time. While employees' right to work would be guaranteed by the Board, the employer could only secure continuity of employment of a particular worker by putting workers on to their normal (non-subsidized) payroll, and would thus have an inducement to do this. Such limitations would be designed to protect the conventional labour market from the distorting effects of these special subsidies by standardizing their impact between firms and by imposing some disadvantages to firms (in terms of continuity and stability of employment) from employing workers on this basis.

The conditions under which workers would be eligible to register with the Board and become its employees require careful consideration if it is to be a supplement to the existing free labour market and not a general replacement for it. It might be that workers would become eligible only after a period of six months' unemployment, in order to ensure that the Board had responsibility for the long-term unemployed rather than for those routinely changing jobs. There is a necessary level of 'frictional' unemployment in any economy. The Board would be required to 'place' all workers properly registered with it, and they would be entitled to the proper remuneration for the work concerned on condition that they performed it properly. The status of 'long-term' unemployed would thus become a voluntary one, since society would have ensured that all who chose to work, could do so.

The second and third prongs of this strategy involve creation of employment via existing public-sector employers, and via direct and specific employment creation programmes. There are more difficult problems here in maintaining a rational allocation of resources given the absence or imperfections of markets. However, there are arguments here too for ensuring that employment decisions continue to be made with regard to the task of the 'enterprise' concerned and its most efficient or productive performance. It is important to recognize that 'wealth' is as much created by public-sector activity (health, education) as by private: this becomes especially obvious when the private and state sectors are providing similar services in competition with each other as in these two cases. While public-sector organizations should have available to them access to subsidized employment, this should be deployed in accordance with their proper institutional goals, and not degenerate into the making-up of jobs that produce neither use- nor exchange-values. This is to preserve the idea that work should of its nature involve contributions of value, and should be organized productively. We should not be seeking to create an economy of 'public assistance'; among other things this would undermine belief in the public sector as a producer of real values. To this extent public monitoring bodies such as Community Health Councils (sadly now weakened) which represent the interests of consumers of these services provide some substitute for market indicators and strengthen the weak position of the consumers of public goods.

A third category would be the direct creation of work by the Regional Labour Board itself, which would require to have access to state capital or borrowing for this purpose. There may be a necessary distinction between expenditure on labour subsidies paid to existing employers of firms, and additional expenditures on the capital (as well as labour) costs of employment creation where existing employers with their existing capital stocks are not able to take up the full surplus of labour. Capital programmes of this kind are difficult to keep analytically separate from other expansionary capital programmes, but it would follow from the obligation to offer work to all citizens that special capital expenditures would be required. In these circumstances governments would have an understandable interest in funding employment that was labour- rather than capital-intensive, and also, it must be acknowledged, to provide work at the lowest possible rates of pay. It is likely to be the case, therefore, that the majority of the work provided as the residual supply (after private and public sector employers had taken up for their usual activities as much as was deemed appropriate) would be relatively less skilled and labour-intensive. It can be imagined that this fraction of employment creation would tend to be in low-paid service, construction, and environmental improvement work, though other possibilities are discussed below. It would be a matter for political bargaining within given regions and with central government to determine what proportion of the funding would be for work of this kind.

Even in the absence of a general policy commitment to a 'statutory right to work', the force of this argument for employment subsidies in conditions of high unemployment remains. It would contribute to net welfare if government were to compute the costs of its own new capital programmes in areas where there is significant unemployment in a way which deducted from the total the indirect costs of unemployment benefit, foregone tax revenues, etc., for the number of workers who would be employed. This procedure would make significant differences to the projected levels of return on capital of schemes in zones of high unemployment. While there would still be a rational economic basis for discriminating between alternative expenditures, schemes would be economically justified which failed to meet this criterion when the costs of unemployment were invisible.

The availability of work for all who want it would have implications for the conditions under which unemployment and supplementary benefit are now awarded. There would clearly be the possibility (and likelihood) of greater duress in decisions to award benefits if in principle there was always work available, than in a situation where there is a large excess of applicants over vacancies and where it is therefore difficult to distinguish genuine job-seekers from others. It is likely that the guaranteed right to work would involve greater financial and moral pressure to work, expressed less in the persecution of claimants for suspected deception, as is now the case, than in the firmer insistence that job-offers were taken up. Subject to various qualifications and safeguards, the obligation to work in return for subsistence seems to be an acceptable principle. (It should apply to the owners of private property also.) It is hard to imagine any socialist or planned economy which did not subscribe to such a rule; what is problematic is not the principle but its mode of application and enforcement.

Given a general reduction of work, such a principle should allow for periods of educational and 'sabbatical' leave, and also for periods between jobs which allow workers to find jobs based on their own skill. There would of course be continuing income-maintenance for those involuntarily out of work, but for those who chose this situation one would expect this to be at lower levels than working incomes. The arguments for increased child benefit, (and 'infant child benefit' for children under five), involve a recognition that child-care is a form of work, and financial support for this function is an alternative to subsidized 'paid work'. Given that 'residual' work might often be in low-paid categories, it is also critical that the tax and benefit system should be reformed to abolish the 'poverty trap' so that the marginal rate of return for low-paid work should be no lower than for other categories of work. It is crucial to these proposals that it is fairly paid work (after tax) that is guaranteed under this scheme, and not a form of stigmatized outdoor workhouse which in fact might worsen rather than improve the condition of the existing unemployed. The involvement of the trade unions in the management of such a programme is for these reasons also important.

We now turn to the possible forms of agency which could implement the proposed statutory entitlement. It seems desirable that it should be regional in scope because of the variability of unemployment levels and the likely appropriateness of different kinds and scales of measures in regions of high and low unemployment. It also seems desirable that the agency concerned should have a specialized function, of providing appropriate work for the unemployed, so that a specific institution could develop the appropriate expertise. The Manpower Services Commission is now the obvious nucleus of such an agency.

There are arguments for this agency being accountable to a broader institution of elected regional government, such as I propose in chapter four. The reason for this is that employment creation is connected with many other government functions (education and training, public investment, economic planning, public employment). The fragmentation of institutions responsible for labour market policy has up to now inhibited any coherent response to rising unemployment, and a concentration of functions in elected regional authorities might help to meet this problem. Another example of decisions bearing on the level of unemployment are the possible methods now widely discussed for changing the pattern of employment itself, through a shorter working week, work-sharing, early retirement, increased time for training and education, and so forth. But under present conditions decisions concerning such changes are largely in the hands of employers and trade unions, who have little interest in measures whose beneficiaries will be not them but the unemployed and the public at large. How are divisions such as these between private and public interest to be resolved?

One might envisage that a regional authority with extensive spending powers and with regional economic planning functions would consider its unemployment problem in the following ways. It would know, given a statutory obligation to provide work, that it would have to find work for a given number of unemployed over a period. Its public expenditure budget, its economic planning strategy in relation to private employers, its education and training policy, and its own policy as a major employer, would all be relevant to its strategy for resolving this problem. Some of these levels of intervention would be ways of reducing the burden on its specialized employment creation department, the Regional Labour Board[13]. It would wish to ensure that this department had a manageable task, and economic planning within the authority would have to construct a strategy by combining the different measures available.

Central government would also be faced with a predictable scale of demands, for employment subsidies and capital grants, to meet the full cost of providing work as entailed by statute. It would also have grounds for relating its decisions in education and training provision, retirement arrangements, child benefit and maternity leave, and its practices as a large employer in terms of the length of the working week or year, to the size of the unemployment problem. The obligation to provide work for all would constrain both central and regional government agencies to adopt a kind of economic and social planning, relating different elements of public policy to one another, which is very different from current practice.

While there are arguments for a regional level of organization of the Labour Boards, and also for other aspects of economic and social planning, there would also be advantages in the involvement of more decentralized and local agencies in employment creation.[14] The opportunity to mobilize unused resources does provide the possibility of creating new public and social goods, as well as goods provided on the market. The funds available to Regional Boards could be 'bid for' not only by private employers but also by co-operatives and by voluntary and neighbourhood associations. Resources could become available to fund socially useful production by worker-controlled enterprises,[15] which might later become viable in the market or supply the public sector. The long-term availability of some funding for public purposes at the neighbourhood level might help to overcome a lack of imagination about social goods which is a product of the bureaucratization of central and local government services, and which now widely discredits the idea of socialism. Community arts and recreation,[16] as well as locally based social services for children and the old, are examples of activities involving both capital programmes and paid work which might expect to grow in an economy of 'fully used resources'. The abolition of unemployment ought to bring not only an improvement in the lives of the unemployed, but an enhancement of capacity for communities to improve their real living standards.

One important objection that will be made to this proposal is that it would be inflationary, both in requiring a major rise in public spending and in increasing the pressures of wage-inflation as excess supply in the labour market is absorbed. These potential difficulties can be limited by a number of factors. One is that everyone would be a producer and the burden of unproductive welfare payments would be substantially reduced, not increased, by the proposal. The differential regional implementation of the statutory right would also limit inflationary effects, as I have argued above. While the statutory right to work would weaken the sanction of unemployment on workers engaged in collective bargaining (not remove it, since workers who lost high-wage jobs in particular firms or industries would not necessarily find comparable employment), it could also have beneficial effects on the working of the labour market, from the point of view of economic growth. Workers' current interests in resisting technical change would be lessened by the assurance of alternative work, especially if it was the case that their Regional Labour or Regional Planning Board was committed not only to provide 'statutory work' but also to maintaining a regional economy appropriate to the skills of the workforce. While the restoration of a universal work ethic might seem an implausible objective for the 1980s, in practice this proposal for 'fair shares in work' makes imaginable a positive ethic of work, combined with a likely reduction of average working time initiated by public-sector employers.

Since the removal of the threat of mass employment would strengthen workers' bargaining power, a wider planning of incomes would be a necessary correlate of introducing a statutory right to work. It seems to me that the planning of incomes would be an acceptable trade-off for universal rights to employment. Socialists have sometimes argued that there would be hypothetical reforms in return for which incomes policies might be justified, and in practice have been prepared to settle for rather minor gains, as in the 'Social

Contract' of the last Labour government. A statutory right to work seems to me to be an appropriate condition: a legislative guarantee of work for all would justify some other measures of planned control of the labour market. The unemployed have been made to pay for the current recession, and it is realistic to recognize that some redistribution of resources towards them (through taxation to pay for capital programmes, for example) would be necessary if unemployment is to be abolished. Greater prosperity should ensure that such sacrifice would be temporary, and the greater resources provided for public goods in such a system (can anyone now imagine that the private sector will by itself lift the British economy out of its decline?) should make possible some more promising future for socialist perspectives. It is likely that balance of payments controls would be necessary, in Britain's economic plight, to meet the import demands that would follow full employment, but this may now be a necessary condition of any foreseeable revival of the British economy. (There is an obvious unrealism in separating programmes for the British economy from its difficult international setting, but this is inevitable if one wishes to begin from a single problem.)

This proposal for a statutory right to work is suggested as a feasible element for a medium-term socialist economic policy. While it concentrates on specific measures of regulation of the labour market, it has some implications for the possible socialization of capital. One must be pessimistic, on past experience, about the possibilities of Labour's existing economic strategies achieving substantial control over, or direct socialization of, capital. Planning controls, nationalizations, or new state investments of the National Enterprise Board-type all historically run into immense resistance from British capital, whose cooperation invariably seems vital for Labour's wider expansionary aims. This will be even more the case with the more radical forms of enterprise now being proposed on the left for cooperatives or worker-initiated and worker-controlled enterprises. One advantage of a statutory obligation to create work is that it would provide some 'push' as well as 'pull' for the public provision of capital, creating space in which public and worker-initiated enterprises could 'bid' for the capital funds to create the jobs required.

The proposal also seeks an ideological initiative at a difficult time. It seeks to pre-empt hostile denigration of the poor and workless by proposing that the state, rather than providing inadequate benefit for those able to work, instead ensures or provides properly paid work. It seeks to link the social needs for more goods and services (the reconstruction of cities, for example) to the abysmal waste and deterioration of worklessness. It would make it possible to redefine the problems of 'law and order', as a natural consequence of mass poverty and redundancy, and make real solutions seem possible. It seeks to return British politics to the language of universal rights and citizenship, in terms of which most of its historic achievements have been won.

It is in some ways a very modest proposal, but it is an indication of how deep the decline in expectations has been that at this point there is scarcely any other on the political agenda that offers a commitment to universal employment. Critical is the idea that access to useful work should be a statutory right, like the vote, or a minimum income, or rights to education, and not a contingent outcome of market forces. It is with this point of principle that a socialist argument against the resurgent politics of unemployment should begin.

NOTES

1. I would like to thank Robin Blackburn, Peter Howells and Gösta Rehn for their encouragement and advice.

2. J. Shackleton's article 'Economists and Unemployment', in the National Westminster Bank's *Quarterly Review* (February 1982) helpfully reviews this literature. There is a fuller symposium on these questions in Daniel Bell and Irving Kristol, eds., *The Crisis in Economic Theory*, New York 1981.

3. Important exceptions are the Community Development Project, whose members did pioneering work on inner-city economic decline, and the economic advisory groups now working for some Labour municipal authorities (London and Sheffield, for instance) on the same problems.

4. T.H. Marshall, 'Citizenship and Social Class', in *Sociology at the Crossroads*, London 1963.

5. Adrian Sinfield has pointed out in *What Unemployment Means*, London 1981, that this division between state welfare and private labour market has tended to remove working life from the concerns of social policy. The split between welfare and market sectors, and its consequences, are also discussed in the final chapter of N. Parry, M. Rustin and C. Satyamurti, eds., *Social Work, Welfare, and the State*, London 1978.

6. I have offered some theoretical justification for this view in 'A Socialist Consideration of Kleinian Psychoanalysis', *New Left Review* 131, January–February 1982.

7. R. Layard, *More Jobs, Less Inflation*, London 1982, reports some relevant research on work-seeking and its relation to the system of unemployment benefits.

8. See, for example, I. Gilmour, *Britain Can Work*, London 1983.

9. This view has been presented forcefully in C. Jenkins and B. Sherman, *The Collapse of Work*, London 1979, and its implications discussed in their *The Leisure*

Shock, London 1981. André Gorz, *Farewell to the Working Class*, London 1982, is also relevant, though it takes a very different view from mine.

10. The miners' strike revealed the deep bitterness aroused by unemployment.

11. Alec Nove, *The Economics of Feasible Socialism*, London 1983, is instructive on these issues.

12. See the articles by Ian Hargreaves, 'Unemployment in Europe', in the *Financial Times*, Jan. 7, 17, 24, Feb. 1, 1983.

13. A far-sighted proposal for a somewhat similar kind of Labour Board was made about ten years ago by a sociologist at North East London Polytechnic, Douglas Young. This was prior to the present high levels of unemployment, and was intended mainly to guarantee income and occupational status to workers displaced by technological change during a transitional period while they learned new skills.

14. Tony Benn has made the interesting suggestion in a note on this paper that not only would local initiatives be important, but individuals should be eligible to apply for funding for particular work projects.

15. The proposal therefore connects with the campaigns for 'socially useful production' initiated by the Lucas Aerospace Shop Stewards' Combine Committee. See Hilary Wainwright and Dave Elliott, *The Lucas Plan* London 1982, and also chapter eight of this book.

16. Robert Hutchinson, *The Politics of the Arts Council*, London 1982, discusses the relative starvation of local and regional arts in the funding policies of the Arts Council.

8

Workers' Plans and Industrial Democracy

This chapter will discuss the political relevance of Workers' Plans, and their implications for the planning and democratization of the British economy. The important initiative of the Lucas Aerospace Shop Stewards' Combine (LASSC) in developing an Alternative Corporate Plan,[1] in response to threats of major redundancies and plant closures by the Lucas company, has received wide attention both within the labour movement and elsewhere. It has given rise to other Alternative Plans, often generated by similar threats of plant closure, and to the establishment of a Centre for Alternative Industrial and Technological System (CAITS)[2] jointly by the Lucas Combine Committee and North East London Polytechnic. (CAITS has since moved to the Polytechnic of North London.) Our intention here is to examine the implications of the alternative plan movement in a more theoretical and strategic way than has previously been done, and to investigate its relevance both to long-term socialist perspectives and to the problems of developing an alternative economic strategy in Britain.

The Originality of the Alternative Corporate Plan Movement

The Workers' Plan movement initated by the Lucas Aerospace Combine is an original development in a number of important respects. The principal one is that, unlike the mainstream of socialist thought and activity in post-war Britain, it is oriented towards production[3] rather than towards consumption, or social 'reproduction' as this has been redefined by Marxists. Whereas social democracy has concerned itself chiefly with income redistribution, educational provision and opportunity, housing and town planning, and the health and social services, as its principal means of achieving greater equality and social justice, the Workers' Plan movement is oriented towards manufacture. It seeks to bring about equality and justice not through redistributing the surplus from a predominantly market system of production, but directly through the choice and control of production itself. This is a necessary change of emphasis, for the programmes of British social democracy have failed on successive occasions to achieve the economic growth on which measures of relative redistribution depended. Had the social democratic strategy succeeded, in the terms argued by Crosland, for example, the outcome might have been a reasonably tolerable social order, on the lines of the Scandinavian societies. But it has not, and we are therefore faced with the need for a more radical consideration of alternatives. The corporate plan movement at least begins to raise some of the issues which must be central to that analysis, as, in a different but related way, has the work of the Institute for Workers Control.

A second source of originality in the alternative plan initiatives is the fact the engineering and design are their principal area of expertise and occupational concern. Most initiatives on the British left, perhaps reflecting a general bias in the dominant British and especially South-East culture, have as their main intellectual source cultural and social-scientific modes of thought, rather than knowledge of technology. In recent years radicalism has flourished in economics, sociology and history, in community initiatives, in applications of the law, in approaches to the family and social services, and in cultural provision. But while the 'alternative technology' and 'ecology' movements (which have some overlap of interests with CAITS) have been a different emphasis, in general one can say that the left has shown the same anti-manufacturing bias as most of British society. Even the Institute for Workers Control seems to have been inspired by a sense of socialist and democratic tradition by a concern for democratic organizational forms and workers' rights, more than by involvement in technology per se.

One might make a comparison with the concerns raised in the Finniston Report about the general status of engineering and manufacture in Britain.[4] That report embodied a 'professional' strategy for engineers, faced with low status and opportunities, and with the costs for them of the general failure of British manufacturing, while the Lucas initiative represents a radical 'unionist' strategy for some comparable occupational groups. Whereas Finniston commends the traditional professional remedies of improved training or 'formation', professional incorporation, and control of entry and standards, the Workers' Plan movement recommends gaining greater control of the production process through extended trade union bargaining. Where Finniston is occupationally exclusive, the Lucas plan is inclusive. Whereas Finniston advocates a more vigorous policy of 'occupational closure' for engineers (following Frank Parkin's terms[5]), the Lucas initiative proposes a strategy of 'usurpation' of powers from capital and senior management. It is a moot question which occupational groups the LASSC represents, on which I have no detailed information.[6] But my impression is that the strength of the Combine has been that it includes, in its broad representation of Lucas employees, many highly skilled engineers and designers. The relative success of the Combine in negotiating with the Company may well be due to the bargaining strength derived from this technological expertise. The high technical capacities demonstrated in the Alternative Corporate Plan are also perhaps an important source of leverage on the Company. Using another idiom one might describe the Lucas Aerospace Combine as representing an important element of the 'cultural capital'[7] of Lucas, as it speaks for members of the design and engineering teams which are one of the company's main assets. This, then, would be an example of the power of Galbraith's 'technostructure',[8] expressed not as he describes through continuing informal (and invisible) negotiation, but through the use of explicit industrial and political bargaining techniques, in alliance with the engineering workforce as a whole.

I may be corrected in these suppositions about the particular occupational strata in Lucas that the alternative plan movement has represented, or about the sources of its bargaining power. The issue is important, if one is willing to generalize a strategy from the Lucas experience, and to identify the 'class fractions' to whom such a strategy might have appeal.

The Goals of Workers' Plans

One can imagine a hypothetical case in which an 'Alternative Plan' proposed by a company workforce was accepted by management and duly implemented after negotiation and revision. The terms in which the Lucas plan was presented do not, after all, appear to disregard the functional requirement of a corporation to have products which make use of its distinctive resources and can be sold profitably in existing or new markets. Although particular weight was given in the Lucas Plan to the preservation of employment and working conditions, notably the location of jobs, these are purposes which corporations often say they would like to heed, other circumstances being equal. And while substantial concern was also expressed for socially useful production, as opposed to production for military purposes, this in some ways only anticipates more long-run and 'ecological' modes of thinking — about energy sources, for example — which may well become increasingly salient facts of a company's external environment. One could have imagined a company response to the ideal of 'social usefulness' which insisted on constraints of profitability, offset only by considerations of image-building and goodwill, but which did not exclude these other criteria of product-choice in principle. It seems that the original Plan was prepared in such a way as to encourage these kinds of response, rather than to maximize differences of value and ideology between the shop stewards and the company. The 'constructiveness' of the workers concerned was widely commented upon, and no doubt accounts in part for the relatively 'good press' which the Lucas Plan received.

We know, however, that the response to workers' plans in this case and in general has by no means been as favourable as in this hopeful scenario. In the Lucas instance, not only was the company hostile, but so were many of the unions, and the Labour government was also covertly negative in collusive defence of the prerogatives of the established union structures. It does not now seem generally practicable to influence companies in the direction of implementing Workers' Plans by direct negotiation, and the British 'de-industrialization' which led the Lucas workers to write their plan in the first place gallops on with increasing momentum. It therefore becomes necessary to examine the wider conditions in which such a planning process might become generally feasible. I put it in this roundabout way to show that the necessity to think out the political and economic implications of the Lucas Plan has been forced on its authors and supporters by harsh experience. It is also worth pointing out that the Lucas Plan was pragmatically conceived, as an attempt to influence locally a market-orientated system in the direction of maintaining employment and a more socially responsible product mix. It was in short a far from utopian document. One should be similarly practical in socialist efforts to undertake 'alternative design work' for the larger economic system.

The following distinctive concerns, implicit in the Alternative

Workers' Plan movement, can be reasonably inferred from the Lucas Plan and other published CAITS documents:

(a): to produce for social use, rather than by the criteria of the market;

(b): to maintain employment, both within particular companies and in the economy as a whole;

(c): to give workers and their representatives a direct involvement, notably by broadened trade union bargaining, in the decisions of the companies in which they work;

(d): to overcome the unrepresentativeness of present trade union structures, especially with regard to the representation of shop stewards and shop steward combines in negotiations with large companies;

(e): to reverse the general decline of manufacturing industry in Britain, and of the economy as a whole.

Economic Intervention by British Governments

We can perhaps usefully contrast the orientation towards production, and especially production for social use, of the Workers' Plan movement, with Labour governments' recent modes of economic intervention. There has been ever since 1947 a marked aversion to 'physical' interventions and controls of any kind. There was Harold Wilson's 'bonfire of controls' in 1947 and the reliance first on fiscal and monetary means of control, in place of physical planning. Subsequently, in the post-1960 period, came tripartite indicative planning of various kinds, through such instruments as the Prices and Incomes Board, the National Incomes Commission, the National Plan, NEDC, and the Planning Agreement system.[9]

Governments in Britain since the war have been committed to the idea of a regulated market economy, differing over time and with each other about the degree and nature of regulation, but with a common commitment to the efficacy of market mechanisms and the role of private capital in principle. It is important to identify the different kinds of intervention practised, and the criteria used to justify them, since this is the terrain on which any new forms of intervention must be argued. We can identify the following:[10]

(a) maintenance of full employment equilibria by fiscal and monetary policy (in accordance with the work of Keynes on the role of governments in influencing the level of employment);

(b) influence on income distribution through the tax and subsidy system, sometimes rationalized as being for the benefit of the poor and of dependants, but in fact also involving substantial middle-class subsidies through, for example, mortgage tax relief on owner-occupied housing;

(c) use of government restrictions, grants and tax-concessions to offset regional and other locational disadvantages;

(d) use of government to maintain universalistic social provision (e.g., in health and education) based on norms of citizenship, in preference to the greater disparities that would result from market mechanisms, although these were allowed to operate for upper income groups;

(e) government investment in and operation of public utilities and certain key industries, usually on the grounds of their non-viability in the private market. There has been much argument about the extent to which such industries are to operate as 'normal commercial concerns' or to incorporate 'non-commercial considerations' (e.g. wider economic benefits of low prices, maintenance of subsidised services, etc.);

(f) government investment in other aspects of 'social infrastructure' than education and health, — for example housing, town development or parks;

(g) government regulation of external diseconomies, through pollution control and similar measures;

(h) use of government resources as a stimulus to economic activity — for example, through investment grants or allowances, research and development funding, funds channelled to innovative companies or for industrial reorganization, employment subsidies, re-training schemes, and so forth. There have been substantial constraints imposed on any net increase in government holdings in profitable private concerns as a result of such interventions, and such have hardly in fact occurred even under Labour governments;

(i) government involvement in tripartite, consensual planning, the object of which has been to achieve voluntary or constrained limitation of market pricing behaviour (of goods, services or labour), and or to improve information available to economic decision-makers, both about macro-economic climates and expectations (NEDC) and about available technologies, markets and so on (NEDC sector working parties);

(j) regulation of agricultural markets, through subsidies, price-support systems, etc.

This list is hardly exhaustive, and considering the proportion of GNP now expended by government and its agencies, it is, not surprisingly, lengthy. It leads us to recognize a paradox, that while the dominant rationale of the British economy remains that of the market, and the dominant power that of capital, the scale and apparatus of government intervention has become very extensive indeed. It is in reaction to the successive growth of forms of intervention that free market economic theory has undergone a revival and provided a coherent ideology for the Thatcher government.[11] This revival is based on the view that the market economy is threatened with ultimate destruction by the progressive growth of government intervention, trade union powers, and universalistic welfare provision. While this might seem an unlikely vision from the perspective of a supporter of recent Labour governments, on a long enough view it may not have been a wholly irrational anxiety.

Workers' Plans and the Mixed Economy

How can one characterize, in theoretical terms, the very complicated combination of market and state-regulatory mechanisms which has evolved in Britain? Part of the political attraction of Thatcherism is its very simplicity: both its appeal as a populist theory, and its strength as a source of policy prescription, however misguided, have been enhanced by the internal consistency of its pure market model. On the other hand, the previous period of 'consensus politics' saw a large ad hoc expansion of state intervention, but without a corresponding theoretical clarification of the logic of mixed systems, or of the criteria for political choices within them. This ideological model of free market capitalism as an ultimate rationale for the system thus remained stronger than actual modifications in the operation of the system might have led one to expect. What is the relationship between the rationales of previous kinds of State or socialist intervention in the mixed economy, and the objectives of the Workers' Plan movement? Why is it that these objectives are so foreign to the character of mixed economy capitalism, and are so original, when capitalism has already become so very mixed and so subject to government intervention in practice?

There are two principal reasons for this. The first arises from the dominance within this system of the norm of 'consumer sovereignty' for final products in the manufacturing sector.[12] Whilst to justify government intervention in the 'social sector' (housing, education, health) collective judgements of value are made, and a planned system is constructed from them, government strategy in the manufacturing sector is to provide enabling support for whatever outcomes the market will generate. The idea of 'social usefulness' or 'production for need' only has purchase in those 'welfare' fields in which government has specifically chosen in general to replace the market, or substantially to modify it. There are of course many forms of dependency of this 'social sector' on the market economy; it is not an autonomous alternative realm of egalitarian, democratic and socialist values. The State education system generally adopts a priority of putting the greatest 'investment' in those pupils who are likely to be the most productive in their subsequent work, by market criteria. The higher education system operates through the Robbins principle which allows for individual students to exercise a 'market choice' of subject and college.[13] The housing market favours a particular conception of family as a consumption unit, and this is reinforced by the construction and allocation policies of councils and building societies. The health system is distorted by the particular power of the medical profession and its traditional prioritization of curative, individual treatment over a preventive, environmental strategy. Nevertheless, in principle and in practice this is a sphere of purposive, planned, collective decision-making, in which at least questions of 'need' and 'social usefulness' can be and are explicitly raised.

But in the 'goods' sector these questions have no purchase at all, except in the negative regulation of goods, services and activities which do actual proven harm. There are important safety standards and controls on pollution through industrial or nuclear wastes, lead in petrol, poisons like tobacco, dangerous drugs, or lethal activities such as drunken or dangerous driving. Yet these are generally seen as intrinsically undesirable interferences with the individual, to be kept to a necessary minimum. In this normative system, individuals are to be left as free as possible to do as they wish, whereas one can imagine an interpretation of 'social need' which would involve a more collective determination of the goods and services contributing to a 'way of life'. This presumption that 'final consumer demand' should be left to determine output, subject only to regulation to avoid particular harm, leaves the norm of 'production for social use' as an anomaly. Social use, by these criteria, is what the market determines as the sum of individual uses, and more collectivist means of decision are thought likely to reduce rather than increase both choice and welfare.

The second important reason for the originality of the Workers'

Plan idea concerns power and control. Mixed-economy capitalism has shown itself extremely sensitive to the maintenance of the prerogatives of capital and of its relative as well as absolute power, more so than one might have expected from some earlier notions of the managerially controlled or socially responsible corporation. The failure of the last government to achieve its Planning Agreements with private companies (an anodyne-enough instrument, one might have thought), the unrelenting hostility to nationalization, the dislike of competitive, State-funded enterprise through the holdings of the National Enterprise Board — all these indicate the great reluctance of capital to share its decision-making powers.[14] Labour governments have by and large accepted this resistance as a fact to be lived with, and the influence they have therefore acquired over private capital has been disproportionately less than the scale of resources which they have poured into it. Governments have operated a whole series of grants and subsidies, allocated often on universalistic and non-selective criteria (such as those of location, or per capita by employee) which do not permit the exercise of purposeful discretion. The failure of the British State to evolve an arm capable of skilled industrial intervention, as apparently exists in France, West Germany or Japan, has been noted by analysts as a major British weakness.[15] The insignificant powers accruing to government from even a majority shareholding in BP become evident in the Rhodesia sanctions affair, and the regulation of financial holdings and the City has been an area of gentlemanly autonomy which was little changed by the Wilson Committee's recommendations. The involvement of trade unions in company control is no more favoured by British capital, as its wholly negative response to the Bullock recommendations showed. While in general public corporations cooperate more favourably with trade unions than does private capital, the Morrisonian tradition of public corporate autonomy has also given no basis for ideas of co-determination with unions, or with consumer interests. Relations between nationalized corporations and the British economic system, despite years of effort and all the ink expended on consensualist ideas, are still fundamentally structured around conflicts of interest. This may explain the willing connivance of the CBI in economic policies which seem only to make sense in terms of the narrowest view of the relative self-interest of capital vis-à-vis other contending interests, and which seem detrimental to the general interest of British national capital.

Trade unions in Britain have been shaped by this situation of adversary relations, and are committed to a conflictual conception of bargaining. For all the framing of the Workers' Plan proposals in terms of an 'extension of bargaining', it seems unlikely that the conception of Workers' Plans can be wholly accommodated within this framework. Workers' Plans are not only about the disposition of labour power, over which workers possess the means to bargain, but about the disposition of capital, over which workers now have no rights or powers. It is one thing to extend bargaining rights to cover the introduction of new technologies and working practices introduced at the instigation of management (as ASTMS has led the way in doing), but quite another to propose to management that it introduces such technologies. This is a function of the control of capital, and while managements may or may not find it in their economic or political interest to accede to such proposals, it goes beyond the current division of power for trade unions to be able to compel them to do so. Investments are about returns to capital, primarily, and workers are not currently sole or joint owners of capital, even in 'public' enterprises. It seems therefore that the Workers' Plan movement is making implicit claims regarding ownership and control which go well beyond existing definitions of the rights to capital. Had it been found within the Lucas Company's interest to accede to large parts of the Alternative Plan (presumably on the basis that the LASSC had correctly judged capital's real interest as well as labour's), this issue of fundamental rights and powers might have been avoided. But it is hard to see that it can be, given British capital's aversion to ceding any of its powers to either unions or the State.

It appears that British capitalism is still a child of the nineteenth century — perhaps this is the reason why Hayek, Friedman and Thatcherism have struck such a resonant chord. British capitalism was *not* established through the direct industrial and financial intervention of the State, like the capitalism of Germany and Japan. Its favoured model is of a free market, insulated from the managerial involvement of the State (if not from its subsidies and regulatory legislation) and confronting the trade unions as bargaining agents for their specific factor of production. The insulation of political and economic spheres is an aspect of this historical formation,[16] nowhere more clearly institutionalized than in the internal division and differentiation in the labour movement between the trade unions and the Labour Party (and the third, now somewhat residual and weak sector of working-class organization, the cooperative societies).

The Insulation of Politics and Workplace

This division of party and union, of which I have written else-where,[17] has the effect of restricting work-based activity largely to the function of bargaining over labour, while confining political activity to a territorial basis. Politics is biased for that reason towards issues centring on residence (i.e., individual and collective consumption) and thus fragments the occupational expertise and solidarities generated in the workplace. The control of capital, other than through wage-bargaining, is a function placed upon the State apparatus, of which the electoral process is supposed to give the Party control, and the effect of this has been through the Morrisonian tradition, to set up yet another alienative apparatus, the public corporation, encountered in the workplace as not usually much different from private capital itself. Of course, the industrial and political aspects of the labour movement are connected, through representation at party branches, at Conference, on the NEC and in Parliament. But while this representation has given the trade unions a substantial measure of influence over the Labour Party, it has left them external to the political process. They have been conspicuously unable to constrain the activities of Labour governments on issues other than those of immediate trade union interest.[18]

This split between the industrial and the political sphere is chal-lenged implicitly by the Workers' Plan movement. Both by seeking influence over the disposition of capital, and by seeking to impose value-criteria on the definition of needs and products, the Lucas Shop Stewards Combine raised issues of economic policy normally reserved for the State. This is a welcome breakthrough in this order of institutional separation, and involves a radical breaking and merging of the categories of the political and the industrial. It is no less political for being implicit, practical and low-key. The more strident demands of the ultra-left are often less radical in funda-mental terms, merely carrying to an extreme, through 'money-wage militancy', the logic of insulated spheres of wage bargaining without political implication. It remains to be seen whether the British system, after its present antediluvian lurch into free market theory, will be able to rethink these fundamental institutional separations, as the earlier tentative flirtations with corporatism indicated some intention to do.

The Meaning of 'Socially Useful Production'

The terms in which the Workers' Plans have made their proposals for a modification of market principles are remarkably confined and moderate, and even reveal the intellectual influence which market theory has over its presumed adversaries. The view, for example, that priority should be given to a maintenance of employment, and the restoration of full employment, is argued on the grounds of the hidden costs of unemployment, as external diseconomies. It is shown that if one counts in the costs of unemployment benefit, redundancy pay, etc., and the opportunity costs of foregone production, unemployment does not even make sense in market terms — the market here being understood in a holistic and ecological way, rather than merely from the point of view of the employing firm.

Similarly, the three areas selected for greatest attention as potential fields of 'socially useful production' are energy, transport and health. These are sectors of the economy already substantially subject to the control of the State, where intervention would require no great reduction of the existing private market sector per se. David Elliott's CAITS paper on *Energy Options and Employment*[19] which shows great restraint in preferring long-run 'economic' arguments to warnings about the physical risks of nuclear power, demonstrates that alternative energy sources can be justified as 'economic' especially if the diseconomies of unemployment are taken into consideration. The National Health Service is already a public concern committed to explicit goals of welfare rather than to market values. While increases in the resources devoted to the NHS, and in production undertaken for it, further the principle of production for social use, these build on a sector of the economy already fully committed in principle to criteria of social need (however defined in practice.)

The practical advantage of stressing these issues of employment, health, transport and energy as central to the Workers' Plan initiatives is that they are already salient public concerns, and permit specific cases to be readily made for encroachments on market criteria. (They should have made it easy for the Labour Government to give support to the Lucas Plan.) But there is also a danger that the more fundamental challenge to modes of economic management and social values implicit in the Workers' Plan initiatives will be blurred by conducting the argument in these pragmatic terms.

The originality of the Workers' Plan initiatives lies in the involvement of representatives of workers themselves in product choice and product design. The idea of 'production for social use' seeks to give initiative and autonomy to workers in deciding what they produce, as well as to 'consumers', whether these are conceived as individuals or collectivities represented by elected governments. Markets make possible alternative choices of goods; the decisions of consumers are affected by what goods and services are made available to them. It is not true that consumers directly determine the range of products they buy: how could this be the case, when there has to be something to choose from before a choice can be made? In market systems, the entrepreneur's design and manufacture of products are themselves a necessary and of course often beneficial element in determining the alternatives before purchasers. They cannot *make* consumers buy things (though choices can be over-influenced by monopolistic practices, advertising, etc), but they define a choice which would not otherwise be there. The availability, for example, of the plays of the Royal Shakespeare Company to theatregoers, of the home equipment range of *Habitat* stores, or of the children's books published over the years by Penguin, depend on the decisions of providers of various sorts, and are not and could not be exclusively a function of 'consumer choice'. It is an unfortunate consequence of 'marginalist' economic theory that it has directed attention towards the process of consumer preference between alternatives, and away from the constitution of the products themselves, in the economic process.

The influence of 'producers' has become even more marked in situations of imperfect and monopolistic competition. In modern economies some producers exercise great influence over the range of products available. Decisions at one point of time, on major new lines of investment, constrain future decisions by consumers and producers for many years ahead. An initial large investment in nuclear power, rather than in energy conservation or renewable energy sources, established a balance of relative economic advantage in favour of nuclear energy which would have been different given another investment pattern. The same is true of heavy investment in highways instead of high-speed trains in the United States, for example.

So to enable workers to participate in choices of what is to be made, is only to extend to them that form of involvement in the process of useful labour which is now confined to a minority of the powerful, or the most highly skilled.

The range of commodities, of various kinds, which are available in a market economy reflects, and must reflect, the preferences and aesthetic values of their producers, as well as of the consumers whose purchases enable them to succeed in the market. Just as, in the process of natural selection, the environment chooses between species alternatives initially established through genetic variation, so in market competition the environment chooses between variants established by the choices of working men and women.

Production is an interactive process, and is never directly 'ordered' either by purchasers or by legislatures. It is true that the choice of what is socially useful or worth producing cannot be made unless 'consumers' *can* choose, by spending their money or by casting their votes. But it also cannot be made unless effort is first put into fashioning the objects of choice, the goods on the table or the promises summarized and arrayed in political manifestos as the 'goods' of 'health', or 'education' or a better environment. What is original in the concept of 'socially useful production', as it has been developed by the Lucas Workers and articulated by Mike Cooley in his *Architect or Bee*,[20] is the idea that the producer's contribution to this interactive process also has a social meaning, and should be part of the conscious experience of all who work.

The power to engage in 'socially useful production' would be, properly, a *limited* power, to determine *what* is available for individual sale or collective decision, but not *whether* it is sold or chosen. The point is not that workers should decide for society what is socially useful, what it *must* have, but that they should be part of a continuing interaction or dialogue between workers and users (often the same people in different segments of their lives) about what is desirable and what is not. This means, one hopes, that workers would choose not to produce commodities which are destructive and harmful. These would then become less available, or more expensive, because of workers' reluctance to work on them. It means too that as the energies of working people are put to thinking about what would be useful, beautiful and desirable, the whole range of goods and commodities would be increased, and needs identified and met which now go unrecognized. The idea that men and women are naturally engaged in a creative relationship with nature and other people through their work was already present in Marx's early work, and in the writings of William Morris. The theme of 'socially useful' production is a modern rediscovery of these insights, in the context of systems of production which are complex and social. As a result of this complexity, involvement by workers in producer-decisions can sometimes only be indirect, through association with others in team decisions or complex design processes. They cannot always be in the form of individual crafts-manship, which was the one most often imagined, for understand-able historical reasons, by Marx and Morris during the nineteenth century.

What the Alternative Plan movement has recognized is that despite these facts of technical and organizational complexity, there are nevertheless crucial moral and aesthetic dimensions to product-choice. These are and should be significant to workers. Morris said that things should not be made that are neither beautiful nor useful. This is the judgement that Lucas Workers were making when they declared that they preferred to make robotic equipment for the disabled rather than for military purposes.

It is an illusion of the market economy, which represents as the whole system what is only one aspect of it, not to recognize that such choices are even now significant to many individuals working as capitalists or their senior managers, even if they are not to the financial agencies that deal exclusively in money values, by the abstract criteria of balance sheets. Whether a person works in tobacco or in fashion, in home-decorating equipment or in foundries, as an architect or a demolition man, is likely to be profoundly influenced by personal, moral and aesthetic pre-ferences. The distinctive meanings of such forms of work are likely to exercise, through the different cultures of occupations, reciprocal influence on the values and development of those who work in them for any length of time. Commodities are culturally defined and resonant, and both their manufacture and their purchase and use have symbolic meanings which it is easy to neglect. The market is an instrument or mechanism, not the end of economic activity. Choices in the market are informed by quali-tative preferences and by aspects of personal and social identity. The idea of 'workers' plans' seeks to make such 'social meanings' more open and to make them the object of choice for everyone.

There had begun to be a wider recognition of the problem of the 'quality of working life' prior to the return to mass unemployment, as the qualitative issues became more prominent on a then more hopeful political agenda. Most forms of industrial work now involve gross human limitation. Mann and Blackburn's[21] study of manual work in Peterborough, for example, reported in 1979 that for a majority of workers the most skilled activity performed in a working day was driving to and from the factory. The desperate need to provide useful work should not make us once more indifferent to the nature and quality of work.

The idea of 'socially useful production' is not a *substitute* for market mechanisms, or for command systems which replace market decisions by those of political authorities. Trying to think of it in these ways leads to irresolvable contradictions between the potential interests of producers, consumers and electors. It threatens to constitute 'producers' as just another special interest, who describe as useful certain products which, in the absence of other criteria, might be useful in reality only to themselves. The crucial insight of the Lucas workers has been less domineering than this. They asked implicitly for the right to be one among *several* necessary participants in the process of product choice, to be included in a system of decision and choice from which workers are presently excluded. It was because they continued to think of the process of production as an interaction, as an exchange of ideas, goods and services — and not as an imposition on others — that their proposals were so reasonable and constructive in tone. And it was because these proposals were so practical and modest in aim that their rejection (by capital, union officials, and Labour Party politicians, in their more and less declared ways) was so significant and depressing a moment in our recent political history.

The idea of 'socially useful production', as it has been developed in the movement for workers' plans, is not an alternative to the role of markets, or of national and local legislatures in determining what is produced. It does not propose to substitute producer-sovereignty for consumer sovereignty or the decision of the electorate. What this concept argues is that all workers should participate as conscious beings (as 'architects, not bees') in deciding what is produced either for exchange in the market, or in response to political choices. Whether the production is of goods or services, whether it is intended for sale in the shops or provided out of taxes as free health care or education, all workers would be able to contribute to the shaping of what is made.

Proposals which see the productive process as an interaction or dialogue between producers and users, as it should be, call for a dialogue in response. We can learn, from the setbacks as well as from the new thinking of the workers' plan movement, that it is not possible to re-make the economic system from the point of view of one interest alone. A vital objective of socialists should now be to see that this debate over the nature and human meaning of the productive process is carried forward.

The Right to Work and Economic Strategy

The failure of conventional mixed-economy Keynesianism in the 1970s, and the unworkability and unpopularity of a centralized State-socialist economic model, have left the Labour Party without a credible economic programme. While the concept of 'meso-economic power', developed by Stuart Holland[22] prior to the election of the 1974 Labour government, did clarify and strengthen the grounds for State intervention in an important way, the consensualist means of Planning Agreements fell short, both in theory and in practice, of an adequate system of economic management. Holland's view was influenced by Galbraith's work on the 'planning system' constituted by large (and especially transnational) corporations, which 'manage' their market environments and therefore undermine the legitimation of this economic system in terms of market sovereignty. The 'monetarist' attack on intervention by the State, trade unions, and the welfare sector was mounted to counter this position.[23] Indeed, it was the defeat of the new interventionist conception within the Labour government, signalled by the removal of Benn from the Department of Industry, which already brought the beginnings of the hegemony of 'monetarism', and its rationale for a more traditional 'capitalist' restraint, and a market-oriented direction of government intervention. One key argument, made notably by Bacon and Eltis and influential while Labour was still in office, was the false equation of the trading, the market and the privately owned sectors of the economy with its 'productive' part, and the characterization of its social expenditure and publicly owned sector as a 'burden' or residue whose disporportionate growth was responsible for Britain's economic decline.[24] Other aspects of monetarism, notably the priority given to the problem of inflation and to the notion of excessive demands on fixed national resources, rather than to the growth of real output, have also been disastrous in their influence. Clearly some radical reconceptualization of these problems, which gives priority to real outputs of all kinds as the only ultimate sources of income and welfare, is fundamental.

I argued in the last chapter that full employment should be made the primary goal of an alternative economic programme. Given the present costs of maintaining unemployed workers and their families, new employment opportunities would actually improve the average welfare of the population. A commitment to full employment would also be a commitment to the highest possible real output, to be allocated by some chosen combination of market and elective government decision-making.

A proposal of the kind made in the last chapter would make it possible for various agencies to apply for employment-creating resources. Such agencies might include companies, who could thus more easily be pressured by their workers to implement alternative plans. But trade unions would be able to become involved as joint applicants for funding under employment-creation schemes. Union participation could even be a condition for such proposals to be regarded favourably.

Realistically, the sector of worker initiatives, like that of co-operatives, is likely for the time being to be a minority participant in any programme of economic reconstruction. This only reflects its currently small size, and the lack of official trade union support for this 'non-economistic' line of development. But the institution of a broader employment-creation programme would add an element of 'pull' from the centre to the 'push' from the periphery, which is now the main role of the Alternative Plan movement. Such an employment programme would provide much more favourable conditions for worker involvement in the development of new forms of production.

One can reasonably propose, in keeping with the objects of employment-generation and reversal of regional and urban decline, an enhanced role for elected local authorities in economic activity. These should be able to bid for resources, to be used on improvements in their current range of services, to be lent to private concerns, and to be invested in cooperative economic enterprises. The local authority sector, being subject to some electoral accountability, should acquire a more important economic role in the market sector as well as in new 'public' or cooperative enterprises. The climate of opinion for such initiatives in conditions of rising unemployment is likely to be more favourable than it has previously been, where the alternative to generated jobs has been the dole and consequent loss of output. One obvious example of an area for such employment-generation, pointed out by the Socialist Environmental Association, would be in the insulation of domestic properties, which should years ago have been organized on a comprehensive street-by-street basis as North Sea Gas conversion was.[25]

Control and Industrial Democracy

The Workers' Plan movement raises fundamental issues for the control of capital, which are unlikely to be advanced only by the exercise of trade union power. Trade unions already often have the customary right and power to set a price on initiatives proposed by management which affect working practices. Disinvestment and closure proposals sometimes come into the category of 'bargain-able' issues, if the remaining areas of activity to which companies are committed allow unions any scope for sanctions. But in order that the product and investment strategies of firms should be posi-tively influenced, there would have to be rights to consultation and joint control of capital not currently provided by bargaining pro-cedures. The question then is: what mechanism might best secure such influence?

This area of argument was opened up by the Institute for Workers Control and its demands for disclosure of information ('open the books'), and by the Bullock Report's[26] ill-fated proposal for trade union (or other worker) representation on the boards of companies. The progress made in bringing these issues to the centre of debate, notably through the work of the IWC with the crucial support of Jack Jones, was one of the major advances of the period of 'corporatist' negotiation of the last Labour government. The model of tripartite co-determination which was evolving in the management of the national economy, and in some ancillary areas of industrial policy such as health and safety and industrial training, was in these discussions extended into the determination of company policy. It has been a great setback that these issues, and a broader concern for the 'quality of working life', have been displaced from the agenda by the defeat of that government and the return of mass unemploy-ment. As a result, political debate has moved backward from the concerns of an advanced and prosperous economy, to the more elemental preoccupations of the 1930s.

Some form of direct workers' representation in the decision-making processes of companies should remain an important long-term objective for socialists, despite other pressing economic problems. This follows from a conception of democracy which encompasses economic and industrial decision as well as political and social issues. British experience suggests that a complex and highly socialized economy cannot be effectively managed in the adversarial style that has usually characterized British industrial relations. The price paid in decimated production and unemployment for the Thatcher government's attempt to combine a bargaining framework with an overwhelming advantage to capital is unlikely to justify itself even in capital's terms. Furthermore, it seems to have accomplished little of that *lasting* change in employees' attitudes and relative powers which it was intended to secure. Governments of the centre or left will eventually have to return to more conciliatory strategies — in the forms of joint determination of economic policy, including incomes — which were earlier described as 'corporatist'.

The Bullock Report recommendations remain a useful point of departure for a renewed discussion of industrial democracy. The experience of the Alternative Plan movement suggests that the arguments for a trade union monopoly of workers' representation on supervisory or other boards are by no means compelling. The problems encountered by the Lucas Shop Steward Combine in negotiating with Lucas could well be replicated in company-based systems of representation if unions gained a statutory monopoly in the representation of workers. Where unions are able to control representation, they are likely to want to preempt direct nomination and representation through shop steward combines, preferring that representatives follow the line of separate trade union interests, and carving these up between unions.

While there are strong arguments for supposing that only union organizations can provide the research back-up and channels of feedback needed by representatives, there is also a case for allowing workplace elections that are formally independent of the union structure, while leaving unions free to nominate candidates and to try to influence the process as much as they wish. In this way, the union functions of defending the bargaining interests of labour would be kept distinct from the role of influencing decisions over the use of capital. While such independent, plant-based representation might lead to a dangerous and unhealthy division among the workforce, open to exploitation by non-unionized workers, intermediary strata, etc., the experience of the Workers' Plans suggests that some openness and pluralism at company level might be helpful, and that 'unity' *can* be mainly used to maintain the domination of the full-time bureaucracies.

It might happen that different functions would in practice be recognized by a workplace electorate and distinguished accordingly. It would not be inconsistent for a workforce to elect to company boards representatives particularly oriented towards company development and able to match the expertise of management in that regard, while continuing to elect to shop steward roles representatives oriented to a narrower concept of bargaining over wages and conditions. Which kind of representative would have the most salience at a given time would depend on local conditions and on the disposition of management. The same individuals can be found to have a different 'sociological' orientation according the structure and role in which they are operating. In a Polytechnic, for example, the forms of representation seen in the union context (oriented towards bargaining and a conflictual approach) and in the context of co-determination (its academic board) have usually been somewhat different in attitude and orientation, even though the electorates overlap substantially.

Influence over the disposition of capital seems inconsistent with an 'economistic' orientation towards wage-bargaining as the principal mode of relationship of workers and enterprises. In this sense the Workers' Plan movement inevitably leads into a consideration of industrial democracy issues, in one form or another.

Pension and Worker Funds

Another means of increasing workers' influence on decisions is participation by trade union or other elected workers' representatives in the management of their pension funds. The arguments for this are not only ones of democratic principle, but also involve substantive economic goals, in that an orientation of financial funds towards industry and the generation of employment, and away from property and overseas investment, would be a desirable corrective to current British practice. The involvement of workers, especially the technically qualified strata most likely to take up this opportunity for influence, might be a means of redressing the excessvely 'financial' orientation of British capital, in a more industrial direction.

Another feasible idea would be a version of the Worker or Wage Earner Fund now being introduced amid bitter controversy in Sweden by the Social Democrat government,[27] at the original instigation of the LO trade union confederation. This proposal, for the establishment of a workers' fund by annual levy on employers, would in time lead to the socialization of perhaps a substantial proportion of capital. In Sweden the total potential holding of Worker Funds has been limited to 15 per cent of shareholdings. This restraint, however, has not succeeded in reconciling private capitalist interests, and the Swedish middle classes more generally, to this proposal, which is seen as the thin edge of a potentially very big wedge. It has thus provoked widespread opposition, extending to big street demonstrations. One of the difficulties the Swedes have encountered is the fear that the Worker Funds would be a means of increasing the power of trade union representatives, and not of workers in the mass. Similar differences of interest, real or imagined, between the majority of workers and the minority of trade union activists have occupied a significant position in recent British political debate. On this issue of the Worker Fund itself, however, a proposal of this kind was made for Britain in 1971 by Jim Skinner,[28] who was then drawing on the example of a Danish scheme. One of the advantages of such a fund is that workers' capital would be held collectively, and thus be a means of exercising influence on company decision-making. If it were merely disseminated to workers individually as shareholders, the effect would most probably be to increase their sense of dependence on firms, and to reduce their capacity for collective action. Alternatively, such share issues could simply be sold for cash. It must be hoped that the Swedish socialists will prevail in their current commitment to this proposal, and that the opposition will in time become reconciled to it, as it has to other pioneering advances of social democracy. Even by the standards of democratic pluralism, some greater measure of joint determination by workers over the disposition of capital would be a vital step towards social justice.

The Workplace and Politics

Despite the fact that it is now more than five years since Labour lost power, there has been little progress made in thinking out new strategies for industrial democracy. Even in the less contentious areas of employment creation, and energy and health policy, Labour has failed to set the political agenda or to work out detailed programmes. The broader problems of ideology and organization that explain this failure are discussed elsewhere in this book. But it is clear that attention to the *political* preconditions of a different economic strategy, and of an enhanced role for workers' plans within it, is now urgently necessary. Not the least of the problems is the outmatching of the intellectual resources available to the left in policy-making by the civil service in government, and by public and private corporations in industrial bargaining. While the Workers'

Plans movement represents a breakthrough in the mobilizing of expertise, and some advances can also be seen in the preparation of trade-union negotiating documents, for example, by the Ford workers and the NUM in recent years, the general situation is one in which trade union representatives lack the resources of skill and time to match State and corporate 'rationality'.

Enhancement of the resources available to the left in these bargaining processes is therefore critical. A distinction can be drawn between areas where workers have acquired some 'professional' rights to determine the shape and nature of the job (such as the education system), and the industrial fields where a more authoritarian subordination of employees prevails. The teaching profession was, to take one case, a major force in the achievement of comprehensive reorganisation, and has so far been able mostly to resist pressures to tailor the school curriculum more closely to 'industrial needs' as employers and government define them.[29] This discrepancy between the political role of the literary and social-scientific intelligentsia, in teaching and the caring professions, and the 'technical intelligentsia' employed in industry, has a long cultural history. It would be beneficial if there were a stronger social commitment among those skilled in design and engineering, especially when Britain's industrial base is a source of such concern. The development of such a commitment is therefore an important priority, as may be efforts to influence the education of engineers (and scientists) towards a concern with social use.

I have proposed elsewhere[30] that the formation of work-based as opposed to territorially based party organization should be considered. The argument, which has deep roots in 20th-century labour history,[31] is that the workplace concentrates expertise where the territorial representational unit fragments it. The workplace is the centre of economic and productive concerns, by definition, whereas the locality is the domain of domestic and 'collective consumer' issues. So the absence of any work-based political association effectively deprives the left of an informed economic 'constituency', and devolves this function on to trade unions whose preoccupations are narrowly economistic and in principle, for reasons already given, 'non-political'. The issues raised by the alternative corporate plans *are* political; they involve the ends and means of economic action and not merely the distributive share to be given to employees. So another way of institutionalizing the production and contesting of plans would be through explicitly political channels, in the workplace. This would establish a separation of 'alternative plan' and 'wage-bargaining' activities different from that already suggested under the heading of industrial democracy.

Another important idea is for the national representation of economic interests through some equivalent of an 'economic' or 'industrial parliament'. This might take the form of a functional second Chamber, representing different categories and electorates of worker, capital-holder, consumer and domestic worker. Such a Chamber would enable plans and policies for areas such as energy, health and industrial regeneration to be proposed and debated in a more open way than is currently the case. Trade unions would be the principal means of economic representation in such a system. There would be benefits from direct union involvement in the political determination of economic policy, even if the market sector remained central in such a system. The situation in which the trade unions are practically oriented towards wage-bargaining, while being brought into various corporatist consultative arrangements 'by the back door', is unsatisfactory. The result is that their role in economic consultation is confined in effect to the determination of incomes policy, and such quid pro quos as they can strike in return for this (such as price control), while they remain marginal to economic policy per se. The current institutional and normative separation of trade union and political representation makes it very difficult for unions to transcend this role, however much they might wish to. (The proposal made in chapter four for a regionally elected second Chamber could perhaps be combined with this idea of an 'economic parliament'. The outcome could hardly be more anomalous, singly or in combination, than hereditary membership of the House of Lords.)

It is conventional in this society that mainly government, private coporations and academic institutions fund and determine the aims of research. It is therefore important to establish the principle that trade unions are also potentially significant clients for research activity. The pioneering CAITS connection with polytechnics is an example in this respect that needs to be taken up and developed as a priority. It entails no more than a pluralist conception of research related to a wide range of social interests.

We must hope that more substantial support and coordination of Alternative Workers' Plans will make possible a concerted challenge from below to corporate decision-making. It is in the absence of informed opinion and pressure from trade unionists that Labour's industrial strategies have so faltered and collapsed in the past, and such a new input would give backing to any reforming government's efforts to achieve a measure of planning. The institutional levels of change proposed in this chapter might be seen as too fundamental, utopian or long-run to be very helpful. Certainly they should not be thought to detract from the importance of the concrete examples of workers' plans being developed, and the movement to encourage these, which are the best arguments for change.

Direct Democracy and the Collective Subject

The Workers' Plan movement is also significant in suggesting new forms of direct democracy. Both the market and the State sector in the present economic system are experienced as forms of abstract, impersonal control by citizens, especially since both are institutionalized in extremely large-scale and bureaucratic organizations. Whereas the work-group, the family and the voluntary association are face-to-face groupings capable of forming collective intentions felt to be personally meaningful, both market and the national electorate are experienced as remote and abstract aggregations. The State sector has come to be widely regarded in this way — this is one major reason for the success of Thatcher populism. Under a regime of increasing unemployment and declining living standards the free market may not retain its present legitimacy as a source of general benefit. There are valid arguments for market mechanisms, as a system of signals making possible exchange and coordination in a decentralized way, and also for areas of centralized and universalistic policy imposed by elected governments. It is utopian and irrational to aim simply to abolish these procedures in favour of a concept of simplistic harmony. However, to recognize the general usefulness of frameworks of markets and law is not to imply that these should be unmediated constraints on working practice. There are alternative forms of adjustment to a more long-run and ecological idea of economic viability, which, as we have shown, does not always coincide with the indices of economic viability signified by profit and loss accounts. Within a framework of law providing for universal education, for example, there are many alternative forms of provision within particular institutions or classrooms. The argument for greater local or plant autonomy in determining what is produced and how, and for the balancing of moral and aesthetic preferences against market imperatives, need not deny the value of various kinds of economic or constitutional 'laws' in establishing a framework of rationality and commensuration. Each of us as individuals after all seeks to exercise meaningful preferences within such determining frameworks; there is no reason why face-to-face collectivities should not do the same. Socialist historians and sociologists have long argued for the recognition of social agency and subjectivity, against the exclusive preoccupation of liberal theory with the individual subject. The Alternative Plan movement is a practical expression of the same concerns and commitments.

'Practical intellectuals' have found, in the work of advising and helping the development of workers' plan initiatives, a less directive conception of intellectual work than the Fabian 'civil service model' which used to be the most influential in the Labour Party. There is continuity between the work of the Community Development Projects[32] of the 1970s, advising community groups, and the CAITS initiatives, advising trade unionists. This valuable model of political work is now being built on by the economic policy units and enterprise boards of some of the socialist Metropolitan Counties.

Conclusion

There is an urgent need to develop positive and hopeful initiatives as alternatives both to the free market and authoritarian populism, and to the limited and failed repertoire of social democratic interventions. The Workers' Plan movement is one of the few such initiatives of recent years which has captured fresh attention, and seems capable of transcending the frozen categories of economic debate. It is important that socialists should continue to recognize the originality and fruitfulness of this new conception, and ensure that it has the intellectual and political support needed for its further development.

NOTES

1. See Lucas Aerospace Confederation Trade Union Committee, *Lucas Aerospace: Turning Industrial Decline into Expansion - A Trade Union Initiative*, 1979; H. Wainwright and D. Elliot, *The Lucas Plan - A New Trade Unionism in the Making*, London 1981; and also for further examples of CAITS's work:
CAITS, *Alternatives to Unemployment*, 1978
CAITS, *Energy Options and Employment*, 1979; Speke Joint Shop Stewards Committee, *Dunlop: Jobs for Merseyside*, 1979

CAITS.*The Future of Employment in Engineering and Manufacture*, undated
CAITS.*Workers' Plans: Cutting Edge or Slippery Slope*, 1979.

2. CAITS exists to further the development of alternative plans, and a programme of publications, conferences, technical product development and advisory help in the preparation of alternative plans has been undertaken since CAITS was established in January 1978.

3. This point was made forcefully by Audrey Wise in a paper, 'Worker's Plans and Labour Governments — Past and Future', given at a CAITS Conference on 17 November 1979.

4. The Finniston Report - *Engineering our Future*, HMSO, 1980.

5. *Frank Parkin's discussion of these occupational strategies is contained in his 'Strategies of Social Closure in Class Formation', in F. Parkin, ed., The Social Analysis of Class Structure*, London 1974, and in his *Marxism and Class Theory: A Bourgeois Critique*, London 1979. Noel and José Parry's *The Rise of the Medical Profession*, London 1976, also has a useful discussion of strategies of occupational defence, which are further analysed in their essay 'Social Closure and Collective Social Mobility', in R. Scase, ed., *Industrial Society: Class, Cleavage and Control*, London 1977.

6. This relates to the general issue of the role of the 'new working class', introduced in France by Touraine, Mallet and Gorz and later debates on class locations and affiliations. Michael Mann, *Consciousness and Action among the Western Working Class*, London 1973, has a useful introduction to the earlier material.

7. This concept is developed by Pierre Bourdieu, for example, in P. Bourdieu and J.-C. Passeron, *Reproduction in Education, Society and Culture*, 1977. It is also discussed by Alvin Gouldner in *The Future of Intellectuals: The Rise of the New Class*, London 1979.

8. J.K. Galbraith, *The New Industrial State*, 1967.

9. For a short account see Trevor Jones, *The Politics of the Corporate Economy*, 1979, and also the final chapter of K. Middlemas, *Politics in Industrial Society*, 1979. A Sociological account of the nature of 'corporatism' is given by J.T. Winkler in 'The Corporate Economy: Theory and Administration', in R. Scase, ed., *Industrial Society: Class, Cleavage and Control*.

10. A More substantial discussion of the role of the State in economic management may be found in Robin Murray, 'Capital and the Nation State', *New Left Review 67*, May–June 1971. Another useful discussion of the role of government in the British economy is to be found in Derek Morris, ed., *The Economic System in the UK*, 1977, especially Chapters 17 and 19.

11. For a summary of the work of the Institute of Economic Affairs in reconstructing this ideology see R. Harris and A Seldon, *Not from Benevolence*, Hobart Papers, London 1977.

12. This can of course be regarded as a largely ideological construction, given the extent to which 'consumer preferences' are the outcome of a social construction of values and are subject to the specific influence of the corporate sector.

13. The present Government's attempts to influence the pattern of course provision in higher education, to the detriment of arts and social science subjects, are an abrogation of this market principle in the provision of higher education. This relies ultimately on perceived opportunities in the labour market and on individuals' relative preferences regarding subjects, potential income, place of study, etc., to allocate educational resources, whereas 'planning' involves imposing assumptions about national manpower needs through central regulation of course provision. It is

curious that this Government has no confidence in the effectiveness of market mechanisms in supplying trained manpower, while it asserts their validity everywhere else.

14. Michael Mann, *op. cit.*, draws attention to the priority given to the maintenance of control by capitalists.

15. These alternative cases were discussed in A. Shonfield's influential *Modern Capitalism*, 1965. Only in France is economic intervention managed chiefly by an arm of the State bureaucracy, whereas in Germany the agency of intervention is the banks, and in Japan the interlocking of leading business families with the political elite.

16. This idea of insulation is discussed in A. Giddens, *The Class Structure of the Advanced Societies*, London 1973.

17. Michael Rustin, 'The New Left and the Present Crisis', *New Left Review* 121, May–June 1980.

18. This failure of unions to influence Labour governments' economic policy is described in L. Panitch, 'Socialists and the Labour Party — a Reappraisal', in R. Miliband and J. Saville, eds., *The Socialist Register*, 1979.

19. David Elliott, *Energy Options and Employment*, CAITS. 1979.

20. Mike Cooley, *Architect or Bee?* Langley Technical Services, 1980.

21. R.M. Blackburn and Michael Mann, *The Working Class in the Labour Market*, London 1979.

22. Stuart Holland, *The Socialist Challenge*, London 1975. Though this book was published after Labour was elected to power, its arguments had been very influential in policy-formation beforehand.

23. Interventionism became vulnerable to attack, in the United States and in Britain on account of inflation, low growth and the unpopularity of welfare expenditures in these conditions. The explanation of this apparent failure is, however, a complicated matter. In opposition to the neo-conservatives, the protagonists of these programmes would argue that they have never gone far enough, either nationally or, following the arguments of the Brandt Report, internationally. Incomes policy has been a characteristic point of breakdown of this system in Britain, signifying a repeated inability (Wilson, Heath, Wilson, Callaghan) to achieve a tenable 'class truce' over an interventionist or corporatist strategy. Whereas a theoretical case for the regulation of incomes, in conjunction with prices and investment, can be made (and is, by Galbraith and Balogh, for example), trade unions and their members have in practice been asked to restrain their powers over wage bargaining when their returns from, and influence over, corporatist regulatory policies have been very limited. Initiatives in this area have never been combined with a sufficiently vigorous, countervailing and expansionist policy towards capital, and the last Labour Government achieved an exemplary succession of errors, not least of timing, in this regard. Monetarism has inherited the fruits of this failure, but while half-heartedness in execution was part-cause of this, an inadequate model and conception of mixed-economy management was also a factor. The 'countervailing powers' described and commended by Galbraith are simply not big enough positively to shape this system, nor do they have adequate popular support and legitimation. The Workers' Plan movement may be able to call in question the logic of the market in a more self-active way, closer to experience, than these corporatist and Statist modes of thinking have been able to do.

24. W. Eltis and R. Bacon, *Britain's Economic Problem - Too Few Producers*, London 1976.

25. A large-scale domestic insulation project, combining employment creation with

energy-saving, would be a good initiative for the Metropolitan County Councils, in cooperation with boroughs managing a large council-housing stock.

26. On Worker or Wage-Earner Funds see W. Korpi, *The Working Class in Welfare Capitalism*, London 1978, and U. Himmelstrand, *Beyond Welfare Capitalism*, London 1981.

27. Dept. of Trade, *Report of the Committee of Inquiry on Industrial Democracy*, Cmd 6707, HMSO, 1977.

28. Jim Skinner, *Collective Bargaining and Inequality*, Fabian Society, 1971. For other Fabian Society publications of the 1970s on the broader issues of industrial democracy and workers' plans see J. Bray and N. Falk, *Towards a Worker-Managed Economy*, 1974; a Fabian Group, *Workers in the Boardroom*, 1976; Alan Fox, *Socialism and Shop Floor Power*, 1978; Giles Radice, ed., *Working Power*, 1978; David R. Allan, *Socialising the Economy*, 1974.

29. Whether the present system of sixth-form specialization and the predominantly academic emphasis of post-16 education is desirable is another issue. The transfer of large parts of the work of the further-education colleges to the Manpower Services Commission is now an unfortunate example of the loss of power by the professional teachers.

30. Michael Rustin, 'The New Left and the Present Crisis', *New Left Review* 121, May–June 1980. Proposals for workplace branches were also made in the Fabian Society's evidence to the NEC on party organization, and in Peter Hain, *Reviving the Labour Party*, Institute for Workers Control, 1980. This argued for work-based branches in the context of a more campaigning party, drawing on the experience of community politics and single-issue movements.

31. For a discussion of earlier versions of this argument see Trevor Jones, *The Politics of the Corporate Economy*, 1979.

32. The Home Office Community Development Projects succeeded in connecting the previously separate issues of industrial investment and disinvestment, and 'inner city decline'. The social problems of the cities were attributed when the CDPs were set up to such factors as the 'cycle of deprivation', poor social cohesion, poor administration of the social services, and other mainly non-economic factors. For the radicalization of these projects through experience see the following: Community Development Project (Home Office), *The Costs of Industrial Change*, 1977; *Gilding the Ghetto*, 1977; *The State and the Local Economy*, 1979.

9

Comprehensive Education after 18

This chapter attempts to outline a socialist programme for post-school education. It is, in the first instance, a response to the immediate crisis in the higher education system brought about by the Thatcher Government's onslaught on its budgets, its priorities, and its autonomy. The department in North East London Polytechnic in which I work was one of the first to be proposed for closure in what was intended to be a pioneering implementation of the New Right's priorities. The failure of that strategy at NELP, and the experience gained in confrontation with it, did much to deepen the thinking about post-school education of all those involved in it. It made apparent, for example, how shallow were this institution's roots and support in the local community, despite all its real and widely proclaimed social commitments. It made its academic staff uncomfortably aware of their own highly privileged position, and of a common gap between theoretical, radical or socialist politics, and educational forms of selection and grading whose conservative and socially restrictive effects were often not fully recognized. But most important, this experience showed those who took part in it that an initial state of mind, among those threatened by contractionist policies, of fear, self-blame and fatalism could change. It was demonstrated that a widely based solidarity, and an insistence on rational and properly argued choices, could achieve a significant change of institutional policy. Even though it was necessary for radicals in this debate also to recognize the need for substantial reforms (they were often more far-sighted about these than their opponents) nevertheless commitment to the fundamental ends of the institution was upheld, and indeed deepened by the experience. This process has possible implications for the many educational institutions that are now affected by crisis on a scale as great or greater than that faced at North East London Polytechnic.

In the context of the Thatcherite attack on the post-war consensus, it is important now to recapture and renew the positive foundations of the earlier programmes of reform and reconstruction, since if there is a popular basis for radical social programmes in Britain it is likely to have some continuities with that experience. In particular, the conception of extended and universal rights of citizenship has been essential to social advance in Britain, and is now one key to the defence of public education and public health services. Thus, post-school education should be advocated as a natural continuation of the universal rights to primary and secondary education. The concept of comprehensive education should extend to the whole educational process, across the lifetime, and not be confined to the primary and secondary years. The virtual limitation of educational rights after 18 years of age to those who now qualify for advanced courses is a major means of exclusion of the majority of people from tertiary education. The concept of universal rights can and should also be used to seek other extensions of citizenship, for example in popular rights over the disposition of capital, and for powers of decision in the workplace.

Yet a defence and extension of the universalist values of post-war social democracy does not in itself provide a basis for further social advance. The Thatcher Government took power as a result of the failures of the post-war political compromise, and of the interventionist Labour and Conservative Governments which had managed it. A profound and deepening economic decline has severely constrained the scope of all social programmes since at least 1964, and there can be no useful consideration of social programmes except in relation to this national crisis.

As we have seen in an earlier chapter, the 'modernizing' programmes initiated by the 1964 Labour Governments were characteristically ambiguous and inadequate, and their failure has discredited much of this form of 'modernizing' and 'technological' political discourse on the left. Yet there was a more substantial political debate about the social origins of the British crisis at that time than has subsequently continued. Some major social reforms — the institution of comprehensive secondary education, for example — were in fact initiated during this period. The agenda of issues raised — the role of the Treasury and the City of London, the character of the higher civil service, the possibilities of economic planning and economic intervention by the State, the role of regional planning institutions, the reform of higher education, and above all the idea of achieving some democratization in the structure and recruitment of the ruling elite — did represent some radical address to the problem of British society which then had a wider resonance than any subsequent programme has done. One significant contrast between that period and twenty years later is that many liberal intellectuals who were then committed to some idea of radical critique and renewal, to implicit alliance with the Labour Party, have subsequently become either overt reactionaries (through hostility to the unions, and a 'more means worse' defence of middle-class standards) or supporters of a restoration of the lost consensus, through the Social Democrats, in terms which so far seem to lack any significant radical commitment. While the Wilson programme of 1964 was not primarily socialist, the left had been able to influence the analysis on which it was based. Now, on the other hand, the alliance of socialists and collectivist liberals has broken down, and socialists find themselves isolated. There is at present an absence of influential socialist definitions of the current crisis, and of possible programmes for its resolution.

A small attempt was made to respond to these problems of political practice in the activities which set me thinking along the lines of this chapter. Socialists in institutions affected by the higher education crisis thought it was essential to develop a more long-term and political response than could be secured by trade union defence alone, crucial as this is. While the Labour movement is central to our view of political change, it was also felt that the Labour Party's own relationship to its various potential constituencies, in different occupational groups and sectors, was often somewhat tenuous, and its policy-making processes (often confined to closed groups of party activists and experts) remote from the publics they sought to represent. For these reasons an effort was made to establish an open campaign to encourage wide participation in the formation of socialist higher education policies. If the Labour Party is in the future to be an effective agent of socialist reform, it will need to develop links of an organic kind with the publics for which it would speak, and the method by which this proposal has been developed was a small example of a specific attempt at an 'organic' form of political programme-making.[1]

The Higher Education System in the Post-War Consensus

Until now, it is doubtful if there has been a distinctively *socialist* approach in Britain to post-school education. Of all institutions in post-war Britain those of higher education seem to have been among the most removed from political controversy, and to have been able to incorporate and absorb a variety of interests without the structure of the whole system being called into question. Even the student upheavals of 1968, which elsewhere in Europe gave rise to substantial reforming pressures, in Britain subsided without significant institutional effects, though to be sure the cultural consequences of this radicalization remain important and have perhaps even been a factor in the present Government's counter-attack on the more radical disciplines. Traditionalists have had the continuing reassurance of their domination of the institutions of greatest status and power, and have been able to continue to colonize new and potentially rival institutions with their own graduates and assumptions. Expansion of the universities, including the foundation of new ones, provided opportunities for many younger and more innovative academics, often in new subject areas and inter-disciplinary modes of work, to establish positions of power and freedom which would not have been available to them in the traditional centres. A new style of educational manager, and a new cadre of tertiary teacher, were given opportunity through the foundation of the polytechnics and the other public sector colleges to develop a somewhat more vocational and practical form of higher education, for a culturally less privileged population. During the long period of expansion, there were seemingly resources and student demand enough to resolve all conflicts of interest. There seemed no sense in battling over the shape and priorities of the whole system, when so many opportunities were provided within it to do all the work that anyone could wish.

Most would see this as a singular and typically British kind of institutional success, one of the most remarkable examples of whiggish adjustment and modernization in the post-war period. The system has expanded significantly to provide the enlarged and technically more sophisticated elite needed in an advanced industrial and bureaucratic society. While the proportion of entrants to higher education has increased less than in some European countries, the graduate percentage of the relevant age group does not compare unfavourably with that of other EEC nations. Only in the case of the United States, which has achieved an altogether different level of mass participation in college education, is the international comparison between levels of higher education provision really unfavourable to Britain. Britain's relative failure has been less in the proportion of over-eighteens in education than in its gross neglect of its post-16-year-old school-leavers. The British economy too seems likely to be handicapped less by the shortage of graduate manpower, than by the low level of education and training received by the majority of its school-leavers.

The considerable expansion in the higher education system from about 7 per cent of the 18-year-old age group in full-time higher education in 1960–61 to about 12 per cent in 1980–81, has been achieved with little disruption to its structures of prestige and power. While additional opportunities have been provided for subordinate strata, the privileged pathways of the elite and the educational experience given to them have scarcely been affected. The leading university institutions, especially Oxford and Cambridge, have remained the routes to top positions in British society, in Parliament, the higher civil service, the professions and academic life, and the business and financial elite. The long series of novelistic representations of this charmed journey have been followed by televisual ones, from *Glittering Prizes* to *Brideshead*, timelessness being as notable a quality of these dramatizations as their specific sense of period. These universities have also retained a little-changed relationship to their dual sources of elite students: the leading public schools whose upper and upper-middle-class catchment has a significant hereditary element; and the meritocratic, mainly middle-class grammar schools, and now to some degree the grammar streams of certain comprehensives. The importance of this dominant position of the leading universities lies not only in the continuing recruitment and acculturation of the centralized British elite (including most of its best-known Marxist critics) but also in the pervasive effects on the rest of the education system, on which Oxbridge weighs like a looming distant monument to the inferiority and missed chances of everyone else. It is surely a striking fact that while socialists have attempted to confront the role of private education in British society, they have given no attention to the way that elite domination and continuity is sustained through the higher education system and have developed no radical programmes to change this.

The dominant codes of this system are those of liberal professionalism, for which the academic profession stands guard both in successful defence of its own powers and privileges and as the custodian of the values of a wider professional stratum. The system is meritocratic, in that it is stratified through competitive entry to an informal yet real hierarchy of institutions, and in that it enforces a fairly rigorous and uniform standard of degrees and credentials.

The status of its leading institutions, and the great influence of the universities over 'O' and 'A' level certification in the schools, ensure that rival educational definitions and routes remain in a subordinate and minority position, as alternative for those defined as less able or disadvantaged. First the University of London Extra-Mural Department, and then the Council for National Academic Awards, have been successful mechanisms for transmitting this established definition of higher education — with the first degree course as its main vehicle — to the non-university sector, which has enabled the system virtually to double in size without fundamental challenge to its exclusionist principles. Yet while committed to the idea of merit and competition, the British system is also organic and paternalist in key respects, and seeks to mitigate the divisive and conflictual effects of competition by deep socialization into its various component structures. In this 'sponsored system', as R.H. Turner has called it,[2] the selected ones are relatively well treated, and if they cannot all do as well as each other, they are at least unlikely to fail at the educational level to which they have gained entry.

Progress in the British higher education system is by age-grade, most graduating within the specified three or four years of a course. The support of students by maintenance grants, by student housing, by normally well-structured curricula, by small-group and tutorial supervision, and by contact with the main body of qualified academics and not a subordinate stratum of temporary teaching assistants, ensure that this is a well-supported process, likely to induce a sense of distinctiveness and even obligation in those who have been exposed to it. Even the curious rhythms of student life, with their long vacations and, in many subjects, undemanding college hours, establish a distance between the experience of students, unregulated by the normal working calendar, and their contemporaries in ordinary jobs.

It is this combination of meritocracy and acculturation which defines this as a distinctively *professional* form of socialization. To endow membership of a stratum with distinctive values and shared assumptions, even shared obligations of service, is the latent purpose of this system, especially marked in its most elite settings. Where other universities and polytechnics use 'A' level grades, Oxford and Cambridge use their own more generalist examinations. Where for normal credentialist purposes, a degree from a good university, or even a polytechnic, will do, elite transmission in Oxbridge is effected also through the Union, through Blues, through political clubs, and through a vast panoply of seductive and idiosyncratic cultural rituals. While other institutions cannot quite emulate this, the new universities were at least given locations amenable to a sense of pre-industrial tradition, and architects and physical resources with which to elaborate some aesthetic sense of community. The polytechnics have little of this culturing activity, but on the other hand have an ideology of pastoralism in their teaching function (sometimes even carrying missionary and settlement overtones) which seeks to tie their students to their work on a different dimension. And of course the ex-colleges of education, small residential, rural, mostly female and protective, had an even stronger version of a 'caring' education practice of which they continue to make a virtue as their courses are diversified away from teacher training.

This system of meritocratic yet also paternalist values has been able to achieve a high degree of legitimacy. Its combination of competition and sponsorship has engendered loyalty in its alumni, in their various subsequent stations in life and this may account for the absence of influential radical critiques of the system. The initial advantages in inter-institutional competition held by traditional universities have been largely maintained, and the competition for entry by students, in these unequal conditions, has reinforced the disparities. The 'Robbins principle' of allowing choice of subject and institution by students was also implicitly an endorsement of the right of choice *by* universities and their departments *of* students. Indeed, while 11+ selection, private education and 'banding' of pupils have been and are vigorously debated in the school system, no 'comprehensive' alternative to the competitive mode of selection for higher education has ever been seriously considered. This freedom of selection has enabled insitutions high in status to reproduce their dominant values in the same way that grammar schools were able to do while they retained their right of selection at entry. (The sexual desegregation of Oxbridge colleges is perhaps one of the few examples of traditional values having clearly to give way before the changing preferences of students themselves.) The competitive sifting of students that characterizes this system, and the subsequent sorting of graduates in the job market, continually re-validate the system, creating an apparently just correspondence between the prestige of institutions and the quality of individuals within them. The pressure of these values is then exerted downwards, through the whole system; the UGC has recently made clear that comparative 'A' level scores can even be used as an *admini-*

strative criterion of institutional merit.

The remorseless processes of stratification which dominate the life of the academic education system in Britain, through 'O' level grades to 'A' level grades and then to degree classifications, ensure that the measurement of the self against these standards is hard to put aside for anyone who wants to stay on the staircase. In Britain, the standards at each level are defined in absolute and not relative terms, which means that the sanctity of a general system of values and meanings is given weight over and against a merely contingent competition within each cohort of one with another. The British elite is still expected to be loyal to some implicitly solidaristic and corporate principles, and not merely to an idea of its members' own competitive excellence. This process places deep internal resistance in the way of any who might resent their ultimate place in this hierarchy. Whatever the disadvantages under which some competitors labour, they are in the end mostly measured and judged by what they can do, and must commit themselves deeply to the values underlying the educational contest to be able to make progress in it. To complain afterwards about its outcome therefore seems to many like betraying one's own highest standards, the very standards which one has tried to reach. Even if it is objectively clear that early privileges count heavily in this competition, who can decently complain about them after the ultimate results are known and destinies settled, many years on? And who wants to risk the additional betrayal of proclaiming educational or family disadvantage as an excuse? It is easier for those with subordinate positions in this elite structure to reconcile themselves gratefully to their lesser privileges. This has been a powerful and effective process of elite socialization in Britain, and it has had the effect of preserving an unbroken continuity of traditional leadership in many sectors of British life.

The importance of common values, acculturation and sponsorship in British higher education marks the domination of a distinctively professional elite, rather than that business elite with whose values the more open and instumental American system is more consistent. As many critics have pointed out, the leading sectors of the system are geared to producing cadres who are culturally rather than technically socialized to occupy high positions, and its values are more congenial to the professions and the civil service, with their strong sense of corporate membership, than to the more competitive world of capitalist enterprise. The system has been marked by a hegemony of a particular kind of professionalism, that of the liberal academic, imbued with an ideology which values education and knowledge above technology or social application. The system has been able largely to protect itself from direct subservience to the State or to business, despite the fact that it is ultimately financially dependent on these external social forces. Educators in Britain have successfully insisted that it is they, not politicians, community-leaders or businessmen, who should control the content of education, and they have until recently persuaded governments to accept this view even while they have legislated and funded a large expansion of their system. The hegemony of a professional stratum, with its commitment to a 'higher' calling than mere industry and trade, is an aspect of a larger failure of the British industrial and commercial bourgeoisie (not to mention the working class) fully to impose its own value-system on a pre-existing culture of aristocracy and rank. Higher education has been a means of perpetuating a closed form of domination: while the forms of rational bureaucracy and the ideology of education itself have gained importance; an idea of exclusiveness, elite membership, and roots in the pre-industrial past retains its cultural force.

Of course the system has been capable of significant adjustment to pressures to meet new social needs. It has, according to the Oxford Social Mobility Study of A.H. Halsey and his colleagues, now met the demand for degree education of the sons of the 'service class' almost to saturation. When the Government called for greater priority to business leadership, the system obliged by developing business schools. The expansion of the social services and collectivist social provision was met with the growth of the social sciences, though this work tended to be left disproportionately to the subordinate polytechnic sector and to be shunned by some of the most prestigious institutions. Over two generations, the universities have responded to the rise of the labour movement by permitting the development of enclaves of 'labour history'. More recently, the academy has been able to respond, not without some severe internal crisis, to the pressures of radical intellectual dissent, and to a more cosmopolitan cultural life. The post-structuralist MacCabe's exile was in the end to a Chair, albeit a remote one. Liberalism has its virtues, and many on the left, aware that they have more space within this system than elsewhere, have feared that the replacement of these liberal values, acceptable to them in the cultural if not in the economic sphere, might well be by something worse.

Not the least success of this system has been to achieve a considerable expansion and proliferation over thirty years while retaining a general quality of higher education, within its own terms, which even its critics agree to be high. The Expansion has been undertaken through procedures which have successfully defended academic standards, and have forced new institutions and programmes to subscribe (by and large) to established academic norms in order to be allowed to grow. The concentration on the three-year honours degree course as the major educational practice of this system — through the financial allocations of the UGC, the 'Burnham grading' of teaching posts, the allocation to students of mandatory grants for these courses and very few others, and through the distinction of funding purposes between 'poolable' and 'non-poolable' courses (a distinction of level of work) — has been a means of avoiding undue dilution or diversification in new programmes of study. Indeed, emphasis on full-time degree work has been increased in recent years through changes in teacher and art education. It has been the policy of the main academic regulatory institution, the CNAA, to enforce comparability of standards between university and non-university degrees. While cautious encouragement has been given to innovation in the 'public sector', the criterion of comparability has been deployed as a limit on new educational practice, especially to avoid the risk of undermining standards. Clearly, inequalities of standard have developed in this period of growth — the unequal allocation of material resources, and the unequal competition for academic staff and students between new and old institutions ensured that this would be so — though there have also been beneficial forms of differentiation of aim and method. But what is most characteristic about the 'British model' is the consistency of academic level which it has achieved across the whole field of higher education. Britain has avoided legislating a formal democratization of higher education, with a bare minimum of material and human support, such as occurred in some EEC countries after 1968. So in its own terms, the system has been a pronounced success, and it is no wonder that its deepest wish is for the restoration of consensus policies with perhaps some gradualist tinkering with the issues of access and rationalization.[3]

The form of expansion of higher education in Britain can be seen as the continuing domination of an elite academic stratum over new groups which it has successfully absorbed. The creation of the Polytechnics by the 1964 Labour Government did represent an attempt to broaden higher education, and to render it more responsive to the interests of lower strata of the middle and skilled working classes, more concerned with technical and vocational education than with acculturation to elite positions. The case for an alternative kind of higher education, creating wider opportunities and closer to the needs of industry, was powerfully argued at this time, which was also the moment at which comparable pressures to broaden opportunities through comprehensive secondary education were having their greatest effect. It is clear now, however, that the main beneficiaries of this expansion were strata who were already relatively privileged. The commitment to enlarge opportunities at 18, rather than to make comprehensive provision at 16, had the effect of allocation resources to the less able children of the middle class, rather than to the majority of working-class children. The systems of academic control and funding we have already described, which emphasized the priority and uniform standard of the three-year degree course over all other forms of provision, ensured that the dominant educational codes were to be more widely transmitted rather than substantially changed. Analysts of the development of the Colleges of Advanced Technologies and the Polytechnics, notably Tyrrell Burgess and John Pratt,[4] have identified a process of 'academic drift' whereby even institutions initially and by Government policy committed to vocational education and extended opportunities found it in their interests to follow the more socially exclusive academic road. This process represents the successful incoporation of a larger (mainly middle-class) stratum into the existing higher education system, and the de facto abandonment of the interests of the larger working-class population.

The New Right's Critique of Higher Education

This post-war history of professional hegemony of higher education and its reflection of the prevailing political consensus explains why it is that the present Thatcher Government does not share the sympathy of its various predecessors for this system. This Government has set out to disrupt many of the leading features of the post-war settlement, including the expanding role of the State, the ever-growing demand for universalistic social rights, the power of trade unions, and what it believes to be the subordination of the values of private capitalism to collectivist, radical and 'cultural' concerns. The Government most directly represents in this complex of attitudes a stratum of the insecure middle class, not generally well-educated, and believing itself threatened by trade unionism, by the demands of the poor and excluded, and by moral and cultural changes. Sections of the skilled and better-paid working class were also attracted to this ideology, not least because they shared its implicit resentment of the privileges and self-confidence of the educated, especially those who had ensconced themselves in the security of the State services. There social strata have no natural sympathy for the values of the higher education system, not being part of the traditional educated British elite. If one takes the right-wing affiliations and commitments of the Thatcher Government at their true measure, its hostility to education is unsurprising.

The New Right regards Britain as a society stalemated by compromises with class forces adverse to those of capitalism. It set itself therefore to redress the balance of these compromises, by weakening the trade unions, by legislation, propaganda and the use of unemployment, and by lessening the role of the State in economic and social affairs. In particular the Thatcher Government has sought to dismantle many State institutions of the 'class truce' or of whiggish compromise. It saw the growing corporate institutions of economic planning as instruments of collectivist and tacitly working-class advance. It saw the institutions of government itself, both local and central, as having become the instruments of collectivist pressure. It perceived a stratum of public officials committed to its own power and position, and using the 'neutrality' of government above social forces and politics to advance itself. The Thatcher Government wants less government, but also government that is more directly the agent of private capital both in the enforcement of authority and in social policies. This is the significance of the attacks on local government, on the ideology and privileges of the higher civil service, on the apparatus of quangos, such as the schools council, on the nationalized industries, on public services, and on the instruments of economic planning. While this Government has had to make many compromises in practice, not least because of the division among Tories about the value of these evolved compromises, there has been an ideologically clear intention behind its own programmes.

Higher education, as we have said, is preeminently an institution of the consensus. It is dominated by a stratum somewhat aloof from the values of business, and substantially insulated from the influence of the business class by its dependence on State rather than private funding. While Lord Robbins, a liberal economist, had proposed in 1963 that the higher education system should be expanded on a 'free market basis', this turns out to have had different consequences from those which the New Right might have wanted. Robbins favoured a student choice of subject and course, on the grounds that this would be responsive in due time to the demands of the labour market for graduates, and because of liberal hostility to any alternative system of manpower planning through education. But Robbins, reporting towards the end of the Mac-Millan Government, presupposed an environment of consensus, in which semi-autonomous universities could respond in their own institutional interests to the pressures of a mixed economy, composed of private and public employers. He was reporting at a time when the MacMillan Government was expanding public expenditure, in the hope of strengthening British capitalism, and higher education seemed a preeminent case for useful State intervention. But the present Government believes that this 'balance' of public and private sectors had already, by then, long since gone awry, and that the demands for labour emanating from State employment, and the ideological perspectives arising from their alleged dominance, have had all too much influence on the shape of education. It is true that a system designed to be responsive to the indirect pressures of the labour market will reflect the demands of the labour market at a given time, and that in the last twenty years public employment has markedly grown. Like other governments lacking the power to achieve their ends through direct intervention in the economic system, the Thatcher Government is tempted to use the education system as its instrument, even if this means tearing up the liberal rule-book and its own theoretical commitment to a free manpower market to do so. Hence the attempt to control more directly 'subject-balance' and what is taught, in an attempt to support the interests of private business through the back door of the higher education system.

Curiously enough, there are good reasons for socialists as well as liberals to support a free choice of jobs, and by extension a free choice of educational programmes by students. The reason is that in choice of job or education, when all have rights of access, each individual chooses for him or herself on an approximately equal basis; whereas in the disposition of capital, given the existing distribution of wealth, most individuals have no say at all unless decisions are made collectively, by some form of elective process.

For a variety of reasons, therefore, this Government has determined to contract the provisions of higher education. It particularly wishes to contain the production of values which it conceives to be hostile to capitalism and business. Social science research is under attack because it is perceived to be inherently collectivist, even in its more neutral and objective forms: it identifies social problems only to propose planned solutions to them. Education in the arts and social sciences produces graduates unsympathetic to business, and mainly seeking work in the already inflated public bureaucracies. The whole idea of education as an inherent good is put in question on the basis (anticipated by various social theorists of a crisis of excessive expectations, such as Daniel Bell) that more education only means more demands and claims on society, and more questioning and undermining of the endangered values of authority and work. New provision — for example for unemployed school-leavers — should therefore be strictly related to employment, and preferably put under the control of institutions committed to 'training' and the immediate needs of the labour market, not 'educators' with their 'superior' and indulgent values.

While the Thatcher Government's perspective and determination are clear enough, it is interesting to see that in this area too it has been forced to make many compromises. In its contractionist policies, it has sought an alliance not with the most vocationalist and industrial sectors of the system, but with the most traditionalist and elitist. The institutions (the new technological universities) which should be closest to its educational ends have been those most severely attacked, since while on the Government's ideological grounds they might qualify for favoured treatment, on grounds of traditional academic merit (measured by prestige in research, 'A' level scores of their entrants, etc.) they rank lowest. While the Government has been willing to attack those unsympathetic to the business ethic in subordinate institutions (in polytechnics, colleges of higher education, arts and social science departments), it has reinforced the power of those who define the terms of the British universities' mandarin culture at its summit. In the end, the defence of privilege, deference to status, and the clamorous arguments of 'more means worse' have weighed more strongly than economic interest. Protecting the relative advantages of the classes the Right believes to be sympathetic to its interests, and worsening the position of its opponents, has in this as in other areas counted for more than the real interests of capital accumulation.

It is perhaps the case that the damage that can now be done by this government to the post-school education system is limited by the fact that, among the interests it threatens in contracting the system, are those of its own potential supporters eager to obtain access to higher education for their children. We should look more closely at the 'consensus', or what is left of it, and examine the positions on the future of the system to be found among those who have supported the main lines of its post-war development.

The Limits of the Present System

While there has been a continuing minority critique of the 'academic' bias of British higher education from some of those most identified with the formation of the polytechnics (Eric Robinson, George Brosan, Tyrrell Burgess, John Pratt, for example), these have not hitherto received very wide support on the left, and especially not among socialists in the universities. Radicals and socialists have found in higher education a relatively hospitable setting in which to do work consistent with their convictions. There has been after all a real development of socialist and Marxist scholarship in the universities in the past twenty years, though the '1968' generation of academic staff probably finds that its formative experience and assumptions are no longer shared by most students. But the knowledge that socialist intellectual work *can* be done, and find an informed audience, certainly discourages radical critique of the institutions within which this is possible.

Socialists have also been caught up in a subtle seduction by the argument of educational standards. They have gravitated to institutions committed to educational extension. Initially these were university extra-mural departments and the Workers Educational Association, providing often voluntary and student-initiated programmes. Then greater state support became available, through the University of London extra-mural degrees in the colleges of technology, and then the polytechnics, institutes of higher education, and the Open University. Teachers in these institutions have welcomed their wider catchment and social purpose, and the opportunity to innovate in course provision and respond in wider cultural and social terms than traditional higher education recognized. But they have most often done so while accepting most of the conventions of existing academic practice. The Open University is radical in its recruitment policy, in its division of educational labour, in its pioneering of distance-learning, and in the content of many of its courses. But it has reinforced the idea of the degree course as the dominant educational practice and has even unavoidably, through its technologies, given fresh emphasis to the idea of education as transmission, passively taken in and reproduced by students. The CNAA has in a similar way offered an exchange to the academics whose work it has validated.It has conferred legitimacy on their own programmes, and on many of their innovations, in return for obeisance to a general notion of 'comparability' which ought to have been called into greater question in the first stages expansion.

Yet for radicals especially, the issues have been difficult. Not only have they become committed through their own experience, quite properly, to the standards of scholarship and teaching by which they have been taught. They have also had reason to believe that any-thing less, as an education for the working class and the disad-vantaged, would be selling them short. Within the existing struc-ture, the choices that have been made to innovate only within these allowable limits have been mostly rational and in good faith. The system has also been liberal enough to allow these educational socialists and social democrats to work as a significant and influential minority, especially on the expansionary fringes of the system. This relationship has been another success of incorporative liberalism, and it is ironic that a system that has worked so smoothly, with so little generation of dissent or disruption, should now be an object of government fear and suspicion. One might argue indeed that a general effect of the absorption of radical intellectuals into the expansion of employment in higher education has been to cut them off from any real contact with the disadvan-taged. Intellectuals, whatever their ideology, become sealed from the wider society by their own privileges, and can even be made ready targets for populist mobilization. In these ways the radical intelligentsia has been incorporated into an enlarged and privileged state-employed profession, under the general hegemony of a broader professional stratum many of whose values it in any case shares. This is an aspect of a wider symbiosis of interests between the educated salariat and the expanded state services of the post-war period, created with the crucial support of working-class interests. It is interesting to note that in the 1979 General Election, which first returned the Thatcher Government to power, it seems to have been the working-class rather than the middle-class com-ponents of Labour's former class alliance that abandoned it in greater numbers. Radical academics have until now found it difficult even to think about the terms of their incorporation into the system, or about the need to argue systematically, as socialists, for another kind of educational structure.

The 'bad conscience' of the higher education system has been most expressed in anxieties about equality of access, as well it might.[5] It has been demonstrated that the proportion of the children of manual workers in higher education has barely changed in thirty years of expansion and is now even declining. The proportion of girls entering higher education has remained also disproportionately low, especially if one recognizes the subordinate status of teacher education which many girls have chosen. Some ethnic minorities are scarcely represented at all in the higher education system, and the chances of entering higher education also vary considerably depending on the region of the country from which potential entrants come.

But the definition of this problem as one of 'access' has the limitation of appearing to assume a general satisfaction with everything in the system except the unfortunate and presumably contingent fact that the majority of the population does not get near it. This state of self-satisfaction in higher education is very general, for reasons that we have already described. But it is crucial that lack of 'access' is a systematic and not a fortuitous property of this system. The mechanisms we have described by which 'standards' have been upheld — priority to three-year degrees, standard entry requirements normally requiring two years full-time study after 16, mainly academic educational programmes, an ethic of individual advancement and competition — are mechanisms of selective *exclusion,* as well as means of stratification and academic domination within the higher education system itself. The concept of 'higher education' to which we earlier drew attention bears an implicit restrictive assumption, since if 'higher' is given its conventional post-'A'-level meaning, the term presupposes the whole filtering procedure which has brought the access problem about. Clearly the efforts of those, in the SRHE, the Leverhulme seminars, the Times Higher Education Supplement, and elsewhere who are trying to initiate debate about access should be supported. But there is the danger that this particular starting point is chosen just because it leaves unquestioned and unproblematic everything about higher education except the social origins of its students. The problem, thus defined, easily translates into the problem of relatively deprived *students,* and the remedial measures of grants and bridging programmes which might help them to overcome a bad start or lack of motive. This, as socialists have been quicker to appreciate in other areas of education, distracts attention from the alternative problem-definition, which is that it is the institutions and the curricula that are fundamentally at fault and not the pupils.

One difficulty for radicals within the higher education system is that this point calls into question the norms on which their own privileges are based. The arguments for 'equal educational opportunities' and 'equal access' presuppose a perfect meritocracy as their ideal, where educational success will depend only on talent and motivation and not at all on social advantage. This is the norm that academics like to imagine they have lived by, though many will have had hidden social and cultural subsidies to help them along the way. But aside from the fact that environmental and cultural advantages are inherent in the system's present academic form, there is the problem that even if they were not the system would still be, in socialist terms, obnoxiously stratified and unequal. The privileges accorded through credentialism, and the advantages given to the secure and highly paid members of state bureaucracies, including the academic profession, are no less class advantages because they depend on function and skill rather than inheritance. A system of inequalities should be no more acceptable to socialists, or to the working class, because it is legitimated by examinations and not ownership of capital. To this end there should be a root-and-branch problem for socialists in a system that allocates the opportunity to obtain education, and the personal development and powers that follow it, by reference to these particular meritocratic and credentialist talents. The system should be unacceptable to egalitarians not only because it is socially biased, but also because it is biased by its own definitions of educational value, tightly linked as these are to bureaucratic and professional criteria of merit and skill. Of course it has been understandably difficult even for radical academics to contemplate sawing away at the branch on which their own profession has been so comfortably settled, especially since even standards which appear to legislate for inequality nevertheless seem in other respects to be necessary to any imaginable modern society.

Yet academics have recently been given a powerful reason for reconsidering these fundamental issues, as they are faced with contraction and diminished opportunities. 'Access' began to become a pressing issue once the DES published figures in 1978 predicting a falling number of 18-year-olds, and therefore of likely higher education entrants in the 1980s and 1990s. Middle-class recruitment suddenly became a problem because its source seemed to be shrinking. The exclusion of the majority of the population, and especially the children of the working class, from higher education, as the main limit on the form of expansion chosen in the 1960s and 1970s, has meant that there will probably be a declining student base for the system for the next two decades. It is clear already that the radical and experimental sectors of higher education are going to be most at risk in this contraction. Suddenly, the academics have reason to look hard for more working-class supporters and customers of the post-school education system. This now gives some political feasibility and potential support to the task of developing a comprehensive post-school education programme, and it is to these problems that we now turn. We begin with an attempt to define some basic principles.

Principles for a Comprehensive Post-School Education Programme

1. The idea of education as the means of developing the competences, cultures and powers of individuals and communities should be restored to a central place in a socialist vision of the future. The opportunity to pursue such development after compulsory schooling and through life should be defined as a universal right, to be available through forms of education appropriate to different capacities and needs, and not restricted only to those with specifically academic attainments, or social advantages.

2. The present academic domination of British education should be recognized as enforcing the domination of British society by a closed upper-middle-class elite, and the exclusion from an equal say in it of many subordinate social groups including the working class. It should therefore be an objective of the comprehensive reform of the post-school education system to open it up to more democratic control, to more equal access, and to a greater plurality of working definitions of skill, education and culture.

3. The failure of British society to provide adequate post-school education for about 60 per cent of school-leavers, and the low and socially biased rates of participation in post-18 education, should be seen as economically, socially and humanly disastrous. It is unlikely that Britain can achieve either economic or political development in a world of advanced skills and high expectations without equipping its population with the best possible level of education, and this should therefore be a major economic and social priority.

4. The social bias built into the British education system leads to vast wastage of ability as a result of the lack of commitment to education especially among the working class but also among groups defined by gender and racial discrimination. This is damaging both to the individuals and groups concerned, and to society as a whole. It should be a priority of a comprehensive post-school education policy to seek to redress these relative dis-

advantages, and to ensure that hitherto disadvantaged groups benefit to a more proportional extent from future policies. This suggests that at the present time a concentration of resources on the 16+ age-group and on improved educational outcomes in the schools is the most urgent social priority, recognizing that improved education at these earlier ages will generate demands for more education for older age-groups.

5. Despite its elitist and narrowly academic character, there are elements of distinctive value in the British higher education system, notably its tradition of effective care for its students, and its generally high intellectual standards. Care should be given in reforms of the system to protect these good qualities where they exist.

A Universal Right of Post-School Education

There are good reasons, from the point of view of individual freedom and the provision of needed skills, for allowing the provision of post-school education to be determined by the choices of students, as the Robbins Report argued in its academically restrictive way in the 1960s. To give an entitlement to a period of grant-aided full- or part-time education to all those over 16, of a kind to which they are suited and qualified, would establish a universal opportunity for post-school education and ensure that this was adapted to a variety of educational needs and not only to those of the most academically successful or privileged. Such a commitment of principle, for example by the Labour Party, to a comprehensive form of post-school education would be an important step and would encourage the process of rethinking of the forms of post-school education that will be needed if this commitment is to be made a meaningful reality.

An important proposal of this was first made by Oliver Fulton.[6] This advocated an entitlement in principle to four years' funded full-time study for all those over 16, to be taken consecutively or in separate units. It was suggested that this might be economically more feasible if the third year of existing degree courses was funded by loan, and certainly it may be necessary to recognize that increased opportunities for the majority may have to involve some constraints in the support now available to the most successful minority of students.

A universal entitlement to post-school education would require

the development of appropriate programmes and forms of qualification, both for entry to and completion of such courses. While
existing entrance requirements to degree courses are unduly formal
and stringent, and should be widened, nevertheless a large proportion of comprehensive past-school educational opportunities
will have to be on courses of different kinds from existing degrees
and adapted to different educational needs and aims. Many current
proposals for increasing access to existing courses should be supported (for example, more flexible entrance requirements, easier
entry for mature students, 'bridging courses', and especially grants
to 16–18 year olds to encourage working-class take-up of education). But the object of defining a comprehensive right to post-
school education is to insist not merely on wider access to the
existing range of courses, but on the development of a broader
range of educational provision.

The development of a range of post-school educational programmes, on a full- and part-time basis, would clearly require a
major educational effort. But just as it has been possible to achieve
a substantial expansion of existing degree courses and their equivalents, with high educational standards, in the past three decades,
so there is every reason to think that growth could be accomplished
with a wider range of programmes. In the advanced further
education sector, this was achieved through a combination of
market incentives to individual institutions, and central regulatory
and approval mechanism, and similar methods could be looked to in
the future. In the United States a highly decentralized and market-
led system has been able to provide for the educational needs of half
the 18-year old age group, and there is no reason why this should be
impossible, over a period, in Britain.

The timetable and procedures for the implementation of such a
universal right are matters requiring much detailed debate. There
seem good reasons for making this entitlement available in the near
future for a wide range of adults, through day-release, study-leave,
or sabbatical schemes for example, rather than conferring it at some
future date on all who have just had their eighteenth birthday. But
since the demand from so large a potential public might well exceed
the available resources (both in terms of overall funds and a feasible
rate of development of programmes) it would have to be recognized
that all potential demand could not be met at once. This has been
the case, after all, with the Open University. There would be some
advantages in providing a steady build-up of provision of this universalistic kind, so that the education system could learn how best to

offer it. This could be accomplished through a progressive increase in funding available to colleges for these new programmes. It is important that entitlements to post-school education should be available in part-time as well as full-time modes; there would be real economies in providing funding and other support for this. Education should be available in recurrent, discontinuous courses of one or more terms, for example, over many years, and not only in the current five-year continuous form of 'A' levels plus degrees. There are already great educational benefits to be observed especially in polytechnics and advanced further education colleges from the presence of older, more experienced and part-time students. The continuation of education in later life should also become increasingly important, with a considerable life-expectation after normal retirement age and the probability of earlier full or preferably part-time retirement for many people. The opportunity to begin an educational programme in the last decade of work, which could then provide a focus of interest and development after retirement, would be a great enhancement of life for many. A national credit transfer scheme would be one step towards the more flexible and student-orientated provision that will be necessary in a comprehensive system. A system of credit-accumulation, so that certain work at sub-degree level gave credits towards degrees, would further increase flexibility, and it would also be desirable for students to be able to study for degrees more intensively, making completion in less than three years possible. A much closer relationship of adult education programmes to the rest of the post-school education system would help the development of comprehensive post-school programmes, since much of the relevant experience and expertise exists in that sector.

Strategies for Developing Comprehensive Post-18-year-old Education

At present the system of funding of post-school education mainly rewards advanced academic work and severely inhibits any other kind. As Gerald Fowler has recently pointed out, the system now actively discourages part-time degrees (despite their potential economic advantages) through under-funding them relative to full-time work.[7] But the designation of only 'advanced' courses as 'poolable', the confining of mandatory grants mainly to degree and degree-equivalent programmes, and the restriction of Dip.H.E. to

a two A-level entry, are examples of the present exclusionist procedures. The concentration of 'advanced' work in separate institutions has a similar effect, cutting 'higher education' off from the
majority of its potential customers, and also from its potential
supporters and cultural communities. The availability of grants for a
wider range of part-time and full-time courses, and the broadening
of the range of courses that could be funded through the advanced
further education 'pool', would encourage institutions to broaden
their range of work in a more comprehensive direction. Institutions,
especially if their existing student demand dries up, will respond to a
different set of market incentives.

The proposal of a universal right of access to post-18 education
implies that programmes and courses will become available to meet
the full range of interests and abilities of the adult population —
adult literacy and vocational re-training programmes, for instance,
as well as degree-level courses. But consideration needs to be given
to the relationship of new forms of 'comprehensive' provision to the
existing academic system. It is important that there should be
linkage between the different academic levels of the system, so that
access to opportunities arising from higher qualifications is as open
as possible.

There are two main strategies available for developing 'comprehensive' forms of provision. One is to encourage, through funding
and student grants, the development of a network of non-degree or
sub-degree courses, from which progression to degrees would be
possible. This was the route that should have been pursued through
the Diploma of Higher Education, but was cut off through the
requirement of degree-equivalence, especially in the minimum
entry qualification. Such development would require new financial
incentives for institutions to provide such courses, and some new
validating and approval procedures to ensure their standard and
credibility. The disadvantage of this method is that because sub-
degree courses have by definition a lower status, they may have
difficulty in attracting students and in achieving a sense of distinctive value.

An additional strategy would be to loosen the existing constraints
on the academic definition and standard of degree courses. This
would be to recognize that while one of the benefits of the CNAA
system has been to maintain a high and uniform concept of a degree,
the cost has been a continued restrictiveness and academic bias of
the higher education system in Britain. It has prevented the development of courses with, for example, more of a craft orientation,

and forced existing practical courses, for example in art and design, into a more academic direction. The only way in which this objective could be accomplished would probably be to abolish the CNAA's present role in course validation, instead devolving on to individual institutions or consortia of institutions the right to develop and award their own degrees. The CNAA could continue in an advisory role, or could have the functions of validating institutions rather than their courses. It has moved some little way along this road in its Partnership in Validation proposals, but one of the reasons why progress has been slow and uncertain may be the assumption that while responsibility should be devolved, the standards enforced through validation should remain essentially unchanged. A more radical proposition would be to insist that 'standards' (which are in any case relative to the professional and academic convictions of those who enforce them) should be more pluralist, and be allowed to vary over a larger range.

Some programmes will be more academic than others, and within a programme of any given type it will be meaningful to talk about progression from lower to higher levels. But the established designation of one kind of tertiary education — the academic — as generally 'higher' is inimical to the idea of comprehensive tertiary education, and it would be better if some more pluralist designation were used.[8]

This pattern of much greater variation in the definition and content of a 'degree' has been one means by which the United States system has been able to expand to include so large a proportion of the school-leaving age-group. It would allow the adaptation of courses to a wider range of vocational needs; while one can point to many examples of CNAA support for innovative and progressive degree schemes, it should not be forgotten that the *general* effect of its procedures has been to encourage conventional and 'safe' academic programmes as those most likely to ensure validation. It has had particularly conservative and restrictive effects on curricula in certain subject-areas. Because mandatory grants and 'Pool' allocations could remain attached to a more flexible definition of a degree course, the funding mechanism would not itself be the main instrument of change. Instead, this would be effected through a weakening of academic control, through the course validation system. There would be increasing differences in degree status, in such a situation of pluralism with institutions encouraged to find students at 'their own level'. But these would not be as clear-cut and categorical as they would be if one encouraged a separate development of 'non-degree' awards as the main channel of expansion.

There is no doubt that such a proposal would be met by a great deal of heart-searching and opposition. The British university and now CNAA degree is a sacred object, held in understandably high regard. The CNAA subject-boards are regarded by many polytechnic and college teachers as their allies, often supporting academic standards against the imputed philistinism, cost-cutting or prejudices of their higher managements. But it must be recognized that this system has had its costs as well as its benefits. While Britain has a high quality tertiary education system, it also has a very small and elitist one. If one wants to see a significant extension of education to large additional sections of the population, one will have to accept a greater plurality and range of what is provided: this seems inescapable.

The continued domination of the existing academic elite, which has now incorporated many academics in the advanced further education system, does not seem compatible with comprehensive post-school education. Perhaps the CNAA system has done its job, in protecting standards in the initial substantial phase of expansion. Maybe these standards will now have to look after themselves, in a more open market, on the American pattern.[9] It seems therefore that both the proposed strategies should be pursued: the concept and range of degree courses should be enlarged, but many other programmes should be developed for students not able or not wishing to study for a degree.

The Diversification of Curricula

The development of a comprehensive system of post-18 education must have implications for curricula and forms of knowledge and culture, as well as for the structures in which education is provided. While the 'standards' of academic courses are real, they are bought at a high price in the devaluation and neglect of other human skills and accomplishments. Early subject-specialization in schools, the undervaluation of work which involves doing and making rather than knowing things, approaches to creative forms, like writing, which emphasize comprehension and judgment rather than competence or imagination in production, and an ethos of individual competition — these are all examples of distortion in the curriculum imposed by the existing academic structures.

There is in any case some hypocrisy in the assertion of academic standards against the claims of extended education, in a disregard of the non-educational functions which in fact determine many of the procedures of higher education. In practice, the needs of credentialism and the bureaucratic sorting of manpower take precedence over intrinsic educational values. The dominating competition for grades from GCE Ordinary Level up to degree honours classifications produces an instrumental reduction of the educational task, to something like cramming, and the enforced subservience to it of teachers and students diminishes the range and individuality of what they can do. Significantly, the highest levels of the system find it desirable to lessen these constraints. The most elite forms of higher education, in Oxford and Cambridge, offer the widest spectrum of educational experiences, mainly extra-curricular, but still central to the benefits these institutions confer.

They are in a sense more comprehensive in their conception of education than most intermediate-level institutions, since they seek to educate in a way of life and not merely specific skills. There is a similar breadth of definition of education, which has been to some extent relieved of grading pressures by the development of comprehensive schools. Art, music, the development of social capacities, and work appealing to children's own interests have been able to evolve as a result.

Teachers as well as pupils are tightly constrained by credentialist procedures. The importance of grading constrains even the work of university teachers, who are in part engaged in the reproduction of their own academic values, and in imposing them on a population of students many of whom have other needs which are neglected and devalued in this process. But as least university and other higher education teachers have the power to develop their own curricula, which the GCE system removes from even the academic elite of school teachers. Through the control of GCE the universities are able to impose their own selection requirements on the whole system, and this is now one of the decisive forms of exclusionist control which needs to be challenged. It is realistic to see such procedures as a form of what Frank Parkin has described as 'closure': that is, preferential access to positions of social and economic advantage for the children of those with accumulated 'cultural capital'.[10]

The conjuction of our highly academic education system with predominantly middle-class recruitment is not fortuitous. Higher education is now chiefly valued as a passport to superior jobs, and a system which so grossly favours the children of the educationaly privileged is transmitting class advantages just as much as the inheritance of wealth. This is one reason why post-school education should be a fundamental issue for socialists.

Education might become accessible and attractive to a wider range of people if its curricula were more responsive to students' choices and needs. Within conventional degree courses, it is often found that students' most personal work is their best, and the opportunity to do this work, in individual and group research projects for example, also has the effect of creating a less one-dimensional hierarchy of competence: intellectual capacity is not the only quality which can contribute to good and original work. The development of the idea of 'independent study' in some institutions has been an important crystallization of an alternative way of thinking about education, as is the practice of schools of art and design.[11] The diversification of provision should encourage such differentiation of curricula and learning.

A crucial part of a comprehensive education strategy is the lessening of university control over school curricula. It would be desirable, as Tyrrell Burgess has proposed, to replace GCE examinations with carefully moderated school-based assessments, of a 'Mode Three' kind, which would allow much greater variety of educational programmes.[12] Both teachers and pupils would gain greater control over the educational process by these means, and there are arguments for involving other community interests in this process. It is relevant to note that qualification for college entrance in the United States is achieved through a national Scholastic Aptitude Test[13] (the SAT) and a High School Diploma providing a transcript for each pupil. This seems to be more open in its effect than a national GCE system, giving more emphasis to students' basic aptitudes and individual qualitites, where the British system requires conventional and specialized academic achievements.

Knowledge and the Popular University

Socialists would hope that a comprehensive post-18 education system would provide access to knowledge and the means of cultural creation to the whole population, and not merely to the present educational elite. It is clear that trade unions, though with twelve million members and deep interests in industrial, economic and social issues, now have virutally no access to the intellectual and research resources of the higher education system. The Industrial

Research Unit of Warwick Univerity was recently accused by the Rothschild Report of bias towards trades unions. Is it conceivable that a research institution could be comparably accused of bias towards business? One hopes to see extensions of the rights of workers to information and participation in the workplace. Such rights will themselves generate a need for educational and research provision. The entitlement to post-school education might well be claimed in some instances by groups seeking education in a co-operative way, as well as by individuals, and trade unions (including those with members in educational institutions) should become involved in developing new programmes for their members.

'Knowledge' is shaped by the institutions that have control over it. Important recent critiques of the selective and partial structuring of 'knowledge' in different fields need to be taken into account in any socialist education programme. These critiques have centred on such questions as the application of science and technology and its characteristic biases; the gender bias of many areas of academic work, including the arts and social sciences; and the marginalization of workers' points of view on industrial and economic matters. In the 'cultural disciplines' the main object of socialist critique is a pervasive elitism in which the conservation and transmission of a tradition, for example in high literature, in a passive 'critical' and consuming mode, takes precedence over broader and more actively creative ideas of cultural work. These assumptions can be held sometimes in the strongest forms by theoretical radicals and even Marxists. But against this there has been a minority tradition of self-guided study and research (the feminist movement has been one recent setting for such work), and it should be one of the main purposes of tertiary education to equip students with the self-confidence and skill to continue their own education outside the formal teaching process. But of course the grading systems of higher education often take away as much confidence as they instil, and habits and skills that they particularly disregard are those of co-operative work. A general conclusion to be urged from these debates is the benefit of a more open and pluralist approach to knowledge and culture. Increased access to cultural means should be a priority for socialist policy. Cultural concerns have been central to socialist and Marxist debates in the last twenty years, and these have been reflected in many oppositional initiatives (alternative journals, bookshops, theatre groups, etc.). But this activity has so far had little impact on the more centralized mass media of the press and broadcasting, and an agreed programme in these areas is now an urgent need.

A more democratic idea of culture and education requires an imaginative leap — it is hard to imagine what one does not have, and has never known. A different idea of the university should be part of this more democratic conception. If more people made use of colleges, at different stages of their lives, and to do things which they chose for vocational and other purposes, the prejudice against education and intellectual life which now isolates many socialists would lessen. A beginning would be made if the generous facilities possessed by universities and colleges for recreation as well as study were made more available to the communities in which they are situated. [14]

British society now needs a period of positive reconstruction and a serious debate about its various crises, to avert its continuing decline. The institutions of higher education should be as central as the mass media and the political parties to such discussion. There is a natural link between the advance of popular education and the achievement of a more informed and democratic society, but this has long been disrupted by the exclusivism and privilege of British educational provision. If radicals in the higher education system were able to overcome these barriers in their institution, they would find the anti-intellectual climate of other public debates also changing for the better. The idea of an organic relationship between intellectuals and emerging classes in society, influentially propounded by Gramsci, has implications for the practice of socialists working in education. While a comprehensive post-18 system will require legislation and state funding, it will also depend on the initiatives of those who work in higher education.

Unemployment and Post-School Education

It is clear that the claims of post-school education will have to compete with many other priorities such as improved pupil-teacher ratios, which are important to any general educational improvement. Nevertheless the development of large-scale unemployment in Britain and elsewhere in Europe, caused by long-term technological changes as well as economic mismangement, does have implications for educational policy. It makes necessary a more radical consideration of the interrelationship of work, education and leisure than is currently discussed. It becomes desirable to envisage various forms of education taking up more time in people's lives than is now the case. Clearly this should be by people's own choice and will in part be related to changes of career and updatings of skill. Since capital investment will probably continue to displace workers from material production, through the use of high technology and control systems, the opportunity for useful work will be found increasingly in activities concerned with human relations, in personal services, social care and cultural development. This will also provide the opportunity to improve such services. It should be possible to enhance considerably the levels of skill and creativity that can be generally achieved, through increasing the time and care available to individuals. How far people can develop their capacities is dependent in part on the relationships available to them in which learning is an object. The vision of socialism in which societies care for their members, and in which creativity is valued as a common quality and not only as an attribute to be admired in exceptional individuals, could now be envisaged as a practical possibility. Some of the additional costs of extending education, where its effect is to make use of previously unused resources and to reduce the overall level of unemployment, will be only notional costs, or constitute a redistribution of the burden of existing economic arrangements from the unemployed, who now bear the heaviest share of these, to taxpayers in general. While taxation to provide for a longer average period in education — which would reduce the size of the available labour force at any given time — might not be universally popular, the present sacrifice of the interests of the unemployed to everyone else's relative benefit is contrary to social justice. Increasing the numbers engaged in post-school education would be a beneficial and potentially popular means of reducing unemployment.

The Social Bases for Educational Change

One of the arguments of this chapter has been that the higher education system in Britain is dominated by a narrow academic elite, closest in its values to the liberal professions and the higher state bureaucracy. The role of the leading universities, especially Oxford and Cambridge, in providing elite cadres for the major national centres of power, and the concentration of these in London and the South-East, has the effect that the universities support the hegemony of a national upper-class social elite. The internal stratification of the universities, the concentration of the best students, and the academic influence and patronage of the best institutions ensure that the countervailing influence of provincial centres is limited. The polytechnics and other colleges of 'public sector' higher education have never established remotely comparable status, level of social recruitment or placement of graduates, and they perform a subordinate function in this class system.

Relatively weakened by this system, and by much else in the organization of British political and cultural life, are the peripheral regions, whose institutions suffer from the creaming away of able pupils to national centres, and from recolonization in the other direction by academics trained in those centres. Other relative losers are business interests, which have little direct influence over most higher education curricula, and indeed have frequently critized the irrelevance of college education for their needs. Much smaller still, of course, is the influence of working-class organizations such as trade unions, which have only a marginal and poor-relation status in higher education through institutions such as Ruskin College. Since English political parties are limited and weak in their scope of activity compared with some European countries, higher education has been until recently insulated from direct political influence. While the polytechnics are formally subject to total government control, in practice it seems that their own educational managers and academics have been able, for most purposes, to fend off any intended local government intervention in educational matters, and to use their national recruitment and their dependence on national funding and validation to defend themselves from local interference. The Thatcher Government's greater responsiveness to business ideology is one reason for its unusual willingness to move against the autonomy of the higher education system, as we have discussed above.

This insulation from social pressures constitutes a problem for academics of the left. On the one hand, a predominantly liberal hegemony is relatively congenial to them and probably discriminates less against the left than most other forms of control would be likely to do. On the other hand, existing forms of control do seem to be associated with the system's restrictiveness; it is in the first instance *academic* values that are being enforced in higher education. It is proposed here that this liberal self-government is now purchased at too high a price in social exclusion, and that the risks of opening up the system to the pressures of outside interests — which may include business, political parties, and a more open market of student demand — have to be faced in order to achieve the benefits of a comprehensive system. It is probably the case that only when the advantages of comprehensive tertiary education are perceived by many different interests will it be likely to come about. It is notable that a previous phase of expansion, when the polytechnics were established, was legitimated by a combination of vocationalist and industrial aims with appeals for opportunities for the disadvantaged. Ways in which the system might be made more open to social pressure include more effective local or regional control over the universities and advanced further education sector; entitlement to tertiary education for students seeking less academic forms of education; and greater freedom for new institutions to confer degrees, even if these institutions might be funded not by the state but from voluntary, trade union or business sources.

Academics have come to believe in the unqualified virtues of a monopoly of tertiary education by the local or national state, as part of their own embedding in the state bureaucracy. Whether this arrangement serves all social interests as well as it has done their own is less clear.

There are obvious risks in any change. A more pluralist system might well, for example, increase the influence of private business interests, more than any other. But the North American system is more exposed to these pressures, yet also more open and democratic. It is unfortunate that the most universalist tertiary education system in the world is in the most capitalist country, but this does not mean that its lessons need not even be considered by the left. It should be the case that in a society with a more even balance of class forces, a more open and pluralistic system would have a different outcome; perhaps this is why the British system adamantly sticks to elitism.

What does seem certain is that no major change will occur in British higher education that is not pressed from outside it, probably from a political agency. One reason for the importance of the labour movement to the argument of this chapter is that no other social force in Britain seems likely to have the will or interest to bring radical change to such a conservative system as that of higher education. Since this system seems deeply implicated in the maintenance of the British social elite, and since progress towards a more democratic and pluralist society is necessary for a socialist outcome to the British crisis, there are urgent reasons that go beyond the educational for seeking educational change.

Comprehensive Institutions of Post-School Education

The proposal to establish a universal right to post-school education and therefore a much greater diversity of provision has implications for the shape of the institutions in which this education is provided. The existing structure is one which, on the basis of a fairly consistent degree award, has a marked and severe stratification of institutions in terms of prestige, average qualification of entrants, career destinations of graduates, material resources, research, and the density and quality of cultural life. In particular, there is a marked gulf between the sector of advanced further education and the universities. The polytechnics were established with a form of radicalism characteristic of the Wilson Government — more an echo of an earlier radicalism of the provincial and industrial middle class than of socialism — but they had some kind of founding commitment to useful knowledge, education for the disadvantaged, and vocationalism. The division between these two sectors had a rationale similar to that of the tripartite secondary system of 1944, with the difference that the polytechnics correspond to what a larger technical school sector should have been, and not to the secondary moderns which were in fact the majority pattern. But in both cases the philosophy of 'parity of esteem' disguised a failure of egalitarian nerve and political will. There was no way, given the structure of advantages and competition in which the two sectors were contained, that parity of esteem could be achieved. The cost of this stratification and division is the insulation of the university sector from pressure to be more responsive to social and educational needs. Universities overwhelmingly continue to recruit 18-year olds from the middle and upper classes, on a basis of competitive academic achievement, and recent UGC policy has reinforced the incentives for them to do so. A further cost is the impoverishment of environment, culture and recruitment in the 'public sector'. The object of moving the orientation of the most highly educated in British society in a more technical and practical direction is not achieved if only a subordinate professional and semi-professional class receives its education in this way. Yet evidence on the pattern of elite recruitment shows this to be so, and there continue to be equally serious differences of opportunity between a few older universities and the universities in general.

Some differentiation of functions between kinds of institutions can be desirable, and there may be no good case for creating by administrative fiat conglomerate institutions to undertake every possible kind of work. Even the comprehensive school programme has to some degree involved confusions between an architectural and administrative idea of universality and integration, and the educational practice which has often been somewhat different. Nevertheless, some major measures to reform the present system of stratification, and especially the creaming of the most highly-achieving students into two or perhaps half a dozen institutions, must be attempted. The British social elite cannot be rendered more democratic, open and pluralist until its uniform and narrow kind of educational formation is ended.

The most feasible change in this direction would probably be to increase the relative advantages of leading regional institutions as against those of the Oxbridge–London triangle. It seems that to strengthen regional institutions might at this point be the most effective means of increasing the influence of subordinate social strata, as well as having other cultural benefits.

In the United States, there have been, as a reflection of economic and political competition between geographical regions, several major centres of academic leadership, often demonstrating different patterns of organization and priority. The United States is in certain respects correspondingly a more open and democratic society. It would be desirable to create a situation of greater parity of cultural resources between English regions too, in which educational institutions could have an important role. A strategy for this is proposed in the following section on forms of control. We have in mind that the allocation of students to institutions might give greater weight to regional origin, much as allocation to secondary schools pays regard to the pupil's local authority of residence. The national cultural and educational resources of Oxford and Cambridge might, on this basis, be given over to a greater degree to post-graduate and adult study, where a national 'streaming process' would be less serious for the general pattern of elite recruitment than is the case with immediate post-school education. Another advantage of this policy would be to interrupt the smooth pathway between leading public schools, Oxbridge colleges, and top jobs, and ensure a greater diversity of experience, at least, for these privileged pupils. This may well turn out to be a more acceptable strategy for weakening the privileged role of the public schools in British life than prohibition, which will create much difficulty within a liberal political climate of ideas.

So far as the broader issue of the pattern of institutional provision is concerned, it is proposed that a diversity of regional patterns should be encouraged to develop. While it should be a matter of national policy to establish rights to and means of extended post-school education, it might well be left to local and regional bodies to decide whether new forms of education take place in existing or new institutions. Similarly, there could be variation in the mutual relations of existing higher education institutions. Given regional control of the whole of post-school education, which we discuss below, the pattern could be expected to vary between a division of institutions similar to that which now exists nationally, and at an opposite pole the creation of unified comprehensive universities for post-school education in which many forms of post-18 education would take place. Socialists might prefer the latter, but it seems sensible to recognize in advance the violent feelings which a universal attempt to 'comprehensivize' universities would provoke, and to seek more varied and consensual solutions which could be put to the test of practice and time.

The Control of Post-School Education

Finally, we consider the means and institutions for the control of post-school education. There is already a state of turmoil and incipient centralization in this area, as the present government seeks to impose contraction and rationalization on the system. Before this new system consolidates itself, it is therefore important to propose alternatives. Furthermore, while it would be premature to formulate detailed administrative proposals, there is a general direction that it may be useful to suggest.

The dominant tradition of the left in Britain has sought social reform through the central state. Clearly a programme could be envisaged which sought on a centralized basis to implement the changes proposed here. Some major national policies on educational entitlements and funding, would in any case be necessary. However, the recent history of central government intervention in this sector is not promising. It is not obvious that the opportunity for a centralized strategy of a socialist kind is likely to occur in the short-term, or if it did that the means and understanding would exist to carry it through with sensitivity and consent. Nor is a local government solution, which has recently been proposed by Tyrrell

Burgess,[15] in our view convincing. Local authorities are mostly too small and ill-equipped to devise a strategy for post-school education. They seem likely to function at best as financial holding companies, within which virtually autonomous institutions can respond to the market. This was the pattern of public sector expansion in the past two decades, and exposure to market pressures is probably one of the main advantages of a radically decentralized system from the point of view of its advocates. But so many local authorities are already involved in public sector higher education that rational coordination and efficiency in the use of resources would be difficult to secure. The system has in the past been relatively expensive and wasteful, and some regard to efficiency will have to be paid. It is hardly conceivable that the existing local authorities could obtain overall control over the universities within their boundaries as well as other colleges, yet some measure of political control of the whole system seems essential to bring about a significant change in its dominant priorities.

For these reasons, and in order to achieve the objectives set down in this programme, it is suggested instead that the control of all post-school education, including both university and 'public' sectors, should be vested with regional educational authorities. These should have the power, within a specified framework of national policy and funding, to develop what they regard as appropriate forms of provision. Each one would control several major institutions, and could therefore develop an overall strategy for this sector, with an adequate technical capacity and expertise for its management.

This proposal is engaged in the context of a general regionalization of elected government, along the lines discussed in chapter four. The creation of stronger, and necessarily professionalized, elected regional administrations would strengthen the political dimension of decision-making in Britain, and would thus be an augmentation of the collective powers of ordinary citizens as opposed to those of large private capital. Such changes would provide a means of enhancing the weight of the interests of the subordinate classes in society, but in a mode that would require the negotiation of broad social alliances, and of specific forms of consensus, and would avoid the costs of centralized bureaucratic power. The role of institutions of post-school education and research could be central to such a development. As cultural means in general have been central to the growth of nationalist identity in Scotland and Wales, so a cultural regeneration of regional identities in England is also long overdue. Clearly, to link a strategy for the reform of the particular sector of post-school education to a major constitutional reform of government may appear to be a case of a small tail attempting to wag a very large dog. However, since this chapter attempts to relate a strategy for post-school education to many wider issues — unemployment, social equality, elite-formation, the nature and quality of culture — such connections are unavoidable. The creation of a universal and open post-school education system less stratified than our existing structure, does imply many major social changes, and new institutions would be needed to implement them. The development of a new level of political authority, and the political will that might emerge from it, may be necessary to an educational reform which would have the desired effect of breaking up and democratizing the elite control of British society.

In more narrow terms, one could envisage a regional form of control of post-school education alone, without reference to any wider elective system. The establishment of regional consortia of local authorities was one of the proposals recently made for the control of the local authority sector of post-school education, and it would be feasible to envisage a broadening of this to include university institutions. Certainly the abolition of the binary division, and the subordination of both main kinds of higher education institution to a common framework of policy, is essential to our proposals, and even a solution through appointed or nominated regional post-school education authorities might make this possible.

A regional form of control would then allow for an efficient allocation of resources, for the development of strategies for universal access with the many new forms of provision this would require, for the lessening of the dominance of the major national institutions, and for the development of a greater cultural diversity. There should be sufficient scope for regional decision to affect the structure of institutions, the priorities of expenditure on different sectors and levels of education, the allocation of students, and through a regional element of research funding, the priorities of research and cultural development.

Comprehensive Education and Cultural Democracy

The radical and socialist movements in recent years have been marked by a commitment to small-scale self-activity and self-expression. This concern, and its related forms of informal and non-hierarchical organization, have characterized groups based for example on neighbourhoods, on workplaces, and on links of gender. Concern for the quality and means of mass communication has been another important radical theme, representing the obverse critique of authoritarian control and cultural monopoly. The structures of tertiary education are closely linked with the universal possibilities, or otherwise, of self-expression and communication. It is necessary to think out and work for a form of post-school (and school) education which supports and makes possible cultural democracy, in place of one whose controlling purpose is the reproduction of a social and cultural elite, and the subordination of society to its values and ways of thinking.

This connection of comprehensive post-school education with the idea of a society in which creativity is generally encouraged and respected is perhaps the most fundamental issue in this whole debate.

NOTES

1.See for further developments of these idea J. Finch and M. Rustin eds., *What Is to be Done About Higher Education?* Harmondsworth 1985. This book is one of a series initiated by the Socialist Society in conjunction with Penguin Books.

2. Ralph H. Turner, 'Modes of Social Ascent through Education', in *Education, Economy and Society*, eds. A.H. Halsey, J. Floud and C.A. Anderson, eds., *Education, Economy and Society*, Free Press, 1961

3. The SDP Green Paper on education and training, *Foundations for the Future* (1982) proposes just this.

4. In T. Burgess and J. Pratt, *Policy and Practice: The Colleges of Advanced Technology* (1970); and J. Pratt and T. Burgess, *Polytechnics: A Report* (1974). See also the more favourable account of the development of the public sector by Peter Scott, *The Crisis of the Universities*, London 1984.

5. *Is Higher Education Fair?* edited by David Warren Piper, JRHE 1981 (papers presented to the Society for Research into Higher Education's 1981 Conference) provides recent information on access and bias.

6. In the SRHE–Leverhulme collection, *Access to Education*, edited by O. Fulton. SRHE 1981.

7. In his essay in the SHRE's *Institutional Adaptation and Change in Higher Education*, edited by Leslie Wagner. SRHE 1982.

8. This point was made very forcefully by Eric Robinson at a recent Campaign for Higher Education Conference.

9. M. Trow, 'Binary Dilemmas: An American View', *Higher Education Review*, Vol. 2, no 1, 1969.

10. He discusses credentialist forms of exclusion in his *Marxism and Class Theory: A Bourgeois Critique*, London 1979.

11. Experiments in 'independent study' at the University of Lancaster and North East London Polytechnic are reported in Keith Percy and Paul Ramsden, *Independent Study - Two Examples from English Higher Education*, SRHE 1980.

12. In his essay in D. Lipsey and D. Leonard, eds., *The Socialist Agenda*, London 1981.

13. Important questions about aptitude tests and their effects on achievement are raised in C. Jencks and J. Rouse, 'Aptitude v. Achievement — Shoud We Replace the SAT?', *The Public Interest* 67, Spring 1982.

14. Albert O. Hirschman has argued in 'The Welfare State in Trouble: Systemic Crisis or Growing Pains?' *American Economic Review* 70, May 1980, that dissatisfaction with the personal services provided by the Welfare State may be due to their uncertain quality. The rate of expansion of provision has temporarily outrun the expertise needed to provide them at a high standard.

15. Burgess's proposal is in the volume cited under 7 above.

10

Towards a Feasible Socialist Foreign Policy

In this chapter, I attempt to trace the formation of foreign policy in Britain to its foundation in class interests, and to define a feasible socialist foreign policy in relation to the constraints and opportunities which are set by this framework.[1] I am aware that this is not the customary approach to such matters. On the left most people wish to make a broader and more universal appeal on foreign policy than appears to be possible on a 'class basis'. The threat of nuclear weapons especially seems to make it appropriate to invoke the interests of the entire British people, even of civilization itself, in support of alternative defence policies, and class is often judged to be a narrow and divisive standpoint by comparison. On the right it is also found convenient to cast policy orientations in national terms — only the reference here is to the apparent military threat from the East and to abstract political principles (freedom versus totalitarianism) rather than the benefits of capitalism as such. Since, however, the conflicts of the military alliances are, in my view, related to class interests and to the political institutions and governments that represent them, I will argue that a focus on these more general ethical or human appeals, from both left and right, in some important ways occludes the realities. A further displacement arises through the separation of defence — especially the technologies of defence — from foreign policy itself. But once these questions are grounded in the underlying interests that various policies seek to defend and advance, it may be possible to achieve a more unified and realistic understanding. In this way, the objectives of foreign policy may be linked to the goals which socialists would wish to pursue in their domestic strategies within a single State, such as Britain.

In the current debates over defence there is an important displacement from the broader field of political and ideological conflict, both within and between states, to the narrower though still large issue of military defence. The principal objective and raison d' être of the NATO and Warsaw Pact alliances is not to repel an anticipated invasion from the other side, which neither camp can consider to be a likely prospect. The main purpose is rather to maintain an approximate balance of forces, by which each side seeks to prevent and deter the exploitation by the other of any local weaknesses that might arise in its own camp, among its Third World allies or dependents, or in non-aligned territories. It must be recognized that the most likely danger to the unity and cohesion of either camp is one which would have its origin in a breakdown of order within a member state, which might then be liable to exploitation from outside. While this may seem an improbable contingency at this particular moment within NATO, it should be remembered that in recent years the political direction of many of its component states has seemed in doubt. Portugal, Greece France (in 1968) and Italy (in the period of the 1970s, when the PCI seemed near to achieving participation in the central government) are the most obvious examples. Nor should one forget the panic caused among certain circles in Britain by the trade union militancy of the early 1970s ('Is Britain governable?', etc.) or by the progress of the Bennite left inside the Labour Party after 1979. Ruling classes have long memories. The anxiety of NATO policy-makers must be that if a serious political disruption occurred within a member state at a time of local military weakness vis-à-vis the Warsaw Pact, it might be possible for the East to exploit the situation and detach a portion of the Western Bloc, at least into a state of neutrality, and perhaps into the East's sphere of influence.[2]

Conversely, the Russians have every reason to be concerned that if one of the melancholy succession of risings or movements of opposition within Eastern Europe were accompanied by military weakness, the West would actively encourage the 'liberation of a satellite country'. For both sides the principal value of large conventional forces, and of the supporting nuclear deterrent, is that they inhibit an opponent from seeking to exploit such occasions, by applying pressures or threats to which the other side is afraid to respond. This is the reason too why neutral countries such as Sweden or Yugoslavia, bordering the blocs, retain significant defence forces, and show conspicuous willingness to resist any military pressure that might be brought to bear on them. They also probably fear not so much direct invasion, but the capacity of (in this case) the USSR to intimidate them sufficiently to enforce compliance with its political goals.

Recent history in other parts of the world, described for example in Fred Halliday's *The Making of the Second Cold War*, supports this view of the dynamics of East–West conflict. Where either side appears to enjoy a local military superiority (Central America in the one case, Afghanistan in the other), it feels free to intervene in support of allies and clients, and its main adversary is reluctant to become directly involved. Each side prefers to use national proxies (Israel or Syria in the Middle East, for example) rather than become directly committed, and also seeks to sustain local factional forces within states which are the focus of conflict. Where neither side enjoys a recognized predominance or zonal sphere of influence, conflict becomes more unpredictable and volatile.

What the two camps defend in this global field of conflict, particularly at the peripheries of each, is not so much principles as powers. It is therefore not surprising that the basis of material and class interest in this conflict is mystified, and that the struggle is presented to the general population in terms of moral absolutes and the threat of invasion or annihilation. It is also true, however, that these systems of opposed forces behave rationally to a degree, in that where there is a relative weakness, each side naturally takes advantage of it. (Halliday demonstrates this cogently in relation to the Third World.)

There is also rationality, from this point of view, in seeking a position of strength. The Americans appear to have gained confidence, since the later years of the Carter administration, that they have the economic and military potential to achieve superiority over the Soviet Union, and are trying both to demonstrate and to impose this. Recent interventions in Grenada and in Lebanon are examples of this more forward strategy. It may be that the original Russian decision to deploy SS-20s targeted on Western Europe was an attempt to achieve a local nuclear superiority in this theatre, to offset increasing relative weakness in other zones, and in the global balance of nuclear forces. If this was the case, the strategy has so far misfired. Doubts about whether the Americans would in fact be prepared to risk their own destruction in defence of Western Europe initially led Schmidt and other political leaders to insist that a new generation of American missiles should be based in Europe. Although some of the consequences of this are now widely regretted — as it has become another aspect of the USA's evident quest for military superiority, and of its abandonment of detente — the decision to support the missile installation has so far been sustained in Western Europe, for the most part. Once deployment was opposed and contested from the left, it became a self-fulfilling test of Western resolve and cohesion. Most Western European governments would probably have preferred a negotiated settlement over the missiles, but they were unable to exercise sufficient influence, not least on their American ally, to bring this about.

Since the rise of the first Campaign for Nuclear Disarmament in the late 1950s many socialists in Britain have supported a socialist neutralist foreign policy. Sweden, Austria and Yugoslavia have offered alternative models to inclusion and subordination in the NATO Alliance, and the further renunciation of nuclear weapons, or of any role in nuclear weapons systems, would probably increase the security of Britain from potential nuclear attack, Britain's geographical situation is an obvious advantage from the point of view of security, and makes improbable any direct military threat to it from the East. Neutrality would also enhance the freedom of British governments to pursue independent goals in foreign and domestic policy, though it is another question whether Britain would thereby acquire greater influence in world politics. In general, the states outside or on the periphery of the military alliances seem to be freer to diverge from the dominant political patterns of the blocs than are those which are central to their military defence. There is no more reason to expect such a position of neutrality to be accompanied by a move towards authoritarian government in Britain than has been the case in Sweden, Ireland or Austria — especially if it were accomplished in a spirit of consensual nationalism which, given the balance of political forces in the UK, is the least unlikely basis for such a development. Neutrality would not obviate the need for defence forces, for the reasons given, and would be unlikely to save resources. But it would increase the independence and perhaps the worldwide influence for peace of the United Kingdom, which might then achieve some of the leverage of a relatively powerful independent in the conflict of the two blocs.

Now, while this option might be abstractly and indeed practically supported, it seems a most improbable outcome of the present political balance of forces, both within Britain and in the West as a whole. This is because the defection of Britain from the NATO Alliance and the Western military camp would be felt to weaken the relative position of the West vis-à-vis the Warsaw Pact, in a unilateral and to many most unwelcome way. It would cause major difficulties to the Western defence system: not so much because of the role of UK-based nuclear weapons, but because Britain makes an important contribution to NATO land forces in Europe (the British Army of the Rhine), to its sea and air forces, and to its communications system. There would be great alarm among other West European States (especially West Germany), which would be afraid of finding themselves in a worse position to incur the risks of military conflict and thus to resist pressures from the East. This could lead to a wide range of outcomes: from a drive to coerce Britain back into the NATO system, through increased armament by its remaining powers, to further defections from the Alliance or attempts to negotiate a more stable truce with the East. But the USA in particular would probably interpret a British move into neutrality in much the same way that the USSR would view a similar step by Poland, or East Germany, or Czechoslovakia. Nor is this only a question of the external pressure that can be brought to bear on a nationalist and neutralist British foreign policy. One should not underestimate the degree to which the ruling classes in a state such as Britain, with its multinational economic ties, now endorse and identify with an international class interest. Any move to uncouple Britain unilaterally from the Alliance system would (and does) plainly meet very powerful and broadly based opposition within Britain.

The difficulty is that the objective consequences of such a shift in Britain's military and foreign policy position would be somewhat different from the original projection. Even though there were no intention of increasing the relative strength of the Warsaw Pact over the West, or of making Western Europe more susceptible to Eastern pressure, a power of the order that Britain still represents could not leave the Western Alliance without having, and certainly being perceived to have, such an effect. It is the likely impact of any such shift in the military and political balance which leads intelligent opponents of the peace movement, such as Conor Cruise O'Brien, continually to draw attention to the different scope for dissent on either side of the East–West frontier. If, it is argued, the independent peace movements in the East *were* able to achieve a disengagement of their states from the USSR comparable to that which the British peace movement might seek to achieve from the USA, then it might be a very different story. But they can't, and won't, and so it is necessary to resist the unavoidably and even unintentionally one-sided arguments of British 'neutralists'.

These issues are well understood by dominant class forces in Britain and the West. They believe that a dismantling of the Western military alliance by defection into neutralism would bring about a serious relative weakening of the capitalist world. Whereas such changes in a single country might be containable, depending on how they were brought about and under whose political leadership, the wider consequences would certainly be unpredictable. These are thought to be unacceptable risks, and are fiercely resisted by political decision-takers from Denis Healey rightwards. Even the CND leadership has had to take into account the strength of opposition to neutralist positions, and has therefore sought to pursue a process of cumulative disarmament within the Alliance structure, initiated by important unilateral steps, rather than oppose Britain's continued membership of NATO. The fact that Western populations are mostly unattracted by the model of 'actually existing socialism' presents an additional difficulty for a position which might seem indirectly favourable to the East. Even democratic socialists whose long-term aim is the dissolution of both military blocs have to take heed of the resistance and instability that might result from threats to the existing balance of force.

Having raised these problems, I would now like to consider whether there is a more feasible basis for a socialist foreign policy for Britain, one which might achieve broader support and provoke less ferocious opposition and anxiety. To approach this question, it is necessary to look at the differences of class and national interest which divide the states of Western Europe from the USA, as well as those which unite them. Whereas, faced with a risk of subordination to the Communist bloc, all Western governments without exception (including the neutrals) will accept de facto American domination, the exclusion or diminution of this risk would make the differences between European and American interests much more apparent. The countries of Western Europe, unlike many US allies in other spheres of influence, are all now electoral democracies of one kind or another. Yet their systems of electoral representation reflect a higher degree of overt class division, and a stronger level of working-class consciousness, than exists in the United States itself. The West European states are each committed through their political system to class compromises of a more or less explicit kind. While these secure the maintenance of a predominantly capitalist system of production and distribution, they have also constructed or conceded a substantial area of state intervention in the economy, and sometimes in the system of production itself. They have sought to incorporate trade unions into economic management to a greater extent than the United States has done, and they have more extensive systems of welfare spending. West European working-class parties call themselves socialist or social democratic, and sustain serious opposition in some cases to capitalist definitions and powers. In Mitterrand's early nationalization programme, for example, or in the current conflicts in Sweden over the innovation of worker-owned funds in private companies, there is or has been the potential for serious inroads into capitalist power. Even the regulations of the EEC represent in some areas a relatively advanced form of class compromise, in the recognition of social and civil rights of various kinds and in the provision of funds for economic development in backward regions.

This underlying class base provides at least the ground for a different economic strategy from that being pursued on a global basis by the USA. Historically the politics of class compromise has depended on economic expansion, and on the generation of increments of wealth which could allay social conflict. The phase of neo-Conservative reaction in the West, which began in the late seventies, arose from a realization of the costs, to capitalism, of a politics of concession, as the roles of the state, welfare spending and trade unions underwent significant growth, and as people generally became more conscious of increased rights and possibilities. But this reaction was intellectually and politically developed in the society with the historically weakest commitment to any socialist alternative. Even now, the credibility and self-confidence of Thatcherism in Britain probably depends on the success and survival of its American big brother.

The interests of capital are also relatively distinct in the West European nations, and have by no means been fully homogenized through the development of multi-nationals dominated by American parent corporations. This distinctiveness has been manifest in many conflicts — over steel and other areas of American protectionism, over the high rate of interest now maintained in the USA by budget deficits and the effects of high defence spending, over the Euopean commitment to and interest in East–West trade, and over the refusal of the Americans to support the further creation of international credit on a neo-Keynesian basis. The interests of workers, and even of the managerial class whose jobs and salaries are much less mobile than the capital which employs them, are more closely tied to the national deployment of capital than are the interests of the owners of capital, for whom what matters is the rate of return on investments, not their geographical location.

The inability of the West European powers to sustain a major imperial military presence, the Falklands and Chad interventions notwithstanding, also suggests a divergence of interests regarding the Third World. Whereas the Americans are now determined to assert their own power, and the control of comprador capital, by establishing local military superiority and inflicting tough financial sanctions on governments which behave contrary to market disciplines (and to the line of American policy), the West European states are more inclined to favour market expansion and, at least in some cases, international reflationary measures of mutual interest to European and Third World states. There is also a perceptible difference of ideological orientation, the more 'social democratic' domestic politics of European states making them more liberal and conciliatory towards revolutionary regimes such as Nicaragua or Cuba. Their preferred strategy is to seek liberalization through trade and aid, rather than to support counter-revolution by armed force.

West European States are now evidently fearful of heightened military tension, and suspect the Americans of being willing to take risks with European lives and territory which they do not intend to take with their own. They are also in general less 'ideological' in their view of the Soviet Union, preferring to define and resolve conflicts, for example over Afghanistan or Poland, in the more old-fashioned terms of traditional territorial interests and equilibrium rather than through appeals to moral principles and ideological mobilization. There is a clear West European interest in the expansion of trade with the East, which still offers one of the major new potential markets for Western capital. The Americans, by contrast, fear that such trading relations will both strengthen the East, and produce an integration of the interests of Eastern and Western Europe which will be to the political and economic disadvantage of the USA.

There does seem, then, to be the basis for very considerable divergencies of policy between the USA and its West European allies, so long as they are not exposed to greater risk from the Eastern bloc. The fact that these differences are still muted (the Americans have, for example, had to make few concessions in return for the go-ahead on Pershing II and Cruise) is to be explained by the chronic disunity of the West European states, and the acute weakness which this imposes in their dealings with the USA. They have no concerted economic policy, and so the superior productive capacity of the West European economy as a whole cannot be brought to bear on the situation. They have little independent defence capability — none under common European command — and are therefore particularly toothless participants, or spectators, in arms negotiations with the USSR. Their weakness vis-à-vis the USA illustrates the consequences of a military imbalance — consequences which are usually considered only in relation to the East. They have only the feeblest joint institutions of policy-making and government, and rarely present a common line on international issues. Finally, the Common Market is now in a state of acute political and financial crisis.

This analysis suggests that whereas neutralism is probably an impractical and non-feasible objective for Britain alone, because of its reduced weight and its deeply conservative internal climate, the balance of class and political forces in Western Europe as a whole may provide objective scope for a general move towards greater neutrality. However, the relative weakness and disunity of working-class movements and parties in Western Europe is such that this could only be achieved if they won support or at least connivance in such a development from other social forces, probably including some sections of their national capitals. It may seem implausible that any sections of capital should tolerate international realignments that would strengthen the position of their class opponents. But this depends on a balance with other threats that are perceived to exist. Undue risks of nuclear warfare, or of defeat in economic competition with the USA, Japan or the newly industrialized countries of the Pacific Basin, might be felt to justify preventive counter-action even at the price of some pragmatic alliance with domestic opponents. There are precedents, not all fortunate, for national class alliances of this kind — for instance, social imperialism before and during the First World War in Germany and Britain, the mobilization of the democracies against fascism during the Second World War, and the Keynesian class compromise of the post-war period. Another factor is the extent to which regional or national economic decline is felt to present more of a long-term threat to the existing social order than would a compromise with the domestic working class.

European capital is now held back by the underdevelopment of its means of state-political coordination, the EEC having achieved little more than an internal free trade area. One might describe this as a contradiction between the integration of economic forces at a continental level, and a primary petty nationalism still governing the relations between states, of which the destructive arguments over British payments into the European budget were a prime example. In the one case of economic integration at the level of the state (the Common Agricultural Policy), this has been achieved in favour of backward sectors of agriculture, rather than at the more important level of budgetary coordination or investment in new technologies. Furthermore the financial institutions of the capitalist system are dominated by rival capitals — mainly American — which, themselves threatened by trade competition, show little concern to promote European economic revival.

One can thus posit a common interest, stretching across many social strata in West European nations, in a greater assertion of regional independence vis-à-vis the Americans. But given the inhibiting effects of disunity and petty nationalism, the left — and the working-class and radical movements more generally — have a potentially pivotal role to play. The more advanced sections of European capital, and certainly its service classes, may have objective need of the support of the working-class movement to enforce a necessary modernization of its system of government, through the kind of class compromise that was initiated after 1945. The technocratic elite that took the initiative in the earlier phase of European integration has found itself without a substantial social base, as the financial sector has maintained or reasserted its control of economic policy in West Germany and Britain, and as nationalist interests, stimulated by the example of Mrs Thatcher, have remained uppermost in EEC policy-making. The insular, anachronistic and ignorant positions of the British left during the entire period of debate over EEC entry have made their own significant contribution towards blocking the process of European integration and independence. Since the outcome of the British policy of keeping all options unfettered has been the unopposed reassertion of American hegemony and the unravelling of many of the social advances of the Keynesian period (including substantial public ownership), it can be seen that this foreign policy has been a classic case of backing the wrong historical horse.

The possible elements of a socialist foreign policy oriented towards Europe may now be briefly enumerated. On the economic plane, concerted budgetary expansion and enlargement of the EEC funds available for investment and reconstruction should be the principal objectives. This would after all do no more than restore the system of deficit financing to Western Europe which is now being covertly practised by the Reagan Administration, to its own and America's advantage. The 'housekeeping' issue of Britain's budgetary contribution to the EEC should be swallowed under the much larger one of how to bring about wealth and job creation. A net budgetary contribution would be worth paying if the average rate of growth of the whole EEC zone, including Britain, was significantly increased. A more detailed economic agenda has been valuably set out in a recent volume edited by Stuart Holland.[3]

In the field of foreign policy, the left should reassert the objectives of detente and improved relations with the East, making it clear that these should be sought on a European plane. There is an economic basis here, in the need for the West Europeans to develop markets in Eastern Europe to counterbalance the expansion of American and Japanese markets in the Pacific. But there is an important political objective, too, of reducing tension and by this means encouraging liberalization in Eastern Europe. Any improvement in the human rights situation in Eastern Europe will be a product of better East–West relations, and attempts to make this a precondition of closer economic links or arms control can only be counter-productive. The West European peace movement has reasons of principle and moral independence to insist on the rights of its counterparts in the East, but it would be playing into the hands of cold warriors, East and West, to make wider progress dependent on the recognition of those rights. Just as there is a common interest among West European states in expansionary economic programmes towards the Third World, so there is an ideological interest in the support of reforming regimes in the Third World, which make more tenable some 'third way' between the opposing constraints of dependence on the USSR or on the USA.

Defence Policy

An effective assertion of European interests in the economic and political spheres will require greater responsibility for defence. In any case, little progress towards economic independence of the USA is likely to occur unless the fears of a consequent de facto enhancement of the USSR's influence are allayed. A shift in emphasis towards conventional defence, and the creation of nuclear-free zones in Northern and Central Europe (of course on both sides of the East-West frontier), are well-established intermediate aims of the peace movements, and they are in many ways consistent with the goal of greater West European independence. But there are also good reasons to support defence cooperation among West European states, in both the resourcing and the command of their forces. For example, it could be insisted that so long as nuclear weapons remain on European soil, they should be subject to 'dual key' control through a West European as well as an American command system. The independence that the Americans retain from the machinery of NATO decision-making should be asserted by the Europeans themselves, particularly with regard to veto powers.

Nuclear weapons constitute a crucial difficulty for the development of a more independent European policy. There could be wide support for a conventional and purely defensive re-structuring of Western Europe's military capability, as has been proposed in a number of recent studies.[4] What is less plausible is that support could be achieved for the complete exclusion of nuclear weapons from any connection with West European defence. I refer here not so much to the physical location of nuclear weapons or their support systems on West European land, but to the last-resort dependence upon a nuclear deterrent system. While one can argue that total reliance on conventional systems and on civil and passive defence is a feasible policy, it will be strongly urged on the contrary that Western Europe would be exposed to nuclear blackmail in any local confrontation in which the potential losses to Western Europe would be greater than to another power, probably the USSR. This kind of contingency, arising in some Cold War 'frontier situtation' which might or might not be on the physical East–West frontier, is the main rationale of the military systems of the two blocs.

Given this limitation, two options other than total unilateral nuclear disarmament would be available to West European policy-makers. One would be to maintain a minimum seaborne deterrent of their own, perhaps comprising the British and French deterrents suitably Europeanized. The second would be to retain a scaled-down reliance on the Americans, on a joint-control basis. The advantage of the latter course is that it makes possible a root-and-branch opposition to British and European nuclear weapons, though at the cost of a tacit dependence on American nuclear forces in certain hypothetical contingencies, with all that that might entail for continuing American hegemony. The advantage of the former option — a minimal European nuclear deterrent — is that it makes possible a fuller decoupling of Western Europe and America, though at the risk of stimulating the nuclear rearmament of Western Europe itself. If, as is not at all improbable,

Western Europe were to fall under the sway of right-wing governments in, let us say, France, Britain and West Germany at the same time, this would present a not inconsiderable risk, and would be greatly feared and resented by the USSR.

Continued reliance on a minimal American nuclear deterrent is consistent with arguments against British nuclear weapons and the presence of nuclear bases in Britain, but it acknowledges the widespread fear, repeatedly shown in opinion polls, that a wholly conventional or neutralist defence policy could leave Britain ultimately defenceless. The Labour Party's current commitment to remove nuclear bases from Britain, while remaining within NATO, effectively takes this position. It is possible to argue, within this framework, for a 'minimum deterrence' strategy, and for the various intermediate steps towards this, such as a nuclear freeze, 'no first use',[5] and the retention of 'mutual assured destruction' in preference to the current destabilizing intent to establish a so-called defensive capability (anti-missile missiles, 'star-wars', etc.) whose probable real goal is American strategic superiority over the Soviet Union.

Such a position may well be incongruent, however, with the aim of greater independence from the United States. The West European governments encouraged the siting of Cruise missiles for fear of a local nuclear imbalance with the East, and because of their doubts about the continued reliability of the American commitment to Europe. A programme of greater European political unity which first required the abandonment of all existing European nuclear weapons (including those of France) does not seem plausible. Nor are the Europeans likely to gain greater influence over American policy from a position of total dependence. The contributions which they could directly make towards military de-escalation — removal of US bases, reduction of defence expenditure and so on — would diminish their own defences, and risk antagonizing and provoking the withdrawal of the power on which they depend. Initiatives are particularly difficult for European countries acting in isolation, which are then subject to the pressures of 'divide and rule'. For these reasons even an aroused West European public opinion has recently had no success in its attempts to slow down the arms race. De-escalation on this view is left to depend on American public opinion, which has not moved far in this direction. This strategy might, however, be helped by closer alignment between the peace movement in Europe, and the 'nuclear freeze' movement in the USA.

For all the dangers of initiating a further round of nuclear armament, it may have to be recognized that greater European autonomy and influence will only come about if the West European governments retain some control over a minimum nuclear capability. It would be most sensible for this to be held under joint European command, as a seaborne system which would be compatible with negotiated withdrawal of all nuclear weapons from European land. The independent British and French deterrents would thus cease to be national forces. Such an arrangement, and a commitment to adequate conventional forces, would require a more independent West European role within NATO.

This position is consistent with a strategy of conventional defence supported by a last-resort nuclear deterrent capacity. The suicidal consequences of nuclear war are fully apparent in Western Europe, which has neither the will nor the resources to seek strategic superiority over the East, and a strong conventional threshold force seems the most crucial safeguard against the unlikely event of an invasion. Being much weaker than the two great military powers, the West Europeans have an objective interest, once their own security is assured, in measures of general disarmament which would lessen this relative disparity and displace rivalry on to other fields of political and economic competition where they are stronger. A limited European defence option, though open to many objections, might therefore be the most realistic way of pursuing greater autonomy and influence vis-à-vis the two major power blocs.

If a balance of power with the East could be maintained through conventional forces and a minimal last-resort nuclear deterrent, it would become rational for the West Europeans to press for the reduction of the enormous and dangerous excesses of nuclear armaments, which make a negative contribution to security. As the campaigns against Cruise missiles in Western Europe, and for a nuclear freeze in the USA have both shown, the most persuasive political arguments, even for those who accept the logic of nuclear armaments, centre on the unstable and dangerous excess of weaponry, far beyond the more extreme needs of 'mutual assured destruction'. If the peace movement were to shift the emphasis of its attack away from deterrence per se to this growing 'excess' of deterrence, it might gain the broader support it needs in order to achieve the policy changes which have so far eluded it.

A more lucid recognition by the peace movement of the relevance of the concept of 'balance' with the East, and of the importance of greater unity within Western Europe, might point towards some working agreement on specific disarmament and disengage-ment initiatives with those serious 'multilateralists' who have now become disturbed at the direction of Western policy and the arms race more generally. Such initiatives could in some cases be 'unilateral' (e.g., on Cruise or Trident), where they tended to initiate a virtuous circle of disarmament and trust. At present, the differences between radical and pragmatic currents of opposition to the dominant nuclear strategy make it difficult for either to gain enough public support to change defence policy. This problem is replicated, within the Labour Party, in the difficulty of reaching a workable compromise on foreign and defence policy which will not fall apart at the first hostile question, as it did so disastrously during the 1983 election campaign. An authentic agreement of this kind is a precondition of any advance within Britain in the foreseeable future.

Some will feel that any consideration of compromise with nuclear deterrent systems is a betrayal of principle, and that absolute re-nunciation is the only morally tolerable position. But even if this were attainable in Britain alone, nuclear arms would continue to threaten the world. The thesis that a 'nuclear winter' would follow any major exchange has closed off any single-nation escape routes, and compels us to address the problem in its full human dimensions. There is an unhappy choice to be made between seemingly ineffec-tive arguments from moral absolutes (asserting our own personal responsibility to have nothing to do with these weapons), and arguments for lesser evils which might bring some amelioration and reduction of risk. Although any compromise with the appalling logic of the nuclear deterrent seems monstrous, the primary moral responsibility may be to support those positions which are most likely to lessen the general danger of nuclear war.

Broader Issues of European Socialist Policy

At the political and institutional level, it is clear that commitment to a European-oriented foreign and economic policy would require the radical strengthening and democratization of European political institutions. In particular the power of the European Par-liament, now minimal, and the responsibility of the EEC Com-mission to Parliament rather than to the Council of Ministers, would have to be asserted over the powers of national governments, and some progress encouraged towards a federal system. Such new powers would strengthen parties over executives and assist a process of mutual learning and cooperation among parties of the left which has scarcely yet begun. The question of which powers should be concentrated in the European Parliament and the Commission, and which should remain with national Parliaments, is a technically complicated one that cannot be further explored here. Electorates will in any case want to see positive economic and social results from inter-governmental cooperation before they will be prepared to concede much formal sovereignty. But the existence of universal suffrage across Western Europe, and the fact that socialists are able to organize in support of one another, provides a democratic opportunity to equal the much more powerful links between national corporations and governments.

Within the context of a more significant legislative role for a European Parliament, it will be necessary to draw up specifically socialist programmes of common rights on such questions as employment, education, health and social security. One can imagine a process of levelling upwards, in which the best practice in any one nation is taken as the desirable norm for the entire region. At the cultural level, the socialist idea might gain a much-needed renewal from comparison of alternative social institutions as these have been developed in other countries, in the same way that in recent years the context of socialist and especially of Marxist thought has been transformed for the better by a less insular approach. It does not seem possible to engender hope in a socialist vision from within the increasingly marginal and defeated experience of British society. Socialism has depended in the past on the idea that it was the way of life of the future, made possible by new productive possibilities. Identification with the combined possibilities of one of the most advanced areas of human civilisation may make possible some recovery of confidence. At the practical level, socialists could hardly be better engaged at the present time than in widening their acquaintance and understanding of their neighbouring societies, through exchanges and meetings, and in making real the common tasks of a European socialism.

The attractions of political work in an expanded European dimension should not be overlooked. It should be possible to work through local authorities, trade unions, and colleges, to give greater meaning to exchange programmes with continental counterparts. Political parties and organizations could also sometimes be involved, so that European solidarity may come to have a more personal meaning for activists. It is important this should be a widely available possibility, and not confined to a small jet-set of functionaries or intellectuals. Foreign policy, as some European Nuclear Disarmament initiatives have recently shown, can have its own programme of grassroots activity.

Initiatives to strengthen the European dimension of socialist policy will also require some leading political figures to gain attention and respect beyond their own country. Willy Brandt is one example in this respect, and some Labour politicians will have to master the skills of continental as well as British communication, through television for instance. Of course the tendency of British Labour leaders in recent years to compete with Mrs Thatcher in the strident assertion of British national interests is hardly compatible with this goal.

The argument in this chapter has deliberately referred to minimal aims that might attract wider support than from committed socialists alone. This connects with my view that in the present weakened state of the working-class movements in Britain and Western Europe, progress will only be achieved through a reconstruction of class alliances in which the working class (broadly defined), parts of the salaried service class especially based in public enterprises, but also even sections of national and regional capitals, can cooperate to restore the economic growth and active state policies of the period prior to the present reaction. A crucial issue for a class alliance is, against what is it allied? In this case it should be the continued domination of mobile international capital and finance, concentrated in Britain in the City of London. It was the failure to subdue this interest which was decisive for the defeats of the Labour governments of the 1960s and 1970s. A modernisation and democratization of British society can no longer be achieved on a national basis, least of all in Britain's state of acute weakness, but requires a West European plane of action. Success at this level might then create the conditions for further advances towards socialist democracy, and for corresponding developments in due time in Eastern Europe.

NOTES

1. An earlier version of this chapter was presented at a meeting of the Europe Working group of the Socialist Society in London. I am grateful to the other members of this group and also to Joseph Schwartz for their helpful comments.
2. These are the reasons cited by Michael Howard for the original formation of

NATO. See his article 'Western Defence in the 1980s: Conditions for Consensus', *Foreign Affairs*, Spring 1983.

3. Stuart Holland, ed., *Out of Crisis: A Project for European Recovery*, Nottingham 1983.

4. See, for example, *Defence without the Bomb: The Report of the Alternative Defence Commission*, London 1983, and G. Prins, ed., *Defended to Death*, Harmondsworth 1982.

5. One of the most influential recent arguments for a 'no first use' commitment by NATO was made in McGeorge Bundy, George Kennan, Robert McNamara, Gerald Smith, 'Nuclear Weapons and the Atlantic Alliance', *Foreign Affairs*, Spring 1982.

11
Afterword

In the General Election that took place in the Spring of 1988, Mrs Thatcher was eventually defeated. The dominant issue was unemployment, as it had been for two or three years prior to the election, since the end of the miners' strike. Although Mrs Thatcher had in 1987 introduced substantial tax cuts, and a much less substantial capital spending programme, with the declared aim of 'tackling unemployment now that we have conquered the problem of inflation once and for all', this was perceived by most as an unconvincing and cynical operation. Having staked so much on her 'prudent housekeeping' approach to government spending, Thatcher found it difficult to reverse course just before an election. Unlike Mondale in 1984, the opposition parties in Britain did not denounce the pre-election budget deficit as irresponsible, but said it was too little and too late. As so often before, the election was won and lost in the two or three years that preceded it, and not during the campaign itself.

While the Labour Party's share of the poll rose by 7 per cent over the 1983 level to 35 per cent, this was not enough to give it a clear majority. The Liberal/SDP Alliance also gained 2 more per cent of the national vote, and there was evidence of considerable vote-switching where Alliance or Labour candidates seemed to have the best chance of winning. The Liberals made more of the running in the Alliance than in 1979, finding it easier in the more strongly anti-Thatcherite climate, and David Owen was made less effective by his earlier endorsements of aspects of the Thatcherite philosophy. Steel's explicit willingness to discuss coalition with Labour probably encouraged Alliance party voters to vote Labour in areas where Labour had previously come second to the Tories, especially where there was an SDP rather than a Liberal candidate. Since Thatcher and her supporters for the time being retained their dominant position in the Conservative Party, there was little alternative to some kind of coalition. The Labour Party used the alternative option of a minority government, followed by an early dissolution to force optimal terms out of the Alliance.

Employment and the Economy

Employment policy was the first priority area for government action, since it was mainly on its failures in this area that the Conservatives had been defeated. There were now nearly four million unemployed, and there had been further inner-city riots in 1986. The most radical step taken by the new government was a commitment to provide a year's employment to everyone who had been registered unemployed for over six months. The Government decided that some declaration of principle of this kind was required, especially if it were to succeed in obtaining the cooperation of the unions for some kind of de facto incomes policy. Regional Employment Commissions were set up, on a tripartite government–industry–union basis, to develop productive employment. These Commissions were to propose capital programmes (railway insulation, sewer reconstruction, house repair and neighbourhood improvement, railway electrification, upgrading of provincial airports, the Severn Barrage, and so on.) Since many of these programmes were of their nature long-term, and would require more skilled workers in the construction (and related) industries, it was also agreed to link the existing Youth Training Scheme and other new vocational training programmes more closely to the expected manpower demands of these schemes, thus lessening the pointlessness of training where there were no employment prospects attached. The Regional Commissions were also authorized to allocate specified funds for short-term employment subsidies to private firms, depending on the level of unemployment in each region. These subsidies were set at something less than the estimated exchequer cost of each unemployed person, in social security benefit and foregone tax revenues. It was agreed to expand health and community care services, in the context of an expansion of preventive and community medicine. These programmes, which responded to the growing number of old people in the population, were designed to provide a better social infrastructure for the idea of community care. Encouragement was also given to voluntary organizations in these areas, as a low-cost way of improving social welfare that would allow greatest use to be made of the more expensive resources of redeployed professional workers. These policies, and their multiplier effects in the economy, did bring a reduction of unemployment by one and a half million in just over a year.

Measures to promote voluntary early retirement — for example, the right to a reduction of working hours by half at the age of sixty for those who had been in employment with a firm for more than five years — also made a favourable impact on employment figures. The half-time provision introduced a more flexible approach to the final years of work, and was accompanied by a small offsetting increase in part-time employment beyond the age of sixty-five. The introduction of a universal 16–18 education and training allowance, as Labour had proposed in opposition, effectively removed 16 to 18-year-olds from the employment figures.

The Government set up a National Investment Bank, as had been long proposed by the TUC and offered tax-free bonds to the public as a way of raising capital for it. For the first time this provided tax advantages for lending for industrial investment (to a ceiling of £40,000 per person), to offset fiscal benefits which domestic property had enjoyed on mortgage interest and other payments. While one effect of this was simply to divert savings from building societies to the new fund, it did increase net savings and helped to raise the rate of capital formation in the early years of the new government without inflationary effect. Labour gained some credit for the introduction of this idea of popular shares in industrial wealth, having been so badly outflanked by the Conservatives over council house ownership.

On assuming office, the new government devalued the pound, reimposed exchange controls and greatly restricted the outward movement of capital. It took reserve powers to introduce a licence system whereby importers would have to pay a sliding-scale premium for foreign currency purchases, which would vary according to the balance of trade in each quarter. The Government sought to encourage trade competitiveness by maintaining the lower value of sterling against other currencies, but the exchange rate was too vulnerable to non-trade-related speculation to be an adequate instrument on its own. The import licences were designed as a trade-balancing measure, and defended as non-protectionist in the sense that there would be no tariff when trade was in balance.

Economic growth of 6 per cent was achieved in the first year of the new government and 5 per cent in the second (the Thatcher

Government having only managed a level of 2.75 per cent in its last full year). The import licence scheme was invoked after nine months, to head off an impending balance-of-payments crisis.

The major industries denationalized by the Thatcher Government — British Airways, British Telecom, etc. — were taken back into public ownership. The major condition exacted by the Alliance was that a measure of competition with the private sector should be preserved in each case. Since this concession was thought likely to improve the efficiency and thus the defensibility of the public sector in the long run, it caused little controversy.

The National Investment Bank (NIB) was close in its conception to the earlier Wilsonian National Enterprise Board, but there were competing pressures for the allocation of its capital resources. The Government chose to concentrate on 'sunrise' industries and new technologies, giving as one of its reasons the need to assure a proper return on savings to bondholders (though in practice the fixed-interest return was guaranteed by government). It also set up a smaller Cooperative Investment Bank, to encourage worker-ownership, and with some success devolved the task of short-term employment creation to the Regional Employment Commissions, shortly to become part of elected regional authorities. There was widespread recognition of the fact that these investment measures could only be effective over a space of time, and that, at the very least, Labour, with or without the Alliance, would have to remain in office for at least two terms.

Closely linked with the 'hi-tech' role of the National Investment Bank was a considerable expansion of the funds provided for technological research. The Government announced that it intended to divert industrial research capacity from defence to civilian purposes. A new Industrial Research Agency (successor to the NRDC) was given a substantial budget, which could be allocated either on a 'matching grant' basis to private or public corporations, or as smaller grants to academic institutions pursuing technological projects prior to their direct industrial applications. New agencies sought and took the advice of the NEDC sector working parties in the allocation of both research and investment capital. Realizing the shortage of skilled management, especially in the public sector, the Government also introduced funding for postgraduate sandwich courses in a number of institutions, by which economics, business and engineering graduates could take programmes in conjunction with placements in industry, or in public economic agencies. One object of these schemes was to generate a high-quality cohort of managers and planners, especially for the public and government sector. A proportion of places was thus provided for civil servants.

Trade Unions

The Labour Party faced a real problem of how to fulfil the interests of the trade unions while remaining in coalition with the Liberals and the SDP. An incomes policy was made a condition of the formation of the Coalition, but the TUC, battered after nine years of Thatcherism, was prepared to accept this (under another name) as a trade-off both for the employment creation programme and for the return of the trade unions to a more central public role. (The success of the Australian Labour Government's programme of an incomes policy for economic expansion had anyway increased the attractiveness of this option in Britain.) The TUC negotiated a two-year agreement which provided that wage increases should not exceed 1.5 per cent above the going rate of inflation during that period. There was also provision for a tax penalty on firms who paid over the odds, although in practice this was sparingly deployed. The trade unions were coopted onto the regional employment commissions, while at more grassroots level some energies were diverted into alternative plan initiatives supported by the new Cooperative Bank.

Funds were made available for paid educational leave schemes (short-term block release and day release programmes for trade unionists) and for an expansion of one-year full-time trade union education programmes. These were related to the idea that trade unions should develop a more positive role in industrial planning and management. While no majority existed in Parliament for the repeal of legislation requiring ballots for strike action, or for the allocation of funds for political purposes, the improved status of the trade unions under the new government, and a recognition that restraint was vital to the new reconstruction, made it easier for some unions to retain their members' support for political funds. The unions also gained from the increased membership that came with falling unemployment. The requirement of shareholders' ballots to authorize company gifts for political purposes reduced corporate funding of the Conservative Party.

The impotence of the unions under Thatcher, and the number of severe industrial defeats they had suffered during this period, had produced a shift of emphasis to political means of advancing working-class interests. The Government this time wisely chose to spend its early capital on political measures, rather than on inflationary wage rises as Labour had done in 1974. Another factor leading to this tougher government attitude was the less-than-happy experience of some Labour metropolitan authorities with their own town-hall unions.

Important measures in winning working-class support were the Government's first budgets. These removed low-earning groups from income-tax liability, and made the fiscal system somewhat more progressive. There was a small increase in the basic rate of income tax. The Government said that it had little to give away because of the priority of industrial reconstruction, but that it would, unlike its predecessor, be fair. Tax concessions on new mortgages (and after two years on existing ones) would be limited to relief at the standard rate of tax. The Labour Party did not forget in these years that concern for working-class living standards was the precondition of its unity and electoral survival. If inflation was to be contained, it was understood that social justice had to be pursued through the tax system.

The Constitution

It was clear at the outset of negotiations between the coalition partners that Labour was not willing to concede Proportional Representation, and would go ahead with a minority government instead if the Alliance insisted on making it a decisive issue 'at this stage'. 'There are higher priorities,' said the Labour Party, and 'in any case if the electorate had wanted this, they would not have voted for us as the largest single party.'

Agreement, however, was easier on regional and local government questions. Crucial in the decision to establish elected regional and Scottish and Welsh authorities, with considerable powers devolved from central government departments, was the influence of certain politicians from the former Metropolitan Counties, several of whom were now in Parliament. They argued that it would not do simply to restore the GLC and other authorities, since their powers had been grossly insufficient for any serious purpose. 'We made a lot of noise, and the Government took us seriously, but in reality we were hamstrung on everything except public transport,' said one prominent ex-GLC figure. Labour did, however, agree that the new regional authorities should be elected by Proportional

Representation. The main reason for this was to disadvantage the Tories, who were thought likely to benefit regionally from first-past-the-post and a split opposition. On this basis four regional authorities fell to the same coalition arrangements as were now functioning at Westminster. The Regional Employment Commissions became Development Agencies (absorbing the Scottish and Welsh Agencies), and they were a significant force in economic and employment policy, especially in the more depressed regions.

The regional authorities were given limited taxing powers. Eventually a two-tier income tax was to be introduced, following computerization of Inland Revenue; in the meantime, they were to be funded by rate precept, and by large proportional grants from the Exchequer. Regional economic development was the main rationale of the new authorities, together with a general rhetoric of decentralization which made the most of hostility to Thatcherite authoritarianism. The new Regional Employment Commissions, the Development Agencies where these already existed, and the functions of the Manpower Services Commissions were among the functions devolved to the regional authorities. In addition, they had responsibility for arts funding, tourism, strategic land use development plans, some commuter transport, and water supplies. They were also free to undertake any functions not expressly forbidden, under 'general competence' legislation. Payment was allocated for the holders of Committee Chairs, and a fairly generous attendance allowance granted for other Regional Members.

The Proportional Representation issue was left in abeyance for two years, but at the end of this time the Alliance announced its intention of fighting a cluster of three forthcoming by-elections wholly on this issue. Since these did not endanger the Government's majority, and since the Alliance said it would engage in no anti-Labour campaigning other than on this question (Labour had successfully insisted from the first on abstention from anti-socialist speech-making as a condition for Alliance members to remain in the Government), this proved to be an ingenious strategy. Labour lost one seat to the Liberals on this issue, and lost votes in the other two. That decided the issue, and soon afterward the Labour Prime Minister announced that the Government would introduce legislation to provide for the next General Election to take place by Proportional Representation.

The House of Lords was now an embarrassing anomaly. There was support both for some regional representation, and for some more formal representation of industrial and trade union interests in the Second Chamber, so that tripartite economic bargaining could take place within rather than outside the Constitution. One solution, it was thought, might be the replacement of hereditary peers with a new category of fixed-term Upper House Members, who would be nominated by regional assemblies. There was also a proposal for a number of seats to be allocated to approved nominees of the CBI and the TUC perhaps as members of NEDC. The difficulty with fixed-term membership, however, was the uncertain length of Parliaments, and the lack of any predictable relationship between this and the term of office of Regional Authorities from which regional members would be drawn. The logical solution was to introduce a fixed term of Parliament of four or five years, and to allow nomination in these limited-term categories to take place, as in the American Congressional system, both at the full- and half-term points of the Parliament. It was announced that hereditary peers who remained active could retain their own rights of membership for their lifetime, a compromise attributed to Ken Livingstone and to The Lords' defeat of Thatcher in the metropolitan county elections vote.

The Government also instituted state funding for political parties represented in Parliament (in proportion to their share of the vote), and allocated a much larger sum for the staff and office expenses of MPs. It also introduced a new form of short-term civil service contract, to coincide with the life of a Parliament, and declared the intention to use this to increase the expertise and 'industrial experience' of civil servants. In practice, as was intended, this enhanced the role of political appointees in government. Similar measures were taken at the levels of local and regional government. The structure of the permanent civil service and local government officialdom continued only little changed, but these new appointments were a significant means of innovation in high-priority areas, such as industrial development, and in strengthening the planning resources of ministers.

The Government and the Intellectuals: The Re-Invention of the Royal Commission

The Government succeeded in wedding the radical intelligentsia more firmly to its cause than its Labour predecessors had done, both by the recruitment of advisers, and by the re-invention of the

Royal Commission after a long period of disuse under Thatcher. Protesting that it was determined not to 'run out of steam' after one term, the Government quickly moved to appoint a number of Royal Commissions and Committees of Inquiry in areas which is deemed important. One of these was a Royal Commission on the Press, whose terms of reference included the issues of monopoly powers, quality, and democratic access. Its principal recommendations were a stringent anti-monopoly rule — which barred the same company from ownership of more than one national and Sunday newspaper, or more than one local newspaper in a given area — and significant tax-exemptions for newspapers operated as non-profit-making trusts.

Another Commission, reporting on the production and distribution of television and film, proposed a 'public highway' concept of Cable, funded by licence fee, in which the basic technical infrastructure would be supplied through British Telecom. Programmes would be provided alternatively by the BBC or new Regional Public Stations, out of licence income, or by commercial bodies using advertisements on the lines of the existing Independent Television Companies. In accepting these recommendations, the Government announced that it wanted to preserve the existing 'mixed economy' in broadcasting, but with a greater plurality of channels, to ensure that the basic licence fee gave all citizens access to all programmes. It argued that the indirect benefits of Cable, through interactive home-shopping, travel booking, and other information services where additional charges could be levied through the use, not the reception of information, would more than justify the 'free' provision of the basic service. The larger the numbers who had access to these systems, the lower the average cost, it was argued, and the more activity they would generate. It was a classic case of a 'public good'. In addition, the Commission recommended generous government funding of an enlarged National Film Finance Corporation, whose aim would be to secure a long-run expansion, through education, training and direct investment, of film- and programme-making capacity. The BBC and the national theatre companies show that public funding can work, said the Government. This Royal Commission had as members some of the leading figures of recent radical debate on mass communications, as well as practitioners, and by holding public hearings which attracted considerable participation and publicity, was able to generate political debate (distraction, some said) in parallel with the Government's more immediate activities. A significant precedent had been the Cable Hearings of the GLC in 1983.

A Royal Commission was also set up on taxation, which proposed a drastic simplification of the tax and benefit system, and a negative income tax to replace the existing host of means-tested benefits. On the capital side, it argued for a more equal distribution of capital, both individually, through worker share-ownership schemes and regional extensions of the investment bond idea, and collectively, through a greater say in pension fund investment by trade-union or other workforce representatives.

A Royal Commission on the Family, whose membership was drawn from single-issue campaigns in the welfare field, the personal social services, and the churches, and included some prominent feminists, recommended improvements in family support services (day-care, domiciliary care for the old, and an infant child-benefit allowance for parents of under-fives), on the grounds that these would strengthen rather than weaken family structure. It also advocated specific measures to protect women (for example, collection through the tax system of the child-maintenance contributions of deserting husbands). This combination of an active welfare policy, an equal rights approach to gender, and a positive attitude towards the family in its variable forms, won mainstream support and successfully pre-empted neo-conservative campaigns over the family.

The Government also created a Committee on Community and Preventive Health, saying that it wanted to set positive goals for the improvement of public health standards. Such 'benchmarks', it said, will allow us to know how much progress we have made after five years in improving the health of our people. This Committee investigated a range of environmental, occupational and preventive health problems, and made recommendations in a number of areas, including infant mortality and malnutrition, deaths and illness associated with tobacco (no more advertising or sponsorship), road safety (including more stringent legislation for the design of vehicles and on driving and alcohol), heart disease and diet. These were linked with an increase in expenditure on the National Health Service, but were also seen as the most cost-effective means of improving health.

The sixth of this unexpected series of Committees of Enquiry and Royal Commissions (government by sociologists, said some Tories) concerned policing, crime rates and penal policy, especially in relation to inner-city areas. This Commission brought together one or two of the more liberal police commissioners and prison governors, civil rights lawyers, and academics, with some representation from the immigrant communities. It maintained that the breakdown of social relationships was the crucial factor in the generation of crime and disorder. It predictably supported 'community' concepts of policing and proposed attention to the stability and improvement of neighbourhoods as a way of lessening crime and insecurity. It pointed out that the switch from comprehensive redevelopment schemes to piecemeal housing improvement might well already be reducing problems associated with rapid social transition — problems of loneliness and mental illness as well as vandalism and crime. It recommended the strengthening of community cohesiveness through the decentralization of council services, and it supported the establishment of elected neighbourhood councils with small spending powers, in the hope that this would increase community integration. It argued that thought had to be given to the quality of relationships established between teenagers and teachers and other involved adults. This required research into the effects of the impersonality of very large schools, and much better staffing ratios (perhaps involving the use of auxiliaries) might be needed in the most difficult areas. It urged attention to the design of public space, including council estates, to prevent areas of dereliction. The social role of the concierge was commended to improve the safety and sociability of tower blocks. There was also an interesting suggestion for the appointment of neighbourhood street wardens, perhaps out of the police budget as a low-cost form of community policing, or under the jurisdiction of elected neighbourhood councils. These would have the role of patrolling a few local streets, getting to know the neighbours, and reporting on 'suspicious circumstances'. They would have lapel radios, to enable them to call for help and to protect them from assault, and residents would be encouraged to tell them when they were going away. Like lollipop men and women, the report said — the posts might suit retired people (anyway in quieter areas). It seemed a way of strengthening community ties and information, where these were lacking.

The report argued for a preventive law and order philosophy, stressing the documented cost and futility of imprisonment and other custodial sentences. These might be necessary deterrents, the report said, but they certainly do no good to the inmates. The key point, the Government added later, was whether preventive measures could reduce crime rates, and it set up a fuller and more public monitoring system. by local government area, to test this.

The Government meanwhile took steps to reduce the prison population and attempted to redirect resources in the direction of preventive action. The problem in pursuing this preventive approach to health and social order was how to make statistical improvements as meaningful to the public as the individual case of a heart transplant or exemplary sentence, which gained more media attention and distorted resource allocation. In taking problems of 'law and order' seriously, the authors of the Report attempted to turn conservative anxieties focused on the decline of moral community into support for positive social policies.

These various reports and investigations captured public attention through the use of public meetings, and especially radio and television, for their hearings. They were seen as long-term agenda-setting and educational devices. The Government wanted to avoid charges of secrecy and elitism (it had legislated on Freedom of Information, sensibly entrusting this issue to a Liberal Cabinet member) and therefore favoured such ways of achieving greater openness. Some thought it would be a harmless diversion for radical intellectuals to involve themselves with these long-term programmes instead of with the contentious problems of the present. At all events, these committees did generate a momentum of new issues and recommendations, and showed that this venerable constitutional instrument could be adapted to more democratic times.

Northern Ireland

Only limited progress was made in regard to Northern Ireland. The Government announced that in principle both Catholics and Protestants in the North should have the same rights to self-determination: the problem was how to interpret this in such difficult circumstances. The introduction of regional government provided the need and opportunity to do something. What the Government did was to set up two Regional Authorities: one, including West Belfast, which would have a Catholic majority; and a larger one with a Protestant majority. The intention was to co-opt the SDLP more fully into the structure of government, on the basis that it would now gain control of some significant state power for the first time. A crucial issue was security, since without some security powers the West (Catholic) region would be hardly credible. The compromise adopted was that each of the two authorities was given some control over local policing in its region. The RUC was divided into two sub-regions, coinciding with the elective boundaries, each with an Assistant Commissioner required to work both with his regional authority and under the Northern Ireland Police Commissioner who had responsibility for non-local police work. The intention was to appoint substantial numbers of Catholics to the West regional police authority, and a smaller number in the mainly Protestant East (since this retained some Catholic population). The Western authority would be free to set up its own discussions on local government and cross-border matters with the Republic (including security matters, but excluding sovereignty for the time being). Crucial to this whole experiment was whether the mainly Catholic authority would preempt and reduce support for Provisional IRA para-military activity, or whether it would be a means of tacitly supporting it, as opponents feared.

It was felt that for the first time the Catholic party committed to peaceful change had the resources and powers with which to win the support of its electorate. It was also thought that some movement of populations might take place to bring about more homogeneous communities, now that pluralism rather than integration was declared to be the underlying philosophy. The existence of two authorities with distinct populations also provided a readier means of aiming at parity of conditions of the two populations, regarding employment and income levels, education, health standards, and so on. The Government made clear that the Protestant population, in order to preserve its autonomy, would have to acquiesce in the Catholics' attainment of a significant measure of self-government, equalization of standards, and closer relations with the South.

Foreign Policy

The new government was able to reach agreement on a philosophy of *minimum* nuclear deterrence, combined with the preservation of military 'balance' with the East. It was established that the only nuclear weapons to be retained on British territory would be seaborne, and that the objective was to transfer these as rapidly as possible to joint European command. The peace movement was persuaded to acknowledge this as at least a step in the right direction by the commitment to remove Cruise missiles from Britain within six months. As the Defence Secretary said, 'one good thing about having missiles on trucks is that they can go out as quickly as they came in.' Agreement was also reached that no nuclear weapons would be deployed on US or British aircraft based in the UK. The international climate had fortunately improved, partly as a result of a realization that the arms burden was damaging Western economies and the political stability of its government even more than those of the Eastern bloc. Moves to economic decentralization in the USSR following Chernenko's departure from the scene had also brought some improvements in the Eastern bloc economy, where there was considerable unfulfilled potential blocked by inefficiency. (And more room for rapid improvement than in the West.) This in turn produced a greater pressure and stimulus for competing economic expansion in Western Europe. The return of a minority SPD government in West Germany, dependent on Green support or abstention, made it imperative for the West to adopt a more conciliatory stance towards the USSR in Europe, and also made a more expansionary economic approach possible in the EEC. While some tangible progress was being made in limited arms reductions, the Government was not much attacked from the left on defence issues. The official departure of Cruise was the occasion of a large peace festival. These developments also produced more positive attitudes in the Labour Party towards the Common Market.

How Did the Government Succeed?

The Government succeeded in holding together for four years, and went to the country in 1992 under the new PR system. Labour improved its share of the vote by a further 3 per cent to 38 per cent after this period of fairly popular and constructive government, but of course, under the PR system finished up with a lesser number of seats, though still as the largest single party. 'If we hadn't gone over to PR, we would have won outright', said left critics, but it was clear that the election results could not be fairly extrapolated to such a situation. After the 1992 election, the SDP and the Liberal Party merged.

The most important factor contributing to the Government's success had been the radically reduced expectations brought about by the Thatcher years. Themes of re-integration of the community, of decentralization and democratization, and of consistent but slow rebuilding of the economy, succeeded in maintaining majority support. After so many years of strident possessive individualism, the country was now receptive to a more ethical and integrative approach. Living standards of those in work rose only slightly in the first three years of the Government (more rapidly in the pre-election period), but there was a substantial improvement in the living conditions of the previously unemployed, and necessary capital formation in both the public and private sectors. The Labour Party gained in organizational strength through the establishment of public funding for parties, and through the new regional author-ities, while the TUC won greater authority through the Govern-ment's return to 'tripartism'. The Government attempted to meet criticisms from the left of 'bureaucratism' and 'corporatism' by providing for trade union participation in the regional development agencies and training bodies, and by giving some support to workers' cooperatives and buy-outs of divisions of private com-panies threatened with closure. But the main effect of Labour's dependence on the Alliance was the impossibility of restoring the trade unions' former privileges. To this extent Thatcherism had had a lasting effect. Together with internal changes in the Labour Party after 1979, this strengthened the role of party vis-à-vis trade unions in the labour movement. The more political and corporatist role the trade unions had taken in the more stable European social demo-cracies (Sweden and Austria, for example) came to England as the best option available after the hammering they had taken from Thatcherism. On the other hand, 'monetarism' had been wholly discredited, and the Thatcher defeat allowed the Government to give priority to the production of goods and services, over the financial sector.

The Government succeeded in appropriating some populist themes that Thatcherism had made its own, particularly democracy and 'letting the people decide'. It achieved this through a return to greater autonomy for local government, and through regional and local decentralization. But its emphasis on the values of com-munity, on the concern for life in preventive health and care schemes, and on social support for the family, also engaged with some sentiments that the right had most effectively orchestrated in the previous period. The commitment to investment and growth, and a continuing rhetoric of efficiency in the public services, paid tribute to the revival of market values, though the Government's employment creation schemes and mildly redistributive tax policies were attacked for lessening incentives and washing public resources. It turned out that the earlier alliance of working-class egalitarianism and 'new middle class' public rationality was still viable against a background of Thatcherite devastation.

The Coalition was surprisingly less liable to retreats on policy than the previous Labour Governments had been. Because policy differences were argued between competing parties, rather than in the secrecy of the Cabinet, it proved possible for the Labour Party to hold its leaders to their declared policies. While Alliance 'intransigence' was exploited on some occasions as an excuse by the Labour right to abandon positions they did not want to defend anyway, Labour generally remained aware that it had to look after its own constituency first. The Prime Minister's position was also weaker under this more pluralist arrangement, which gave the left more leverage, within the overall limits of Coalition policy, than it had most recently had. Labour was to some extent protected by its Coalition partners from accusations of socialist extremism (once it had been clarified that the Government aimed to last the full term, and that its members would not openly discredit each other). Reversals of Thatcher legislation, notably over public ownership, were carried through in key sectors. The key gain for the Alliance, and especially the Liberals, was the adoption of Proportional Representation, and for this they were prepared to make significant concessions. The advantage to Labour of delaying PR legislation until late in the Parliament was that the Alliance dared not risk bringing down the Government until it had been passed. This bargaining card enabled Labour to take a strong position within the Coalition, and the benefit of this was a significant recovery in its share of the vote.

It was not, as some on the left said after the second election victory of 1992, socialism, but at least it was a move forward again.

Index